D1831957

Malabar in Transition

Malabar in Transition

State, Society and Economy in Malabar, 1750-1810

M. P. Mujeebu Rehiman

KALPAZ

©Author

All rights reserved. No part of this work may be reproduced, stored, adapted, or transmitted in any form or by any means, electronic, mechanical, photocopying, micro-filming recording or otherwise, or translated in any language, without the prior written permission of the copyright owner and the publisher. The book is sold subject to the condition that it shall not, by way of trade or otherwise, be lent, resold, hired out, or otherwise circulated without the prior publisher's written consent in any form of binding or cover other than that in which it is published.

The views and opinions expressed in this book are author(s) own and the facts reported by them have been verified to the extent possible, and the publishers are not in any way liable for the same.

First Published, 2020

Published by

Kalpaz Publications
C-30, Satyawati Nagar,
Delhi – 110052
Ph.: 011-47034999, 9811692060
www.kalpazpublications.com
E-mail: kalpaz@hotmail.com

Printed at: G. Print Process, Delhi

Cataloging in Publication Data—DK

Courtesy: D.K. Agencies (P) Ltd. <docinfo@dkagencies.com>

Mujeebu Rehiman, M. P., author.

Malabar in transition : state, society and economy in Malabar, 1750-1810/ by M.P. Mujeebu Rehiman.

pages cm

Includes bibliographical references.

ISBN 9789353242206

1. Malabar Region (India)—Politics and government—18th century. 2. Malabar Region (India)—Politics and government—19th century. 3. Malabar Region (India)—Social conditions—18th century. 4. Malabar Region (India)—Social conditions—19th century. 5. Malabar Region (India)—Economic conditions—18th century. 6. Malabar Region (India)—Economic conditions—19th century. 7. Anti-imperialist movements—India—Malabar Region. I. Title.

LCC DS485.M35M85 2020 | DDC 954.83 23

For
Professor K. N. Ganesh
My Beloved teacher

For
Professor K. N. Ganesh
My Beloved teacher

Contents

Preface

It gives me immense pleasure to see this book published, primarily because, the out put of my research is getting disseminated to a wider audience, apart from being proud of contributing a small share to the domain of historical understanding of the present society. Previously, I made my loving friends disappointed when their affectionate compulsion on me to publish this doctoral dissertation was turned down, which actually occurred out of my disinclination. However, of late, the remarks of some of my students and young researchers regarding the apparent unavailability of literature on transition process in eighteenth century Malabar, actually made me to rethink and which culminated in the publication of my dissertation in the present format.

I would take anticipatory bail with regard to the revision of the thesis in toto, as it is well known that revising an already written text is rather difficult than writing anew. Accordingly, a thorough revision was not attempted, rather a fine tuning is done with the help of some of my friends, that I hope it has enhanced the clarity in explanation. Apart from that, I have tried my level best to avoid the monotony of reading a research report. A word about the style of writing the non-English terms: that I have not followed the diacritical marks, whereas the terms are included in italics inorder to denote accent variations. Similarly, tables and diagrams are not provided in the assumption that it may hinder the pleasure of reading.

I must record my indebtedness to quite a few individuals and institutions, who have extended to me unreserved help and support throughout the whole process of production of this book, indeed is beyond words. First and foremost, let me express my deep sense of gratitude to Prof. K.N. Ganesh, my supervising teacher, a guru in every sense, for his encouragement, suggestions, comments, and above all, his patience to entertain all my obliviousness. For me, what he was trying to do for years was to inspire his students including myself and teaching what not history was. As a dedicated teacher, eminent scholar and an honest human being, his commitment to students was unparalleled. Interestingly, he never imposed his ideas and positions upon his students, rather loved to equip them in an argumentative manner. If the readers feel anything worthy with regard to this book, it really owes to him and indeed the only responsible person for the mistakes and errors is none other than me. I am also thankful to his better half [Dr. T.K.] Anandi*Chechi*, for whose love and warmth extended to me and also for her 'stories' and food for thought she offered, especially during our annual 'pilgrimages' to the Indian History Congress sessions.

My heartfelt thanks are due to my teachers for graduation and masters, Prof. P. Venu and Dr. K.A.M. Anwar, who actually initiated me into the world of historical research. I am equally grateful to Dr. K. Gopalankutty, former Professor and Head of the Department of History, University of Calicut, whose magnanimity towards me as a colleague added much comfort in finishing off this book in its earlier form. I am grateful to late Prof. S. M. Muhammed Koya and Prof. V. Kunhali, formerly heads of our department for their support to me in the initial phase of my research.

Throughout the course of my research, I had great opportunity to interact with great historians such as Professors Michael Tharakan, K.K.N. Kurup, Lakshmi Subrahmaniam, and Jayaprakash Raghavaiah which have benefited me to get oriented to the the right track of historical research and I am really grateful to them. I am very much glad to record my thankfulness to Kerala Council for Historical Research, Trivandrum and its former director, Prof. P. J. Cheriyan for granting me a fellowship for revision towards publication of doctoral thesis in to a book format. I must thank my well-wisher and a source of inspiration Mr. N. M. Hussain, a scholar and writer who has been compelling me to get this book published at least for a decade.

It gives me immense joy and pleasure to cherish the experiences and memories I had had from the institutions and people in the initial phase of data collection. I am thankful to the Director and Staff of Maharashtra State Archives, Mumbai, Kerala State Archives, Trivandrum, Regional Archives, Kozhikode, Librarian and Staff of Kerala University Library, Trivandrum, Centre for Development Studies Library Trivandrum, Bombay University Library, Mumbai, Bombay Asiatic Society, Department of History Library, and C.H.M.K. Library, University of Calicut, Farook College Library, etc. for their services and co-operation rendered to me during my work. I am really owed to Prof. Jose George, former Professor of Political Science, Bombay University, for arranging me accommodation in Mumbai University hostel during the early phase of my research.

I am also grateful to my friends, faculty members, colleagues and students in various institutions I taught such as Department of History, University of Calicut; Farook College, Calicut; N.M.S.M Govt. College,

Kalpetta; C.K.G. Memorial Govt. College, Perambra, for their love, encouragement and support rendered to me. I am grateful to my colleagues such as Prof. K.P. Velayudhan, Prof. T. M. Vijayan, Prof. P. Sivadasan, Prof. Muhammed Maheen, Dr. K. S. Madhavan, Dr. V. V. Haridas, Dr. Burton Cleetus and Mr.Vineeth R., for their encouragement, love and affection.

I am really owed to the collective of History Research Forum at the Department of History, University of Calicut, where I was getting moulded myself as a researcher and express thankfulness to my friends and colleagues including Dr. T. Muhammedali, Dr. P.P. Abdul Razak, Dr. V. Sreevidhya, Lukumanul Hakeem, Ameen Das, Dr. Ramdas, Dr. Shihabuddeen Poonthala, Dr. SreevidyaVattarambath, Dr. Laina and several others for their encouragement and support towards this writer in various ways.

Dr. A. K. Yoosaf, author and Professor of English, Government College, Mokeri, who has spared his precious time and energy for patiently going through the draft of this book and I am thankful to him for corrections and suggestions. Special thanks are due to my student and young scholar Dr. K.P. Rajesh, for his assistance in preparing maps for this study. I am greatly indebted to my father (*baapa*) and mother (*umma*), who had strongly believed in the power of modern education, whose encouraging gestures prompted me to pursue my studies but really I am not in a position to pay back with any means of rewards except in the form of this book. They instilled in me the spirit of getting engaged with knowledge and also equipped me to entertain any differences, may be of caste, class, religion, ideology or otherwise gender while interacting with others. I wish my *bapa* alive today, so that he would have been the most delighted person to see this book. He was extremely fond of historical narratives in the frame work of his locality, flavoured with a bent towards the subjugated class.I am also bereaved in the immature demise of A. M. Ali, my father in law, who had loved to see the book come to light. My life partner Saleena A.K., along with our children, Janafroz Mirza and Gazanfar Mihan, have been anxious to see the earliest publication of the thesis in the present form and I am quite sure that any formal words of appreciations to them may not be appropriate for their warmth and support, who fondly kept me free from their routine engagements. Last but not least, I am grateful to Amit Garg of Gyan Books, New Delhi, for taking pains in bringing out this volume without delay. I honestly wish this book may generate debates regarding historiography of eighteenth century Kerala, and request the readers to critically engage with the same.

M. P. Mujeebu Rehiman

Abbreviations

EEIC	English East India Company
IESHR	Indian Economic and Social History Review
KSA	Kerala State Archives
ME	Malayalam Era
MSA	Maharashtra State Archives
RDD	Revenue Department Diaries
RJC	Report of a Joint Commission
SPDD	Secret and Political Department Diary
TC	Tellicherry Consultations
TD	Tellicherry Diary

List of Maps

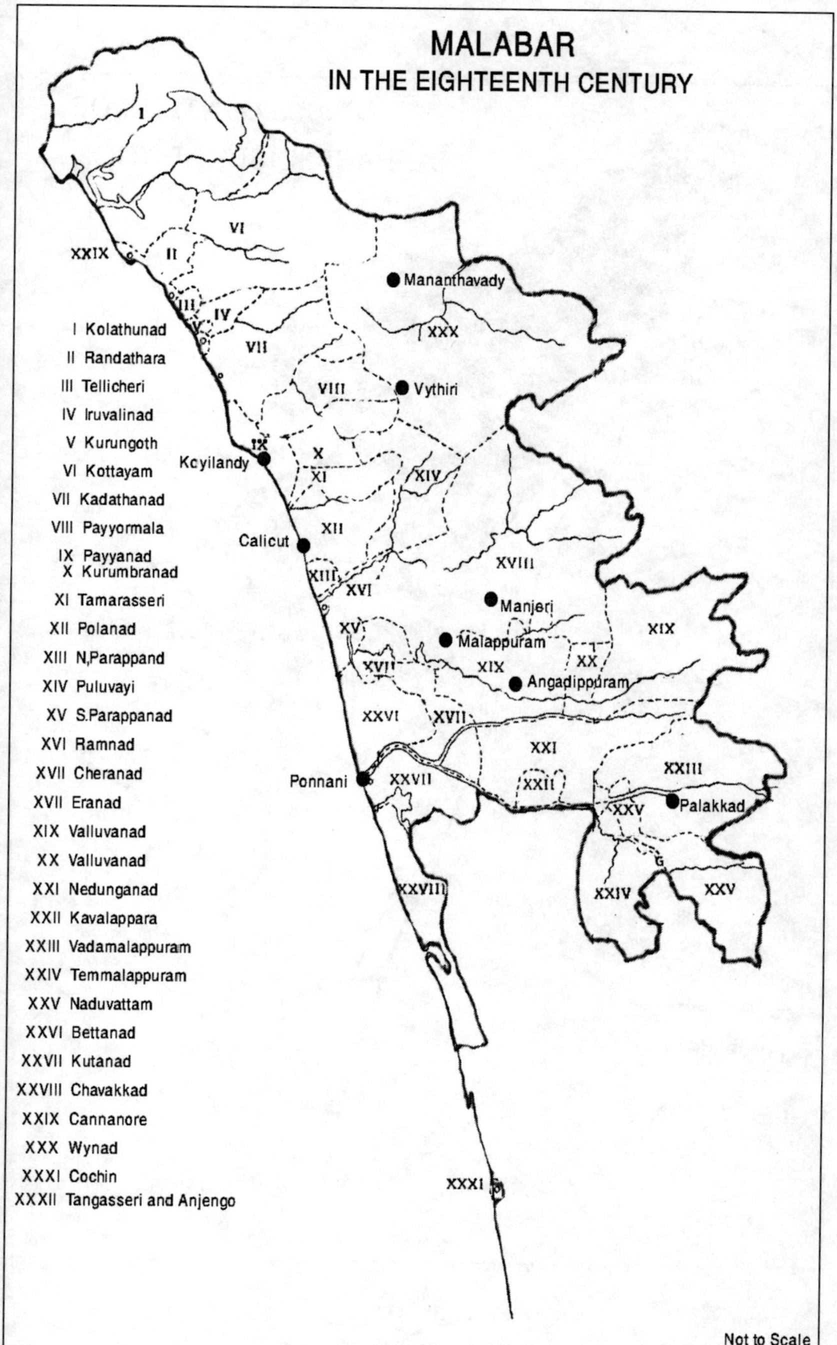
MALABAR
IN THE EIGHTEENTH CENTURY
I Kolathunad
II Randathara
III Tellicheri
IV Iruvalinad
V Kurungoth
VI Kottayam
VII Kadathanad
VIII Payyormala
IX Payyanad
X Kurumbranad
XI Tamarasseri
XII Polanad
XIII N,Parappand
XIV Puluvayi
XV S.Parappanad
XVI Ramnad
XVII Cheranad
XVII Eranad
XIX Valluvanad
XX Valluvanad
XXI Nedunganad
XXII Kavalappara
XXIII Vadamalappuram
XXIV Temmalappuram
XXV Naduvattam
XXVI Bettanad
XXVII Kutanad
XXVIII Chavakkad
XXIX Cannanore
XXX Wynad
XXXI Cochin
XXXII Tangasseri and Anjengo
Mananthavady
Vythiri
Koyilandy
Calicut
Manjeri
Malappuram
Angadippuram
Ponnani
Palakkad
Not to Scale

Map : I

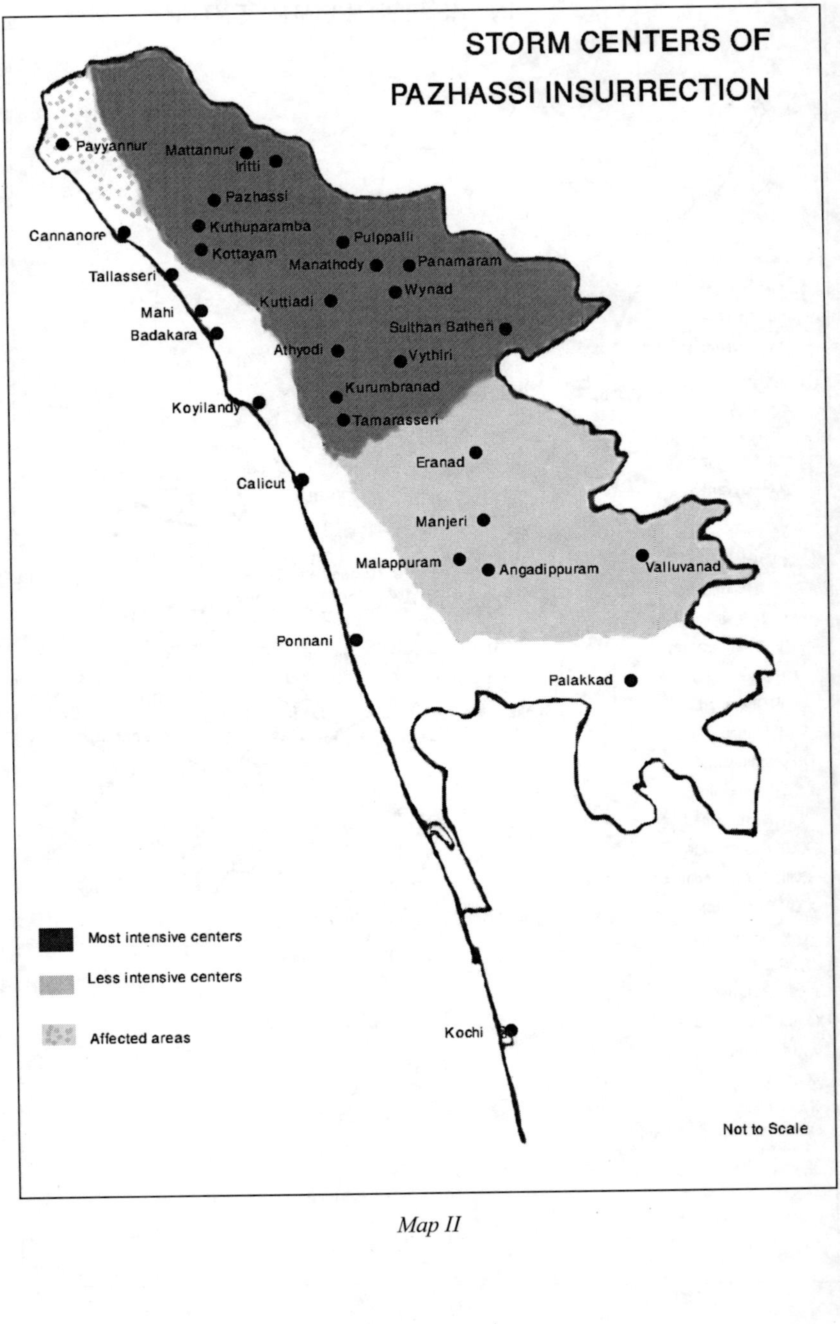
STORM CENTERS OF
PAZHASSI INSURRECTION
Payyannur
Mattannur
Iritti
Pazhassi
Kuthuparamba
Cannanore
Pulppalli
Kottayam
Manathody
Panamaram
Tallasseri
Wynad
Kuttiadi
Mahi
Sulthan Batheri
Badakara
Athyodi
Vythiri
Kurumbranad
Koyilandy
Tamarasseri
Eranad
Calicut
Manjeri
Malappuram
Angadippuram
Valluvanad
Ponnani
Palakkad
Most intensive centers
Less intensive centers
Affected areas
Kochi
Not to Scale

Map II

Introduction

Generally speaking, the eighteenth century in history has been perceived as a period of transition across the globe, due to the manifestations of significant land marks of the emerging new world such as enlightenment, emergence of nation states, formation of industrial capitalism, apart from the ideological baggage of modernity. Its impact upon the socio- economic and cultural domains of the traditional social life was quite sporadic. Though there snowballed significant changes in economy and society by sixteenth century onwards, all of which were loomed large by the second half of the eighteenth century. Geographical discoveries, formation of merchant capital, and scientific revolution etc. were some of the major factors which triggered unprecedented impact on the whole society, prior to the historical processes we discussed previously.

Coming to India of that century, characterised politically by the decline of the ever imperious Mughal state, was leading to the emergence of regional powers subsequently culminating in the colonization of the country. Taking economy for an analysis may lead us to the conclusion that the vicissitudes in the economic scenario too were grave in the sense that there were some major shifts with regard to the domains of agriculture, trade and indigenous industry. Agriculture in eighteenth century India underwent certain drastic changes due to the fluctuations in the world markets, though the reclamation of more (waste) lands, hill tracts, forests etc. could generate high yield of products to satisfy the new global demands. In fact, India was an economy which contributed its share not less than 24 percent in the world market in pre-British times, however later which was narrowed down by around 4 percent . Dislocations in the trading centres and fluctuations in the demands for commodities in the changing socio-economic scenario also made the process complete.

Malabar, in the south-western region of India, was a region very sensitive to all such changes and was subjected to sweeping changes in the society, especially in forces and relations of production. The present book is the revised version of my doctoral research submitted in 2009 to the Department of History, University of Calicut entitled, “Formation of society and Economy in Malabar, 1750-1810" successfully completed under the supervision of Prof. K.N. Ganesh. Here an attempt has been made to explore various aspects of the process of transition of economy and society of eighteenth century and early nineteenth century Malabar. The major objective of this study is to locate the process of change, especially in the ownership right in land in the backdrop of colonial reforms in Malabar. The term Malabar in historical discourses is understood in three different ways. The ancient and medieval chroniclers and foreign travellers used to refer to Malabar as the whole land which is presently known as Kerala. However, for a host of writers, Malabar represents the whole western coast ranging from Gujarat to Cape Comorin as Malabar Coast. Various categorisations apart, it is the third category, that is, the geographical area created by the British as Malabar district, stretching from South Canara to Kochi, where this study has been focused on.

A word about the time span of the study may be worthy: that the study attempts to cover transition in three different phases of the history of Malabar. The first phase, period between 1750 and 1766, represents the traditional or pre - Mysorean social order that prevailed in Malabar. In the second phase, that is from 1766, there heralded a new state and socio-economic fabric under the Mysorean rulers Hydar Ali and his son Tipu Sultan up to 1792, when the British defeated Tipu in third Mysore war. The third phase covers a period from 1792 to 1810, which marks the foundation of the colonial supremacy in Malabar. It was during this time that the British introduced certain colonial regulations in property rights in land and its relation in order to collect revenue and sustain their rule over the province. Indeed, the traditional rights in land and its relations in Malabar were subjected to change according to the western notions of private property. These developments invariably made the erstwhile janmis as the absolute owner of the land and the tenants had to experience a life of extreme servitude and exploitation under the colonial political dispensation. And more importantly, it was a period when the anti-British struggles were undertaken by the indigenous people which endured for several years. Though the resistance from Pazhassi Raja against the British was come to an end by his death in 1805, the Company had to wait a little more (at least up to 1810) to normalise and stabilise its administration, though the fierce resistance came from the indigenous people such as Kurichyas, Kurumbas and Mappilas in the near future itself.

Historiography

A substantial volume of works have been come about seeking to examine the transitional phase of the society in various parts of India, though such attempts are comparatively scanty with regard to the history of 18th century Kerala. Out of those available limited works, one can make a categorisation in the following way: that, the first covers the history of trade; the second focuses on the political aspect and; the third surveys both trade and politics during the period. Ashin Das Gupta's *Malabar in Asian Trade 1740-1800* (1967), a pioneering work of international repute, covers the history of 18th century trade in Kerala, though he uses the term 'Malabar' for the entire Kerala region. He has diligently reconstructed the nuances of the eighteenth century trade like trading communities, trading centres, (which were an untapped area till that time) with the support of the Dutch and the British sources. Yet, being a general study on Kerala as a whole, the work couldn't focus its analysis on the province of Malabar. Interestingly, it could be seen that it was precisely under the influence of the colonial writers/sources that Prof. Gupta postulated that the major causative factor responsible for the decline of trade in eighteenth century Malabar was by and large Tipu Sultan's invasion.

T. K. Ravindran's monograph, *Malabar under Bombay Presidency* (1969), is one of the earlier works related to the British occupation of Malabar. The work thoroughly examines the initial judicial reforms introduced by British in Malabar, when the region was under the control of Bombay presidency, before it was transferred to Madras presidency in 1800. The author actually takes ten years (from 1792-1802) as the period of study which unravels the important changes that occurred due to the introduction of colonial legality in this land. This small work consisting of a single chapter, (with introduction and conclusion) however, doesn't pay attention to social or economic impact of British administration.

As a general survey of trade in the western coast, for students of Malabar history, Pamela Nightingale's *Trade and Empire in Western India, 1784 - 1806* (1970) is a treasure of information with regard to the spice trade/ pepper politics during the early phase of colonial administration throughout the coast. In such a considerably large volume, merely two chapters are dedicated to Malabar, in which the author has highlighted the diverse issues, such as struggles between the French and the British for pepper, political structure of the coast, activities and the private business entrepreneurship of Company's own people like Murdoch Brown etc. However, the highly investigated two chapters are sufficiently informative as far as the students of this field are concerned.

Kerala under Haidar Ali and Tipu Sultan (1973) by Prof. C.K. Kareem can be considered to be the pioneering study on the history of Mysorean presence in Malabar. Such a vast work organized into twenty one chapters presents every aspect of the history of Mysorean period in a simple and lucid language. It was in a way the first attempt from the part of a historian to look at Mysorean period with a sympathetic attitude, in a time when even the so called nationalist writers had been succumbed to characterise Tipu Sultan as a 'fanatic'. No wonder this style of writing history was bequeathed by his supervising teacher the great Prof. Mohibul Hasan, who had authored a monograph on Tipu Sultan as early as 1951. However, the author's enthusiasm to highlight the policies of Mysorean rulers might be assumed in terms of his subjectivity putting aside the scientific methodology of historical research. In fact, the author places each and every argument with the corroborative evidences. Even though the work covers a wider area, the author has not touched many crucial problems, say for instance, the nature of revenue settlement introduced by Tipu Sultan in Malabar.

Prof. N. Rajendran's *Establishment of British Power in Malabar 1664 to 1799* (1979), is a general description of the initial phase of establishment of British power in the coast of Malabar. The book is based upon a strong archival support, which is highly helpful for researchers. *History of Tellicherry Factory* (1985) authored by K.K.N. Kurup is an exclusive study of establishment of the British power in Malabar that highlights the activities of the factory from its establishment to the year 1794. Though Prof. Kurup has done a commendable job by reconstructing the first phase of colonial enterprises in Malabar, what it handicaps is the missing of an indepth analysis of the impact of the British imperialism in Malabar. In continuation to this work, he has published two Malayalam works, namely, *Pazhassi Samarangal* (1980) and *Pazhassi Samara Rekhakal* (2004), which analyse the nature and course of the indigenous people's resistance to the exploitative British state.

Comparatively a recent work on this area is that of a young German scholar Margaret Frenz, entitled, *From Contact to Conquest: Transition to British Rule in Malabar 1790-1805* (2003). The work is categorized into six sections covering an extensive period from pre-colonial social order to the transformative phase of colonial administration in Malabar. In spite of the fact that the book covers the history of a short period between 1790 and 1805, the author has brilliantly portrayed the issues like the conflicts between the Portuguese, the Dutch, the French and the British and the invasion of Mysore rulers on Malabar. The author enthusiastically introduces the 'little Kingdom' model of Nicholas B. Dirks in order to understand the history of Malabar. While Dirks applied this mode of 'little Kingdom' and 'great Kingdom' to analyse the pyramidal nature of the pre-colonial South Indian state, the same model is adopted by Frenz proves to be unfit in the case of Malabar. Another model she discusses is 'contact zone', which again fails to get currency in the discourse on the eighteenth century Malabar.

One of the significant works that deals with the society and economy of eighteenth century Malabar is the doctoral thesis of Bonaventure Swai, titled 'Trade and Politics in eighteenth century Malabar', submitted to the University of Tanzania, Dare-es-Salam (1979). The work attempts to unravel the intricacies of the eighteenth century political structure as well as the colonial intervention in spices trade. In one chapter, Swai examines the roots of British merchant capital in the hinterland of Malabar which may be the first attempt of its kind. But, like many other foreign authors, Swai fails to analyse the complexities of the deeper socio-economic factors in the region. Nevertheless, this study has been greatly benefited by sources of information in many stages of this research. His research papers such as 'Notes on Colonial state with special reference to Malabar in eighteenth and 19th Centuries', (*Social Scientist*, Vol. 6, July 1978), and 'From Kolathunad to Chirakkal: British Merchant Capital and the Hinterland of Tellicherry, 1694- 1766', (*Studies in History,* Vol. 1, No.1, Jan-Jun 1985) also have equal importance.

Sources and Methodology

The major share of the source materials of this work constitute the published and unpublished colonial records collected from various archives across India. The major chunk of primary sources consists of Diaries such as Secret and Political Department Diaries (from 1767 to 1810), Revenue Department Diaries (from 1779 to 1801), *A collection of Treaties Engagements and Sanads Relating to India and Neighbouring countries* etc. are collected from Maharastra State Archives and are of highly historical value. Secret correspondences as well as secret letters of Tipu Sultan, collected from Bombay University Library, have immensely helped this study. Tellicherry consultations (from 1725 to 1750), Letters from Tellicherry (from 1721 to 1751), Letters to Tellicherry (from 1726 to 1750) etc. collected from Kerala Studies Centre Kerala University Library, Trivandrum are also of great significance. Report of a Joint Commission (1792-93), Jonathan Duncan's Report (1794), Minutes of the Board of Revenue (1818), John Shore's Minutes on the Joint Commissioners Report (all from Regional Archives, Kozhikkode) etc. have highly supportive of this study. Apart from these studies, some published Manuals, Treaties and gazetteers also are made use of.

Apart from this, the work has depended upon a few indigenous sources like *grandhavari*s namely, *Vanjeri Grandhavari, Kutali Grandhavari* and *Kavalappara Papers*. Besides, two other valuable sources of the period, but rarely tapped, *Thalasseri Rekhakal* and *Vellayude Charithram,* a contemporary chronicle by a brahmin named Vella have also been made use of. *Vellayude Charithram* nullifies almost all existing narratives of colonilists or of the so called 'nationalist' writers with regard to the Mysore administrator Hydar Ali, by stating that the prime motive of his invasion of Malabar was economic rather than religious. A large corpus of secondary sources such as books, articles and journals are also made use of by the present work.

The present study mainly follows the perspective of historical materialism, with which a close analysis of the transformation of the society, economy and political structure is intended. The author of this book firmly believes that no other frame work is invented so far to strictly locate the changes occurred in the past. The work also follows the standard method of historical research, that collection of archival sources from repositories, analysis of the collected data and dissemination of those data in the form of the report and presently as this book.

Organization

The book is organized into five chapters apart from an introduction and conclusion. The first chapter, namely, 'Society, Economy and State in Pre-Modern Kerala: Some Observations' is a back ground chapter which sketches the characteristics of pre-colonial society, economy and political structure of Kerala in general. The chapter offers an overall picture of the pre-colonial social structure, otherwise known as *janmam-kaanam-maryadai* or feudalism. It looks in to various forms of rights over land such as *janmam* and *kaanam* and also the development of forms of land holdings called *kuzhikkaanam* and *kuttikkaanam*. Appropriation of surplus produce by the elite class, its forms etc. are thoroughly discussed. Pattern of settlement, redistribution and consumption, trade, power structure and its relations are other areas of discussion.

The second chapter, 'Battle for Pepper State: Mysore State's Intervention and Transformation of Society,' definitely is a reconsideration of the Mysorean era (from 1766 to 1792) of Malabar. In the first part, an attempt has been made to critically re-appraise historiographical representation of Mysore period in Kerala history and locates the way in which the period was represented by the imperialist as well as nationalist historians. The core theme of this chapter is the 'pepper politics' of the eighteenth century

Malabar and explores how did the Mysoreans take part in the struggle for monopoly over the spice trade. There are also references to the response of the Mappila merchants and the Company officials towards the Mysore policy of monopoly and establishment of Tipu Sultan's attempt to establish a capital city for his Malabar territory.

The third chapter, 'The British Power in Malabar: Transition to a colonial Structure', begins with a question whether the company had really conquered Malabar by the year 1792. It is true that the company officials at Tellicherry and authorities in Bombay were not confident enough to pursue their colonialist ambitions. However, the company could advance a lot by entering into treaties with the local rulers of Malabar. The chapter gives a description of the Company's motives to attain pepper monopoly and its initial reforms in judiciary. There is also reference to the relinquishment of the trade monopoly and the private interests of the Company's servants like Murdock Brown in Malabar. This chapter also highlights the issues within the company like dismissal of the second Malabar Commission, appointment and dismissal of collectors and early resistance against the British revenue reforms.

The fourth chapter, 'Land Rights and Relations in Malabar: Problematizing British Perceptions,' the essentialist discussion in this book analyses the British projects of introducing new land ownership right and land tenure reforms in Malabar. In the first part it seeks to understand the theoretical moorings of the British to think about the introduction of private ownership in land. Now we realize that the philosophical base of the western thinkers such as Physiocrats as well as John Locke, Mill, and Riccardo etc. had greatly influenced the British administrators. An enquiry about the process of introduction of various settlements like *zamindari*, *mahalwari*, and *ryotwari* in various parts of India and logic for selecting each in particular areas is also attempted. The colonialist perception of land ownership in Malabar has gained a space in the chapter. Apart from that, in order to get an idea of the traditional land ownership right in Kerala, two typical *attipettola karanams* have also been included.

The last chapter, 'Anti-colonial Resistance and Consolidation of British Power,' examines the nature and character of protests initiated by the indigenous people, undertaken especially by the local chiefs such as Kerala Varma Pazhassi Raja and the great warrior Mappila chiefs of South Malabar, such as Athan Gurukkal, Unnimootha Mooppan, Chemban Pokker and Hydros Kutty. The chapter offers a reconsideration of the existing theories on the nature and character of those insurgencies and tries to propose a different observation on the same.

Chapter I

Society, Economy and State in Pre-modern Kerala: Some Observations

What sort of a society did take shape historically in the southwestern coast of India, in pre-modern times? What was the nature of economy that flourished in the region and by which means was it transformed during various phases of time? What was the nature of the political system or state functioning in this land during the period under discussion? The present chapter is an attempt to find out answers to these questions and it further explores various aspects of society, economy and state that existed in pre-colonial Kerala.

Malabar in the pre-colonial times cannot be considered as a separate entity as it obviously shares many common features with other parts of Kerala. Therefore, the account presented here does not claim to be an exclusive elaboration of the features of Malabar district under the British; rather, it necessarily transcends the geographical boundaries[1] and offers a larger frame, Kerala as a whole. Nevertheless, it elucidates the nature of the process and relations of production, the intricacies of the nature of ownership/proprietorship of the land along with the characteristics of redistribution, and role of existing power centres.

Evolution of the Agrarian Society

The society under review, which has often been described as medieval or pre-colonial, is characterised by *jati-janmi-Naduvazhi* system or *janmam-kaanam maryadai*. The role of temple in the formation of socio-economic as well as cultural fabric of the medieval society has been elaborated extensively.[2] The territorial units called *swarupams,* are said to be the products of the existing socio-economic condition. The predominant role of the *brahmins* and their ideology continued to be unchanged and unchallenged even during the time of *swarupams.* As the agrarian settlements were considered to be the base for the establishment of the *swarupams*[3], the study of the consolidation of agrarian society may shed much light on the pre-modern economy and society.

The dominant theory on the evolution of an agrarian system in Kerala goes back to the establishment of the Brahmin settlements during the early medieval times.[4] An agrarian economy had developed under the temple - based brahmin oligarchy in early medieval times,[5] and the agrarian society of Kerala was consolidated by the beginning of the sixteenth century.[6] In such a social setting, there were essentially three broad types of rights on land in Kerala, namely, *Cherikkal* (royal land), *devaswam* (temple property), and the *brahmaswam* (the brahmin property)[7]. Some temple lands were also called as *Cherikkal* as in the case of Thiruvananthapuram temple and Peruvanam temple.[8] Gradually, a hierarchy of land rights was developed, in the form of owners, *Kudiyar* (tenants), and *adiyar* (agrestic bondmen). This kind of a relation was strengthened by caste hierarchy and very influential customs and practices or *maryadai,* which were always designed to keep the *brahmins* and the *Naduvazhis* in the highest positions.[9]

It was the appropriation of surplus land and labour that resulted in the consolidation of a system of land ownership, giving rise to rights such as *brahmaswam, devaswam* and *cherikkal. Brahmaswam* and *devaswam* were permanent tenures as their lands were transferred as *nirattipper* with libation of water. The grants always contained the formulaic expression *aachandra tarame santati pravesame*, [up until the moon and stars exist and prevail through the generations] indicating the permanency of the tenure. The term *swam* (*thommu*) also indicates a form of ownership different from other forms of rights over lands (*avakasom*). The rights over such lands were said to be absolute, which couldn't be violated by existing political forms. Lands directly held by the rulers were called *cherikkal, pandaravaga* or *kandulavu.* They were also organised along similar lines, although the regulations were not as rigid as the case of temples.[10] Such lands provided for the daily expenses of the ruling family in grain, condiments and money and large number of other payments were also acknowledged.

The problem of ownership of land is found to be very complex and perception of which has appeared to be rather misleading. The discussion on the question of the nature of right over land in Kerala has helped the formulation of theories that have been dominant. For instance, Prof. Elamkulam has emphasised the existence of private ownership in land which according to him, began in Kerala long before the Sangam age. The landlords and local chieftains were the *pulayas*, *idayas*, *villavas* and other agriculturists. Ownership was passed to the present class of landholders from them, states Elamkulam, during the period from the ninth to thirteenth centuries.[11] Significantly enough, he traces the origin of the *janmi* system in the medieval Kerala society back to ninth century C. E.

However, M. G. S. Narayanan maintains that, in theory, the entire land seems to have belonged to the Chera king. The governors were his feudatories and as such they enjoyed the lands in their districts in turn for payment of tribute. Prof. Narayanan has emphasized the presence of three kinds of tenure in land, such as *janmam, kaanam*, and *kutimai*, which may be translated as the rights of proprietorship, tenancy and occupancy respectively.[12] According to Kesavan Veluthat, the revenue was fixed by the king, where the interests of the temples were also taken into account. He corroborates this argument by using the Trikkaditanam inscription, which refers to *attaikkol,* the annual revenue.[13] The revenue system that has been highighted here makes us to conclude that there had existed a form of land ownership during the Chera period.

Another view that gained wider acceptance with regard to the period from the sixteenth to the eighteenth century is that the consolidation of an agrarian society during the period was more or less complete. The mechanism by which a technically backward agricultural economy like Kerala sustained the diverse lords and chiefs along with the religious institutions has to be sought in the form of ownership and control of land exercised by the dominant classes. In this context, the term 'land owner' is used to signify hereditary titular rights over land as applied to *janmam* and *swam.* This ownership involves birthright or customary right.[14]

The term *janmi,* equivalent to the landlord, is associated with *janmam* means hereditary right or birth right. The term *janmam* literally means birth i.e., the right that the landlord comes to occupy descent from his predecessor who held the land. Hence, *janmi*'s ownership over the land does not imply any services or dues that he has to pay to an overlord for maintaining his right. The *janmi* loses this right only if he transfers or sells his land and the new owner has to pay rent or dues because he does not come to own the land as a birthright.[15] This birth right was legitimised by the brahmins with their legal and genealogical texts.[16]

According to one of the predominant conceptualisations, the term *janmam* originally implies the life-time tenure and which was applied to the position of temple *uralar*. But they were re-appointed repeatedly as trustees of the temple. Though the appointment meant for a stipulated period, in effect, it was possible that a person could be a trustee for life time (*jivitam*).

However, the rights over property became permanent and perpetual since there could be no practical difference between perceptual ownership rights and life time rights that were hereditary. This development took place during the long war (between the Cheras and Cholas) in the eleventh century.[17]

From the sixteenth century onwards, there were significant developments in the form of ownership of land, and in its relations and pattern of agriculture. Temples became largest *janmi*s in the beginning of the century.[18] The temples and *brahmins* leased out lands to cultivators in order to provide for services in the temple or rent to the land owner.[19] The right of *janmi* over the land was defined by *kizhiyakkam* or tradition and the obligations of tenants were determined by *maryadai* or custom.[20] The underlining fact is that, either *kizhiyakkam* or *maryadai* had no uniform pattern all over Kerala and never had any sort of rigid structures like *kacchams* that prevailed in early medieval Kerala, say for instance, Muzhikkulam *Kaccham*[21].

What the term 'control' actually designates is that the actual control over the process of production and distribution. In such a context, several landholders who may even not own the land would be actual controllers of land. In fact, the lands owned by large temples and individual owners were held by tenants under various forms of lease:[22] where simple leases were the most widespread form of land holding. Most of the tenant cultivators (*Kudiyans*) were simple lease holders. Ordinary lease holders (*paattam*) and the temple or royal servants converted the rent to be paid to the land owner in the form of a service. The amount paid as *paattam* apparently didn't undergo radical change for long periods, and the lands remained with the same men even if the rights on land was changed hands from one landlord to another.[23]

Remarkable variations occurred in a period between seventeenth and eighteenth centuries in the nature of lease holdings, involving cultivating rights for an extended period, called *uzhavupaattam* or *marayapaattam*. Probably the most important change was the growth of the lease-cum-mortgage tenures, which differentiated from *verumpaattam* in a marked way during this period.[24] Mortgage tenures called *kaanam* or *otti* had come into existence in early medieval times itself. Such tenure was based upon paying a particular amount of money as security for obtaining land or any other service for a stipulated period of time.[25] However, this practice was apparently concentrated in south Tiruvitamkur and very few transactions are found in other parts of Kerala.

By the sixteenth century, transactions in land, either by paying security (*artham*) in kind or in cash were on the increase. Land mortgages were initially for a period from three to twelve years and redeemable by the landlord. Later, the stipulated period of mortgage began to increase and during the eighteenth century, lands were being held under mortgage for 36 and 48 years and sometimes even more. The security given for the lands amounted to three fourths of the value of the land but was never equal to its value.[26] Obviously, the land was not at all a commodity to be sold at any cost. The interest on the security was deducted from the rent and realised from the land and the remainder was paid as *micchavaram*. Sometimes an additional amount was supposed to be paid by the leaseholder for the renewal of a mortgage. The extent of land mortgaged became largely by eighteenth century and the security was paid mostly in cash and involved a very large amount. Several other forms of pledging of lands like *panayam* and *padukalam* were developed in other parts of Kerala (especially in Kochi) which proves a noticeable presence of cash payments. A permanent land holding like *chora otti* was in practice in eighteenth century chiefly in Southern Tiruvitamkur.

Along with the mortgage tenure, another form of holding called *Kuzhikkaanam* was developed by sixteenth century, which became a popular form of holding by eighteenth century. *Kuzhikkaanam* was found normally associated with lease-cum-mortgage holdings. *Kuzhikkaanam,* which is referred to the modified, often reduced the share of produce levied on new trees grown in gardens on new plot brought under cultivation.[27] It is a particular kind of assessment extended to lands newly brought under cultivation or trees newly planted, where a reduction was allowed for the initial period when the land was cultivated or trees were growing. The *Kuzhikkaanam* tenure is a pointer to the emerging trend towards the extension of agriculture in the form of *parambu* or elevated land associated with cash crop farming. *Parambu* land (garden land-growing fruit trees and others) and arable lands were mortgaged as *kuttikkooru* and *kuzhikkooru* which were allotments corresponding to *Kuzhikkaanam*[28].

The *Grandhavaris* that belong to a period from sixteenth to eighteenth centuries, especially the *Vanjeri Grandhavari* contains several deed documents highlighting the importance of the emerging *parambu* land and its sources. Extension of a *parambu – purayitam* (household) economy must be perceived against the backdrop of the growing connectedness with the exterior world. Each *parambu* household was self-sufficient with its crops, which actually may have given them an independent identity, from the clutches of the feudal lords. *Adiyars* or agrestic slaves were not attached to *parambu* lands and spread of *Parambu* gradually facilitated the settlement of various groups of artisans. Multiplication of *parambu - purayitam* settlements caused the increase of the collectivity of workers and labourers not fully servile to the land holders.[29] Several occupations became hereditary as a result of growing needs of the *parambu* economy; the best example for which is that of *avakasom* on coconut tree climbing as found mentioned in *Vanjeri Grandhavari*.[30] Hereditary guilds extended their labour power to the land owners as part of the caste obligations and compulsory duties (*Katamai*). But the *kaanakkaars* and *kutiyars* were not the beneficiaries of this labour because these labourers had no obligation to them.[31]

By eighteenth century, almost all services had become hereditary, and *virutti* holdings had acquired a permanent character. *Utamai*, the allotment of share of produce from land or in cash to the royal and temple servants was recognized by eighteenth century. Both the overseers and the overlords siphoned off the surplus produce from the producing folk in various ways. Several forms of dues were in vogue, extracted either by the temple custodians or by the royal coffers. *Kavalpalam* or *Rakshabhogam* was paid to the temple servants (*Changatam*) who were in charge of the protection of land. The newly introduced customary obligations in the form of a number of dues to the rulers were collected either in cash or in kind. The ruler of Venad, for example collected *Rajakaram* during early eighteenth century as an extraordinary cess for maintaining cavalry (*Kutirappanthi*)[32]. The ruler of Kolathunad at the same time collected a cess during the invasion of Bednore.[33] Later on we will have a detailed discussion on various types of dues.

The question regarding existence of land revenue in medieval Kerala remains more or less one of the perplexed problems of economy. Some historians love to believe that land revenue was first introduced in Kerala in the eighteenth century. This perception, according to Elamkulam, is based upon the conditions after the advent of the Portuguese. For him, the land revenue was extant in Kerala till the thirteenth century. By then most of the landed property was confiscated, under *devaswam, brahamaswam* or *Viruthi* rights, which were absolutely exempted from the taxation. Such a view in fact has contributed much in strengthening the belief that revenue system was absent in Kerala from thirteenth to eighteenth centuries.[34] Observation of the medieval chronicler Sheikh Zainuddin actually disapproves the existence of a revenue system in contemporary Kerala. He underscores that there was no form of land tax or revenue extraction in fifteenth or sixteenth century in Kerala, though there were such dues imposed upon traders.[35] However, the output of recent research throws much light on the problem.

Though the references to the existence of a systematic collection of land tax is scarce, we are having ample corroborative evidence to establish the existence of various methods of extraction of surplus produce in pre-modern Kerala. The term *paattam* is often signified as a share of the produce to the overlord, though it is a term for tenure. The share of the produce to be paid by the *paattam* holders was normally a fixed amount.[36] The general pattern was to fix the amount on the basis of the sowing capacity of the land.[37] *Paattam* as a mode of payment is of having similarity to *varam*, usually understood as the overlord's share of the produce. The terms such as *Melvaaram, Melpaathi, Melodi,* etc. signify the collection of a fraction of the produce from different types of land, usually by the rulers, the temples, or chieftains. This differentiation was presumably as *Melvaaram* and *kozhuvaaram* the latter, the share going to the immediate landlord.[38] Some scholars have endeavoured to unravel the intricacies related to the share of the produce and concluded that the dues such as *Melvaaram and Melpaathi* were considered as the owner's share of produce, but were generally enjoyed by the ruling family or the temples which gave the dues the nature of 'rent-tax'.[39] An important feature of this realization of dues like *Melvaaram* is that when it was realised by the temples or rulers, the landholders and cultivators were considered as subjects to the overlords in a customary sense.

Melvaaram and *paattam,* the two forms of rent were generally collected twice a year during the months of *Kanni* and *Kumbham,* i.e., September – October and December – January respectively, in the case of double crop lands, and once, in the case of single crop lands. In the case of *Melvaaram*, the realisation differed from half the total yield to one - fifth or one - sixth of the total yield. Lands yielding *Melpaathi* or *Melvaaram* might have been held on a share-cropping basis. Collection of a fixed amount per crop was more common than the collection of a fraction of the produce.

Default in paying rent was considered to be a serious crime in those days. In such cases, where the cultivators fail to pay the rent arrears the outstanding amount would be collected with the next instalment. Though the instances of imposing double amount on the defaulters and eviction of a regular defaulter was common in the early medieval period, such instances were not reported later on. However, the records from Nanchinad in southern Travancore speak of other forms of coercion as well. One of which was the treatment of arrears as *padukaalam* by which the royal representatives were free to treat the tenants as debtors, inflicting punishment on them including seizure of lands for non-payment of the arrears, along with its interest. Another was the prevention of cultivation in the lands held by defaulters until the rent in arrears were paid. Sometimes a whole village or *desam* would be so prevented from carrying out their agricultural activities known as *desattadai*, or *desamudakkam*. There were additional cesses like *Kachchayavinai* (payment of cloth), *pativukaanikkai* (fee paid by the cultivator, for preparing the document showing his rights on land called *pativu)* etc.[40]

In those days, allotment of the share of produce to the overlord was not simple. Several landlords such as temples, *brahmins* etc. had received a fixed amount as the overlord's share from the same land. The landholder paying the overlords' share might have leased his lands, so that he himself was receiving rent from his tenants. Sometimes, the rent going to the king or the overlord was differentiated from the rent going to the landholder himself, whether they were individuals or bodies like temples, *mathas* (monastry) etc. Thus, the amount to the landholder (*kozhuvaaram,* as in the case of Nanchinadu) also has to be deducted from the total rent. On the basis of the available sources, it may be inferred that a lion's share of the total produce was appropriated by all the over lords altogether. In some cases, even the landholder's share was taken by overlords like temples. But the case of *thanathu* land was quite different, as the rent was collected exclusively by the actual overlord and no other overlord could extract any share from it. However, the form of rent that existed in the pre-colonial times was entirely different from the revenue regime that was introduced by Mysoreans and later taken over by the British.

Some extraordinary payments and surcharges in cash like *kottaippanam* and *Mattalpanam* were imposed up on the people of Nanchinadu, which were called by them as *Vaiyavari* or impossible dues. They had also to make payments for the stationing of army or other extraordinary expenses from time to time. The Padmanabhaswami temple, as well as the rulers of Venad, used to realise the same for time and again. They collected the dues like *Kappukattu Kettirai, Chittirai, Rakshabhogam, kandukalcha, taliappa-nam, piral kuttagai, Kuttadendam, Kottappanam* and *Viseshakanikkai* etc.[41]

There existed the due systems like *Anamurai, chengompu, podiyadi* and *Talaivilai* in the northern parts of Venad. *Talaivilai* and *Talaippanam* were presumably charged from the depressed communities. They were similar to *Innavari* or poll tax on communities like *Nadars* and *Irai Ilakkam* collected from *Shanar* and others. There were other occasional dues like *Purusantharam* paid by families which the head of the property was inherited by his heir, *Adiyarar*, paid for conferring titles, appointments to various posts and *kuttadendam* and *uthirappadu* both were fines for offences. There are also references to *kuppakkalcha* and *melkalcha,* which were among the customary payments.[42] Some other surcharges were generally termed as *adakkuvathu*, including *melalavu, kaikkuli* and *manuchaveetham* normally realised by the people mediating on transactions.

We have ample references to the dues going to the temples in the form of special dues like *Onam Chelavu, Karkataka Chelavu, Chenkompu, Aanamurai, Pulai irai, meni irai* etc. which were also collected by the rulers as mentioned above. When the Navayakkulam temple was transferred to Akkaiyur Devan, the dues collected by the ruler like *Chengompu, Talaivilai, Muppura munnali, Angam, Chungam, Taragu* etc. were also transferred along with temple.[43] The practice of maintaining a royal representative or *adhikari* and tax collector or *Turakkarai* was being continued. Besides, the references to accountants like *Karuvakara Kanakku* and *Pandara kanakku,* who were in charge of maintaining royal dues, suggest that there existed an institutionalized form of collection of revenue by the state of Venad. At the same time, the variation in taxation and some other specificities prompted some scholars to conclude that there couldn't have a centralised revenue department, whose success was presumably depended upon the ability of the accountants as well as the princes to exercise their authority. All these sufficiently validate the existence of a peculiar system of revenue in pre-modern Kerala, though not in a uniform and institutional form.

Pattern of Settlement

The nature of settlement pattern of pre-modern Kerala can be understood primarily from the names of *purayidams* or household sites occupied by the individuals. In fact, we do have very few evidence on occupational structure of the settlements. The *Tharisappalli* copper plates of 849 C.E. refers to the occupational families such as *Ilavas* (toddy tappers), *Vannar* (Washer man), *tacchar* (carpenters), and *Vaaniyars*, literally merchants, but oil mongers in the pre-modern context, who had been handed over to the donee along with the land. The same practice can be found repeated in the Vira Raghava copper plates of 1225 C.E., where the five artisanal workers, *ainkammaalar* were also handed over to the donees. Kollur Matham Plates of 1189 C.E. also suggests the presence of different occupational groups such as oil mongers, potters, and washermen in the settlement. The temple-oriented brahmin settlements had specialist functionaries such as drummers (*uvaccar*) and garland makers.[44] The basic occupational groups of such settlements consisted of agricultural labourers, ritual-cum medicine men, astrologers, washer men and so on. The coastal area was inhabited by the fisher folk.[45] The most common agrestic slaves were constituted by out castes such as the *cherumas, pulayas, kaanakkaars, parayas* etc. along with *malayas, kadars*, and *nayadis* who were major hill tribes.[46] By the extension of agriculture to the hill tracts, these tribes naturally played an important role in the agricultural production.

Redistribution and consumption Pattern

The gradual development of the production process naturally resulted in evolving a redistribution system. Concepts of 'reciprocity' and 'redistribution' can be applied to the pre-modern system of exchange in our society, though not in the very strict sense as formulated by Karl Polanyi.[47] It may be pointed out that the temples, which stood at the centre of redistribution of the rent collected, had played a major role. Besides, they also acted as major centres for transactions in cash or kind. Quite often, the huge amount was spent mainly for construction and beautification of temples, and the personal consumption of their overlords provided the major channels of redistribution of the income coming to the hands of the overlords.[48] There were instances of occasional/customary practices of giving away the gifts to the overlords by the tenants or cultivators as well as the endowments offered to the scholars or priests by the overlords or by the state itself.

Utilisation of rent actually was determined by institutions and individuals - a substantial part of rent was under the control of temples, royal households and institutions like *mathas*. There were some instances of utilisation of *nityanadai chelavu* in some temples and allotment of *Chandra chelavu* for various *koyikkals*. Apart from this, some allotments in cash or paddy were made for specific expenditure in temples such as maintaining lamps, providing garlands, paying wages of the temple servants etc. There were also some allotments for constructing or repairing the shrines. Construction and beautification of houses of the overlords was yet another way of consumption. But the other side of the picture was painfully bleak. The primary producers and artisans groups often failed to meet the both ends together, though they were actual producers both in agricultural and non-agricultural sectors. From the consumption pattern described above, one can infer that there existed entirely unequal distribution of wealth.

Trading World of Pre-Modern Kerala

We have a large corpus of inscriptions and literature that shed light upon the existence of an extensive trade network in Kerala from the very ancient times onwards. The general tendency of labelling pre-modern Kerala economy as a 'self-sufficient' or 'closed economy' is a reductionist way of looking at a vibrant economy and which may be proved to be misleading.

According to Raghva Varier, the pattern of production that developed in Kerala was production for use and production for the market/exchange which was the prime cause of the internal developments in the various sub-regions which led to the growth of trade and trading centres.[49] Kerala's trade was spread in three levels namely, local trade, long distance overland trade and long distance overseas trade[50].

The so-called subsistence-oriented economy had produced surplus in agriculture as well as in non-agricultural production used for procuring the items of need. Certain areas produced a surplus of some articles but lacked several other items which had to be acquired by exchanging of those surplus products. Medieval trade of Malabar was based on small scale farming and handicrafts production.[51] Village markets in regular intervals show institutional forms of this kind of exchange.[52] As found elsewhere in India, the periodical fairs, the *melas,* where only specialized traders met together to sell and replenish their stocks also was a characteristic feature of the local trade.[53] References to medieval texts such as *Unniyati Charitam, Unnunili Sandesam* and *Ananthapura Varnanam* etc. corroborate the presence of a strong and extensive market network in the hinterland. Presumably, barter was the most common form of exchange prior to the wide circulation of money and no considerable change found in this regard.

Interestingly, local trade continued its course without considerable changes for quite a long time. *Athanis* and *Angadis* are repositories of the existence of erstwhile peddling trade in Kerala. *Athanis* were the resting places of the head loads of the peddlers, who could usually put down their loads on the granite slabs fixed way side, and had the drinking water [*Thanneer*] offered by the prominent families in the locality as charity. Those pavilions for water distribution were known as *Thanneer Panthals.* Interestingly, the place names with suffixes or prefixes of *angadi*, such as Putiyangadi, Pazhayangaadi, Melangaadi, Thazhangaadi, Parappanangadi, Meenangadi, Tirurangaadi, Angaadippuram, and with *athani* such as Athaanikkal, Randatthani, Putthanattaani, and the place names such as 'Thanneer Panthals' etc. shed light to the existence of a wide local trade network, usually connecting the ports and hinterlands or the local *angaadis* with the *kadavus* [ferries].

Overland long distance trade was somewhat complex in its functioning and had spread out the whole of South India extending to Bengal in the East and Gujarat in the west. Merchants from the regions of Tamil Nadu, Karnataka, Konkan, Andhra Pradesh, Kalinga, Malwa, Bengal etc. appeared in the interior markets of pre-modern Kerala. The organisation of trading centres called *nagaram* were evolved in the trading emporiums such as Kollam (Quilon), Kodungallur, Thazhakkad, Bhaskarapuram and Pantalayani Kollam during the time of Perumals.[54] Epigraphical records from 9th to 12th century A. D. refer to the existence of some trading organisations like *anchuvannam, manigramam, nanadesikal, patinenbhumi, tisai ayirattu ainnuutuvar* and *valanciyar* etc. which were engaged in commercial activities cutting across the boundaries of the various political regions of South India.[55] Tamil *Brahmins* were one of the active trading groups who supplied the commodities like rice, cotton, silk, fabrics and chillies to Kerala and returned large quantity of spices, especially pepper.[56] Merchants from Kerala are noticed in this period in several inscriptions (13th - 14th centuries) of different parts of Chola Empire. There are frequent references in Chola inscriptions from Tanjore, Tiruchirappalli and South Arcot to *Kutira chettikal* (horse dealers), who seemed to have imported horses from Arabia.[57] Presumably they belonged to the northern parts of Kerala. Chettis, Vaniyar and Kalavaniyar were other groups who actively engaged in trade.

According to contemporary sources, throughout the medieval period, Malabar was having a vigorous merchant class. Groups of merchants had vied one another for commercial predominance. By the sixteenth century the Muslim aristocracy of commerce had retreated just before the coming of the Portuguese. The vacuum of which was filled by the *Konkani brahmin*'s arrival on the coast.[58] Along with the *Konkanis*, the Jews also left their age-long colony of Kodungallur (Cranganore) and they migrated to Kochi and Kozhikode.[59] The Muslim merchant groups like *Kunjalis* and *Karimis* had been engaged in the lucrative business of Malabar. The Christian families like *tharakans* also had played their role in the trade of Kerala. Apart from luxury articles and food grains, considerable amount of metals, medicinal herbs, silk and other fabrics etc. were brought to Kerala. Though details of these transactions are not known, apparently the products were from North.

Malabar had made an imprint on the map of international trade from the very ancient times on. This land was considered to be a place of halt for traders on their way between the West Asia and South East Asia.[60] Al Idirisi of 12th century was the first to call this land as 'Malibar', the land of pepper (*mall* = wealth) which had a great reputation for spices. Large amount of spices including pepper, ginger, cardamom, cinnamon and Malabathrum, spikenard etc. were exported from Malabar. The Arab traders must have been able to get the support of a locally sanctioned group that had access to the regions of pepper and also to the cultivators. 'Trade diasporas' of the Arab Muslims developed on the coast of Malabar, which were perhaps to render support to the Arab traders.[61] The main role of merchants in sea port towns was to act as intermediaries between the producing class and the consuming markets, widely scattered in space.[62]

Malabar had an interesting feature in the domain of overseas trade: the commodities imported from Indonesia and China was exported again without being consumed locally. Local consumption of imported goods was nominal. But, at the same time, the produce which came down from north was, to a large extent, absorbed upon the coast.[63] Trade through the Palakkad gap, at times responded to a demand from the interior. Japanese copper would occasionally be sold to 'the merchants from the hills'.[64]

Those engaged in trade varied greatly in wealth and social status. Merchants such as Ezechiel Rahabi, Haji Yusuf, Nelliappa Chetty, Padaram Chetti, Muccuttum Paquy etc. include in the list of the most affluent merchants of Malabar during the eighteenth century. Those merchants were privileged to operate their business network with a number of associates who normally spread along different ports. They were usually called by various names, such as 'correspondents', 'agents' or with a common name, brokers. The role of these agents was instrumental in procuring the local goods as well as in selling out the goods brought from outside. When the European traders, especially the Portuguese and the Dutch, endeavoured to engage in trade, the duties assigned to these correspondents were varied. First of all, the broker had to keep his foreign associates posted with local news and commercial intelligence. Secondly, he was obliged to assist their vessels when the correspondent's port in all possible ways. Thirdly, he was endorsed to procure local cargo when it was desired[65]. One thing is obvious that the nature of overseas trade and composition of the trading groups had undergone major changes with the advent of the Portuguese in Malabar. Introduction of pass system (*cartazes*) was a great challenge as far as the traditional merchants were concerned. The quest for revenue and the struggle against the Muslim commercial aristocracy were coalesced into an elaborate pass system.[66] The hostility of Portuguese towards Muslim traders had been occasionally regarded in religious terms and the fighting between the merchants became sustained and systematic. Incessant violence and hostility from the part of Europeans caused many traders, who were depending on coastal/overseas trade, to move inland and to invest in agriculture, especially, in cash crops.

Trading Centres: *Chantha, Angadi and Theruvu*

Different kinds of markets such as *anticchantha, aazhchachanta,* and *Nalangadi* were the common market places in pre-modern Kerala society. In addition to these occasional markets, there emerged *angadis/ bazars* [markets of permanent nature] for exchanging goods of daily life such as rice, edible roots, vegetables, fruits, salt, pepper, oil, textiles etc. Barter was the most common form of exchange and petty bargaining was the method of procurement.[67] All the goods were supposed to be brought to the market by head/shoulder load, pack animals and by waters. The markets in interior regions like Tirumaruthur, Tamarasseri, Angadippuram etc. are the evidences of the existence of an extensive trade networks and transport of commodities.

Artisan classes of pre-modern Kerala had their own peculiar sites of settlements called *theruvus*. Accordingly, there were *chaliya theruvus,* where the weavers settled and produced textile goods and *chakkara vanibha theruvu,* where the jaggery manufacturers settled and sold their products, and *kusava theruvu,* where potters exhibited their articles for sale. These streets attracted many people, and in the course of time, were transformed into markets.[68] Those markets had a wide range of goods from food stuffs to craft products.

It is reported that in the regular bazars, fairs were held on special occasions like Onam and Ramzan. It was supposed to be the duty of the chieftains to conduct such fairs aiming at encouraging the trade.[69] A small amount was levied on the articles sold. The fairs attracted traders from various parts of the region. It is believed that the local markets in Malabar were monopolised by the predominent merchant class of Mappilas. Those traders had enjoyed virtual monopoly to procure and sell the commodities such as pepper, cloth, rice and coir in all markets in the region.[70] Though the prime role of the Mappilas in these markets is undeniable, the role played by the Christian traders in the South and the Nair traders' interest in pepper in some areas etc. should not be underestimated.

The articles appeared in the rural fairs and markets included salt, spices and metal objects which were either produced in distant centres or made from raw materials which were not locally available. This type of exchange resulted in the rise of small fairs, markets and towns which were the mediating factors in the distribution of commodities. Place names such as Parappanangadi, Tirurangadi, Angadippuram, Pazhayangadi and Putiyangadi etc. appeared in the medieval period are sufficiently illustrative to conclude that there existed an exclusive network of permanent markets throughout Malabar.

On the basis of the features of the exchange, commodities and locality, Prof. Varier has categorized the trading centres in the following way as rural exchange nodes, periodic fairs where itinerant and specialised traders gathered together to sell and buy commodities, interior markets and small scale *bazars* which catered to the necessities of comparatively wider regions and the big emporia of foreign trade.[71] Likewise, according to some historians, the occasional gatherings like *mamankam* had played the role of a wider market.[72]

Kodungallur is considered to be one of the earliest emporia on the western coast. Though in ancient times Muchiri [Muziris] was mainly a reputed centre of luxury goods[73], in later times there was a marked shift in the products by medieval period. By 13th century, articles of trade in Kodungallur included not only imported luxury items like musk but also jaggery, salt, oil, grains, cloth etc., the necessary items for the daily life of the common people.[74] Places such as Kollam, Kochi, Kozhikode, Kannur and in later times Thalasseri became prominent emporia of foreign trade. The changes in demand of commodities as well as international or regional politics often influenced to vary the importance of trading centre from one to another. Interestingly, the foreign traders considered Malabar Coast as a single unit of trade rather than some specific centres. The earlier centres of trade had retained the features of medieval towns where a farming element was present. The absence of a clear-cut demarcation of rural and urban boundaries was shared by the centres like Kodungallur, Kollam and Panthalayani Kollam. The medieval trade in Malabar was subjected to a process of remarkable changes towards the end of eighteenth century. It is argued that the trade was also subjected to dislocation due to the Mysorean invasions.[75]

Role of Money in Exchanges

Increasing exchanges among the local and overseas traders necessitated the circulation of various types of coins on different occasions. Inscriptions and contemporaneous deeds have often referred to the names and values of certain coins. For instance, Vazhappally copper plate speaks of *tinarum* (dinara), which, to some writers, reached to Kerala along with the *Brahmins* who migrated from the North. Apart from *dinara, palam kaasu* and *kaasu* are occasionally found mentioned in Chera inscriptions. However, the most common regular medium of exchange appears to have been gold of prescribed weight and standard.[76] *Dinarum* in the early medieval times was a multi-purposed coin, that is a coin for giving away the *dana* and *dakshina* and to pay the rent, fines etc. Later it was considered and used to be a coin of common value.[77] More importantly, money in the earlier times was absolutely circulated through the hands of the rich and the big merchants only.

By the latter half of the 12th century, a group of new coins like *achu, kasu, panam, sakala* were found mentioned in the inscriptions. Period from thirteenth to fifteenth centuries witnessed considerable changes in the nature of coins and use of money. It was at this time that *panam* had gained a dual identity, that is, it was understood as a synonym for wealth/money, and as a name of a particular coin. The transformation of *panam* from its first form in gold to lower metals indicates the popularisation of the use of money.

As mentioned earlier, the changing economic and social condition from sixteenth to eighteenth centuries necessitated the wider use of money. Extension of economy highly depended upon cash crops and emergence of new land tennurial forms like *kaanam*, *otti, artham* and various forms of interest etc., suggest that there was considerably wider use of money. Likewise, the emerging *parambu - purayidam* economy witnessed growth of a class of wage labourers instead of agrestic slaves, where money played a pivotal role in economic activity. The contemporaneous records such as *Kootali Grandhavari, Vanjeri Grandhavari* and Kavalappara Papers extensively speak of the coins with regional variations/distribution. *Fanam,* and *vira rayan putiya panam* were circulated in some areas of Malabar.[78] Likewise, *Putupanam* and *panam* were in use in southern part of Malabar.[79] *Kannanoor Putiya panam* was another regional coin.[80] If *panam* had a wider circulation throughout Kerala (Venad, Kochi, Valluvanad, Kozhikode), *tharam* is mentioned as a coin of Kozhikode and Kochi from fourteenth to sixteenth centuries.[81] As a matter of fact, money had been circulated merely between the hands of affluent classes so that there is no meaning to believe that circulation of money was common and barter system was obsolete during the time. Surprisingly enough, even among the overseas companies, there was a custom of doing exchanges partially in cash and partially through barter.[82] However, money had definitely played the role of a catalyst in the process of emergence of a dynamic economy.

Power Structure and Relations: Family, *Jati* and *Swarupam*

The socio-economic process of medieval Kerala was actually under the control of three different power centres, namely, the family, the *jati* and the *swarupam*. Taking family into consideration, we have different varieties of which including patrilineal and patrilocal *Namputiri Illam*, the matrilineal *taravad* and *swarupam* as well as the matrilineal or patrilineal kinship or clan groups. Matrilineal kinship was prevalent among *Nairs* and in some areas among Mappilas and *Thiyyas*. Some scholars argue that matriliny in Kerala was a form of matriarchy and unfortunately both terms have been used almost synonymously. It is substantiated by documents on land transactions of that period, most of the deeds were made in the name of the families. The root of the matriliny, *Penvazhi avakasam* was actually the transfer of rights on a hereditary basis along the family line. Though women were considered to be the titular heads of the families, the legal and juridical functions involving the household were carried out by men.

The typical matrilineal household is characterised by complexities of power hierarchy in terms of the order of seniority, inheritance and segmented pattern of rights and obligations. Indeed, the *tayvazhis* and the *kur* (seniority rank) were always worked as determining factors. Among the gradations within the *swarupam,* seniority was the major criterion for becoming the ruler. This practice was called assuming *Muppu* (Eldership). *Muppu* was at the same time the head of the family and the titular ruler of the territory. The order of seniority (*Muppumura)* within the family was of importance. According to the system called *kuruvalcha,* the *swarupam* would be divided into several *kur* and accordingly the order of seniority was determined among them. The order of seniority was complicated by the emergence of *Tayvazhis*, or mother's lineages[83]. The senior most male member, *Karanavar/ammavan*, who was whether son or brother acted as the custodian of the entire activities of the family and he symbolized the public power. The growing militarisation was the reason for the reinforcement of the public power of the male member. The medieval matrilineal household was essentially patriarchal, with a clear division in power relation between men and women in terms of their role in the public and domestic domains. *Taravads* and *Swarupams*, to some historians, are extension of this family power.

Jati, the second power centre had a influential role in shaping the socio-economic relations in the period under discussion. *Jati* is considered to be an after effect of the existing economic structure centred around the brahmins' land which remained as independent units of production. These units required permanency of labour and naturally, several families belonging to clannish groups must have been permanently engaged in food production as well as other essential functions.[84] Occupational differentiation that evolved on the basis of the growing production relations and ritualistic order resulted in the growth of the *jati* system. Brahmin household had tried to distinguish themselves from others by the rest of the folk, by the ideal of purity and pollution in order to ensure the principle of inequality. *Jati* system cannot be viewed merely as an ideology based on brahminical treatises but it may be looked at primarily as an 'effective' way of division of labour in the pre- modern society. The *jati* had determined even the force and relations of production and centres of power for ages, and in fact had acted as a separate centre of power as well. The institution of *jati* has been very much complex indeed, and having its own distinctions and patterns different from the caste system that existed elsewhere in India.

Seventh, Eighth and Ninth centuries witnessed the large scale proliferation of *brahmadeyas* or Brahmin villages all over Tamilakam. This resulted in the expansion of irrigated agriculture as well as of the new system of relation, eventually led to the super imposition of Brahmin proprietorship over many communal lands which introduced new social relations. There emerged an intermediary caste between Brahmins and peasants. Naturally there was a clear cut separation between the primary producers and the full time non functionaries such as administrators, warriors etc., who were entitled to a lion's share of surplus through their managerial and protective functions.[85] In this sense, the *jati* was made use of for the siphoning off of the surplus by some influential groups. Indeed, it was for the same reason that the caste differentiation was introduced and maintained.

As mentioned before, the *jati* system prevailed in Kerala was a variant form, in which there were vertical as well as horizontal elements. The vertical element was consisted of a ritual hierarchy mediated by brahminical / sanskritic ideology. The horizontal element incorporated various occupational groups, caste groups, and sectors involved in every forms of production and exchange. It was in this way that the *Nazranis* and *Mappilas* were termed as separate *jatis* rather than religious groups. Even the Portuguese (*Parankis*), the Dutch and the English were called as separate jatis. Here we see a departure of Kerala form of *jati* from the so called caste system.

Brahmin landlords, who were the custodians of temple wealth and the proprietors of the village, had highest economic status as well. Those rich *agamic* specialist brahmins gradually emerged as a separate group called *tantrikal* as distinguished from the other sections of brahmins. There were *bhattas, chattas* and *santi* among the brahmins who received *virutti*, the land-lease as reward for their services in the temple. There was a sharp differentiation between the brahmins themselves based on land control, the major landlords among Brahmins, identifying themselves as *adhya* or elite as distinguished from the others, called *asya*[86].

The *Madhyasta* caste *Potuval* was the common man positioned as intermediary between the temple and devotees, who also were acted as the secretary of the temple, both *variyar,* the member of temple committees (*variyam*) had received the *virutti* privilege. Other castes like *marar*, *chakyar*, *nanniyar* etc. were also rendering service to the temples in various capacities.

These castes are generally called the *antarala-jati,* that is the caste between the brahmins and the non-brahmins, who were alternatively known as temple castes.

The emergence of a system of land control called *kaaraanmai* was favourable to some non-brahmin castes, predominantly the Nairs. The class of intermediaries in land, with the rank of and entailing privileges of nobility owing allegiance only to the brahmin landlords, succeeded in asserting themselves in the temple oriented society. The peculiar form of the Nair woman's relation with the brahmin (*sambandham*) was an added privilege for their closeness to the Brahmins. Traditionally, the Nayar was a warrior and non-cultivating tenant.[87] Gradually, some predominant Nair families acquired position of *taravad* with civil and military powers.[88] The astuteness of the Nairs helped themselves successfully utilising the opportunities, and as a result, they became the intermediaries or supervisors of the land with the title of *Kaanakkaar*.

Transformation of craftsmen and artisans (*kammaalars*) to the caste groups also occurred in the same manner, that is, through the process of attaching them to the temple society. Inscriptional evidences refer to *tacchar* (carpenter), *Kollar* (blacksmith), *Kalavaniyar* (potters) *vaniyar* (oil mongers), *vannaar* (washer men) etc. who were brought and settled in the temple village to ensure their service to society. The *parambu* (plot) names like *aasariparambu*, *aasarukandi*, *kollan parambu/thodika*, *thachan kandi/kunnu* etc., exemplify the extensive presence of these crafts/caste groups in a growing cash crop economy.[89] They enjoyed occupancy right over land and this constituted the material incentive for them to be hereditary professional groups, and further, there was no other alternative for them as they were caught up in a social milieu of immobility and functional obligations.[90] Each group had been accepting its annual rights from the concerned overlord as well.[91]

Lower stratum of the hierarchical social order was constituted by the primary producing castes such as *pulayas, cherumas*, and *vettuvas*. They were attached to the lands and were leased and mortgaged along with the lands. There developed the distancing of these *jatis* on the basis of purity/pollution by which their identity was reduced to servility (*atiyayma*) under the landlords/temples. Brahmins could successfully subjugate the *avarnas* primarily in three ways: economically, the *brahmins* possessed the right over their land; ritually, they were kept aloof from the sacred spaces as untouchables; and intellectually, all the resources and medium of attaining knowledge were denied to them.[92]

References to the existence of agrestic slaves and hired labourers all over Kerala shed light on their role in the extension of an agrarian economy. The hired labourers were assigned to do seasonal work on lands such as transplantation of paddy plants and were paid daily wages mostly in kind. The *panans* of Thalassery and *Malayans* and *Kadars* of Kochi and the *Tiyans* in Kottayam worked as hired labourers of Christian and Nair landlords.[93] With the growth of coconut cultivation, the Ezhavas (*Tiyyas*) became an important caste serving on the land. Some among them served the *naduvazhis* as warriors known as *Chekon*, especially in Malabar. Though dynamic in production process, these people were deemed to be polluting castes by the brahmins so that they maintained several folk gods and goddesses in their own *kavus* for worship. This eventually caused to evolve two streams of culture in society, namely, 'high culture' and 'lower/popular culture'. While the upper castes, composed of *janmis* and intermediaries, represented the high culture; the lower castes represented the lower culture.

The state, another major power centre, was characterised by the political authority, which was wielded by extended joint families called *swarupams*[94]. In fact, the early form of medieval state, the Perumal, was necessitated and sustained by the constitution of agrarian social formation under the initiative of the Brahmins. Some scholars trace the origin of the *swarupams* into the *nadus* of the later *Chera* period.[95] After the decline of the later *Chera* state, some *nadus* disintegrated and others became *swarupams*, who were known by the location of the ruling joint family. *Swarupams* were following a matrilineal order and each had a family elder and other members were having given a rank (*mura*).[96] There is a tendency to represent the terms of *muppu* and *swarupam* in a reducible form of the king and kingdom, due to a lack of proper understanding of a period where in the central authority was absent.[97]

Like the former rulers, the *Naduvazhi* power was based upon the extraction and accumulation of surplus from the *nadus*, the regions which were under cultivation. Trade networks and the levies on trade also benefited them. According to the available evidences, the ruler didn't attempt to control the overseas trade in ports directly, but was receiving a share of tolls normally collected by the principal merchants. The most important example is that of the Zamorins of Kozhikode. The port of Kozhikode was under the control of Talachennor, a representative of the *samutiri* and the Kozhikode *Koya*. Similarly, Kollam was not controlled directly, and the prince of Desinganad stayed at Kallada, to the north of Kollam. Similar were the cases of rulers of Kochi and Kodungallur. Tolls from trade were given high importance as they augmented the financial reserves of the rulers, a feature that played a major role in the rise of the Samutiri and the authority of Kolathunad and Venad.[98]

The state system existed during the period was without much pomp or splendour and even without a standing army. More importantly, there was no legal formulation like *Kizhiyakkams* or *Kachams*, the brahminical legal codes, but the ritual and economic role of the temple was noticeable. The *Naduvazhis* were conferred to be the rulers of the land and the managers and trustees of the temples by means of ceremonies such as *ariyittu vazcha* or *hiranyagarbha*. Temple *sanketams* were so powerful, which gave protection to rulers against outside invasions.[99] The services of landlords and militia and the benediction of the *brahmins* were based by the elders to exercise effective control over the producers. Although customary authority ensured the subjugation of the producers, the segmented character of the ruling families also required the services of the *swarupis* to keep the cultivators completely submissive.

Since an efficient system of revenue collection was absent, a large number of small chiefs and landlords existed everywhere, military power was essential for mobilization of resources for the ruler. Thus the ritual power of the *brahmins* and the secular power of the non-brahmins who evolved into the *nayar* caste were the two major arms of the political authority, of the *swarupams*[100]. As mentioned elsewhere, the surplus generated appears to have been utilized for unproductive activities like renovation or construction of temples, palace buildings etc.

In the changing political scenario of the late medieval period, the *swarupams* were attempted to become larger states and some of them had become successful. The following developments such as expansion of *parambu* lands, enhancement in the volume of spice trade with the West Asians or Europeans and the direct intervention of the ruling families in the organisation of trade etc. had contributed favourably towards this trend.

Conclusion

In pre-Modern Kerala, the land was central to the process of production and the relations of production were determined by land. The whole land, came under the heads of *brahmaswam*, *devaswam* and *cherikkal,* was owned or controlled by the influential groups which caused to evolve an absentee landlordism, where the landless sections of people acted as the actual tillers. The rights of *janmam* and *kaanam*, the forms of ownership and control, actually determined the organization of the production process as well. The emergence of a cash crop economy and extension of agriculture to the hill tracts made the economy more vibrant. The presence of intermediary *kaanakkaars* associated with the emergence of a cash crop economy had not paved the way for commercialization of agriculture. It is also important to note that the feudal relations remained unchanged though a money economy was taken shape.

Though the economy of pre-modern Kerala is characterised to be self-sufficient village economy, the trade was a forceful and dynamic factor. There emerged a wide network of local trade, long distance trade as well as dynamic trans-continental trading network linking Western Coast with the western and eastern worlds. The state by and large did not intervene directly in the matters of trade but had attempted to maintain an affable atmosphere for flourishing the trade though it levied toll or taxes. In the new era of trade which was inaugurated by the Portuguese in the sixteenth century, Kerala became part of a world system, which resulted in drastic changes in the existing economy in several ways.

The three centres of power, namely, family, *jati* and *swarupams* shared the actual power over the process and relations of production and the exchange as well. Extension of plough agriculture and the demand for a permanent labour force resulted in the maintenance of *jati* system, In order to sustain the dominance over the labour, the brahmins made the primary producing class in the position of servility. In a sense, the *jati*, which never remained stagnant, was acted as the most effective system of division of labour and an ideology for extracting the surplus.

The actual form of state, known as *swarupam*, was an extended form of the erstwhile *taravad* families. The right to rule was determined by *muppu- mura* and ramifications of which were not so simple. Though the *swarupams* were not strictly based upon *kacham* or *kizhiyakkam* unlike in the case of Perumal state, their political power was normally conferred and supported by the Brahmins. In such a way, the upper castes and the ruling class stood hand in hand in extracting the labour as well as surplus product. Such an age- old socio-political structure was destabilized by the invasion of Mysore towards the close of the eighteenth century, which will be examined in the next chapter in detail.

Notes

1. Malabar, in the modern sense, constitutes the whole northern part of Kerala. But, in the pre-British times, Malabar was understood as the whole geographical area, now known as Kerala. So that in the present chapter, the socio-economic condition of the whole Kerala is taken in to account.

2. Elamkulam P. N. Kunjan Pillai, *Studies in Kerala History*, Kottayam, 1970, p. 32; M. G. S. Narayanan has discussed the features of *sanketam* and its quasi autonomous status in detail in his introduction to *Vanjeri Grandhavari*. See M. G. S. Narayanan, ed., *Vanjeri Grandhavari,* Department of History, University of Calicut, 1987. Scholars such as Rajan Gurukal, is more comfortable to call it 'temple - oriented society'. See, Rajan Gurukkal, *The Kerala Temple and Early Medieval Agrarian System*, Sukapuram, 1992.
3. K. N. Ganesh, 'Agrarian Society in Kerala (1500-1800)' in P. J. Cheriyan, ed., *Perspectives on Kerala History, Kerala Gazetteer*, Vol. II, Pt. II, Thiruvananthapuram, 1999, p. 123.
4. Kesavan Veluthat, *Brahmin Settlements in Kerala*, Calicut, 1978
5. Rajan Gurukkal, *The Kerala Temple and Early Medieval Agrarian System*, Sukapuram, 1992, p. 32.
6. K. N. Ganesh, *op. cit.,* p. 123.
7. It was prevalent even during the time of Perumals, see M. G. S. Narayanan, *Perumals of Kerala: Political and Social Conditions of Kerala under the Chera Perumals of Makotai (800 - 1124 AD)*, Calicut, 1996, p. 174.
8. K. N. Ganesh, *op. cit.*
9. *Ibid.*
10. *Ibid.*, p. 141.
11. Elamkulam P. N. Kunjan Pillai, *op. cit.,* p.325. However, this argument is not acceptable to most of the historians.
12. M. G. S. Narayanan, *op. cit.,* p. 174.
13. Kesavan Veluthat, *op. cit.,* p. 60.
14. K. N. Ganesh, *op. cit.,* p. 60.
15. K. N. Ganesh, 'Ownership and control of land in Medieval Kerala: *janmam - kanam* relations during the sixteenth - eighteenth centuries', *IESHR*, 28, 3, (1991).
16. The indigenous texts like *Keralolpathy* and *Vyavaharamala* played the role of ideological foundation for the brahmins which could early dominate rest of the society without establishing hegemoney. Donald R. Davis has meticulously delineated how *Vyavaharamala* was incorporated by the upper class of Medieval Kerala. See his paper, 'Recovering the Indigenous Legal Traditions of India: Classical Hindu Law in Practice in Late Medieval Kerala', *Journal of Indian Philosophy*, 27, 1999, pp. 159-213.
17. Elamkulam, *op. cit.,* p.348; Appendix to *Janmi Sampradayam Keralathil*, Kottayam, 1959, pp. 103-106.
18. K. N. Ganesh, 'Agrarian Society', *op. cit.,* p. 141.
19. M. G. S. Narayanan ed, *Vanjeri Grandhavari*, introduction, p. xviii.
20. The term *Maryadai* is wiedely found as *desamarachati* in *Vanjeri Grandhavari* (hereafter V.G.), Calicut, 1987; see Doc. No. 27A (A. D. 1581) and No. 344 (A. D. 1599) *Kiliyakkam* is referred in V.G. Doc. 1A, 21 C. etc.
21. See, K. N. Ganesh, 'Agrarian Society', *op. cit.,* p. 146; Muzhikulam *kacham* laid down strict rules and regulations for the conduct of temple affairs and the administration of temple properties. In the 9th century A.D., the *naduvazhis* and

representatives of temple committees framed these rules and regulations on the basis of general consensus after elaborate discussions.

22. *Ibid.*, p. 139.
23. *Ibid.*, p. 142.
24. *Ibid.*
25. *Ibid.*
26. *Ibid.*, p. 143.
27. V. G. Doc. 27A, 28A, 34 A.
28. K. N. Ganesh, 'Agrarian Relations in Kerala: An Overview', in E. K. G Nambiar, ed., *Agrarian India, Problems and Perspectives*, Calicut University, 1997, p.70; See also M.G.S. Narayanan ed., *V. G., op.cit.,* Doc. 21A, 22 A.
29. M. R. Raghava Varier, *Madhyakala Keralam Sambattu Samuham Samskaram* (Mal.) [Medieval Kerala: Economy, Society and Culture], Trivandrum, 1997, pp. 23-32. Though Prof. Varrier mentions the independence of the artisan groups, actually they were depending upon agriculture.
30. M.G. S Narayanan, ed., *Vanjeri Grandhavari*, *op.cit.,* Doc. 36A, p. 19.
31. M. R. Raghava Varier, *op. cit.,* p. 28.
32. K. N. Ganesh, 'Agrarian Society', *op. cit.,* p. 145.
33. Elamkulam, *Studies*, p. 35, fn. 2.
34. *Ibid.,* p. 343; P. K. Gopalakrishnan, *Keralathinte Saamskaarika Charithram* (Mal) [Cultural History of Kerala], Trivandrum, 1994, pp. 270-71.
35. Sheikh Zeinuddin, *Thuhfat al- Mujahiddin,* tr. by S. Muhammad Husayn Nainar, Calicut, 2006, p. 46.
36. The term *paattam* was firstly found mentioned in *Tali Records* as the share of produce. It was actually the rulers' share that was agreed to give away to the temple expense as *paattam*. It was on this basis that there was an understanding that the lands granted as *devaswam* were to be exempted from the tax (*Raja bhogam*). When the right of *Rajabhogam* was transferred to temple or individuals, it naturally becomes *paattam*; see P. K. Gopalakrishnan, *op. cit.,* p. 265.
37. K. N. Ganesh, "Agrarian Relations and Political Authority in Medieval Travancore, (AD 1300 - 1750)", Unpublished Ph.D. thesis, Jawaharlal Nehru University, New Delhi, 1987, p. 127.
38. *Ibid.,* p. 130.
39. *Ibid.,* pp. 130-31. Prof. K. N. Ganesh calls it 'rent-tax' as it is characterised by the features of both rent and tax.
40. K. N. Ganesh, Ph.D. thesis, *op. cit.,* p. 158.
41 *Ibid.*, p. 171.
42 *Ibid.*, p. 172.
43 *Ibid.*, p. 218.
44. M. R. Raghava Varier, 'Socio-Economic Structure', in P. J. Cheriyan ed., *op. cit.,* p. 83.
45. *Ibid.*
46. T. K. Gopala Panikkar, *Malabar and its Folk: A Systematic Description of the Social Customs and Institutions of Malabar,* Madras, 1929.

47. Karl Polanyi, *et. al., Trade and Markets in Early Empires*, Free Press, New York, 1957, pp. 223-23.
48. K. N. Ganesh, Ph.D Thesis, *op. cit.,* p. 176.
49. M.R. Raghava Varier, 'Socio-economic structure', *op. cit.,* p. 99.
50. This classification is by Prof. Varrier, which is cited here for the purpose of elucidation.
51. Ashin Das Gupta, *Malabar in Asian Trade*, Cambridge, 1967, p. 103.
52. *Ibid.*, pp. 99-100.
53. Prof. K. N. Chaudhuri, while classifying the types of Asian markets, highlights these fairs as an important aspect of local trade; see, K. N. Chaudhuri, *The Trading World of Asia and the English East India Company, 1660-1760*, Cambridge, 1978, p. 138.
54. M. G. S. Narayanan, *Perumals*, p. 171.
55. M. R. Raghava Varier, *op. cit.,* p. 100.
56. *Ibid.*, p. 101.
57. M.G.S. Narayanan, *op. cit.,* p. 172.
58. Ashin Das Gupta, *op.cit.,* p. 103.
59. *Ibid.*, p. 104.
60. Geneveve Bouchon, 'A Microcosom: Calicut in the sixteenth century', in Denys Lombard and Jean Aubin, ed., *Asian Merchants and Businessmen in the Indian Ocean and Chinese Sea*, Delhi, 2000, p. 40.
61. *Ibid.*, p. 105.
62. K. N. Chaudhuri, *op. cit.,* p. 139.
63. Ashin Das Gupta, *op. cit.,* p. 139.
64. *Ibid.*
65. *Ibid.*, pp. 106-108.
66. *Ibid.*, p. 6.
67. M. R. Raghava Varrier, 'Socio-Economic', *op. cit.,* p. 100.
68. Johnsy Mathews, *Economy and Society in Medieval Malabar (A.D. 1200-1600)*, Changanesseri, 1996, p. 149.
69. *Ibid.*, p. 151.
70. *Ibid.*, p.152
71. M. R. Raghava Varier, *op. cit.,* p. 114.
72. N. M. Namputiri, *Mamamkam Rekhakal* (Mal) [The Maamankam Records], Sukapuram, 2005.
73. See, *Periplus of Erythrean Sea, Travel and Trade in the Indian Ocean by a Merchant of the First Century,* translated and annotated by Wilfred H. Schoff, Longmans, New York, London, Bombay & Calcutta, 1912, pp. 44-45.
74. M. R. Raghava Varier, *op. cit.,* p. 115.
75. Ashin Das Gupta, *op. cit.,* p.114. He argues that, by the Mysorean invasions, trade in North Malabar ceased to be an attractive profession. This statement can be seen as a part of the general view and demands further research.
76. M. G. S. Narayanan, *Perumals*, *op. cit.,* p. 144.
77. M. R. Raghava Varieir, *Madhyakala Samooham*, *op. cit.,* p. 37.

78. K. K. N. Kurup, ed., *Kavalappara Papers*, Calicut, 1984, pp. 159-160.
79. M. G. S. Narayanan, ed., *Vanjeri Grandhavari*, Calicut, 1987, p. 198.
80. K. K. N. Kururp, ed., *Kootali Grandhavari*, Calicut, 1995.
81. R. Varrier, *Madhyakala*, *op. cit.*, p. 47.
82. Ashin Das Gupta, *op. cit.*, p. 114.
83. K. N. Ganesh, 'Structure of Political Authority', in P. J. Cheriyan, *op. cit.*, p. 223.
84. Rajan Gurukkal, 'The Formation of Caste Society in Kerala: Historical Antecedents', in K. L. Sharma, ed., *Caste and Class in India*, Jaipur, 1994, p. 395.
85. *Ibid.*, p. 396.
86. *Ibid.*, pp. 398-9.
87. K. K. N. Kurup, *Aspects of Kerala History and Culture*, Trivandrum, 1977, p. 40.
88. K. K. N. Kurup, *William Logan: A study in the Agrarian Relations of Malabar*, Calicut University, 1981, pp.1-3.
89. R. Varier, *Madhyakala Samuham*, *op. cit.*, p. 59.
90. R. Gurukkal, 'Formation of Caste', *op. cit.*, p. 400.
91. K. P. Padmanabha Menon, *Kochi Rajya Charithram* (Mal) [History of Kochi], p. 121.
92. P. K. Gopalakrishnan, *op.cit.*, p. 288.
93. For a detailed discussion on agrestic slaves, see Johnsy Mathews, *op. cit.*, pp. 73-75.
94. The following works delineate the process of the state formation in Medieval Kerala, K. N. Ganesh, 'Structure of Political Authority in Medieval Kerala', in P. J. Cherian, *op. cit.*, 1999, K. N. Ganesh, 'Process of State Formation', K. V. Krishna Iyer, *op. cit.*, 1989; M. G. S. Narayanan, *The Perumals of Kerala*, Calicut, 1996, and Bonaventure Swai, 'Trade and Politics in eighteenth century Malabar,' mimeo, Unpublished, Dar es Salam, Tanzania, 1979.
95. Kesavan Veluthat, 'Further Expansion of the Agrarian society: the Political Forms', in P. J. Cherian ed. *op. cit.*, p. 68; Varrier and Gurukkal, *op. cit.*, pp. 255-56.
96. K. N. Ganesh, 'Process of State formation', *op. cit.*
97. S. Raju, 'Organization of Medieval Self forms: *Swarupam* and *Muppuvazhcha*', Lateral Study Series, 15, School of Social Sciences, M. G. University, Kottayam, n.d.
98. K. N. Ganesh, in P. J. Cheriyan, ed., *op. cit.*, p. 227.
99. K. N. Ganesh, 'Structure', *op. cit.*, p. 226.
100. *Ibid.*, p. 227.

Chapter II

Battle for 'Pepper State': Mysore State's Interventions and Transformation of Society

The latter half of the eighteenth century witnessed drastic changes in the domains of society, polity and economy of Malabar which had been evolved and sustained during the pre-modern times. The most significant and sudden impact on the existing system occurred as a result of the expansionist policy of the neighbouring state of Mysore on the one hand and the establishment of British commercial enterprises on the other. The Mysore state's intervention in Malabar resulted in a rupture of the previous state and society, and heralded a new era of socio-economic transformation. The present chapter is intended to examine the way in which the ever controversial problem of Mysore conquest of Malabar is represented both in colonial and indigenous literature and and also to explore the nature and impact of the Mysorean state and its interventions in the society and economy of Malabar.

Interestingly, the existing collection of literature on the problem of Mysore's interventions in Malabar region (including writings/folklore/legends) shares more or less the same pattern of narration, in the sense that the period was characterised by religious persecution by the Mysore rulers, who were essentially bigots. Such a genre of writings was launched by the British writers and unfortunately it was widely circulated by the later historians including the Nationalists[1]. Right from the very beginning of the colonial enterprises of writing of history of India, Hydar Ali and Tipu Sultan, the rulers of Mysore, had been portrayed and represented as the worst of all awful things on the earth. Col. Wilks' *History of Mysore* was a pioneering work in this regard. Inclined to the Orientalist persuasions, Wilks vehemently pronounces the terms such as 'bigotry' and 'tyranny' to characterise the nature of the administration of Hydar and Tipu Sultan. Like wise, Meadows Taylor's dramatic narrative, *Tipoo Sultan*, characterised the warrior as the embodiment of all sorts of wickedness. The following lines are the description of an imaginary camp of Tipu Sultan, where according to Taylor the gravest things occurred. Taylor writes, "it was no uncommon thing to see beyond the precincts of the camp, a row of miserable Hindoos hanging upon trees, who had defied the Sultan's efforts at conversion and had preferred death than change the religions of their fathers".[2] Edward Thompson and G.T. Garrett, generally known to be the liberal writers also found recourse to depicting Tipu as a bigot.[3] Francis Buchanan, who was appointed by the colonial establishment to examine the conditions of the province of Madras, Malabar and Mysore, was a typical writer with "colonial gaze" upon the indigenous people. For instance, we see a vociferous writer while embarking on the much debated issue of conversions during the time of Tipu Sultan's administration.[4]

William Logan, who has always been admired for his liberal views and 'sympathetic' approach, too was not free from the colonialist predispositions, especially when he wrote about the Mysore's conquest of Malabar. Contrary to his much-adored sympathetic attitude to the people of Malabar, Logan use to sensationalise the episode of Mysore invasion and strictly epitomizes colonial narrative with much supportive statistics to highlight the killing of Hindus and proselytization by Tipu Sultan. For instance, he writes, "the country [Malabar] was split into a number of Kingdoms and principalities, a prey to the bigotry of its late Mohamedan conquerors abandoned by its principal landholders, and distracted by the depredations and rapacity of the Mappila banditty" [sic].[5] We see no point in differentiating Logan (in the case of the narratives on Mysorean rulers) from the earlier stream of British writers who stereotypically represented the Muslims in racial terms like "Jungle Mappilas".

It is interesting to note that even a recent study on the Hindu-Muslim relations in North Malabar has been gravely influenced by the colonialist perception of the issues of bigotry and tyranny[6]. According to this study, "in spite of his iron fisted administration and his heavy handed exactions, Hydar had interfered little with the religious activities of his Hindu subjects. But Malabar was now entrusted to a ruler who added religious bigotry to other disadvantages of alien rule". Such a rather innocent and objective statement establishes that the scholars of the present generation also are not free from the spectres of dominant ideas of colonial writers.

Surprisingly, the so-called nationalist (as a more convenient term for indigenous) writers were always fond of following the foot print of colonial writers when foraying into the issues such as religious conversion, bigotry or religious persecution. For instance, K.V. Krishna Ayyar in his pioneering work on Zamorins of Calicut highlights the issues of conversion without making any further enquiries on the colonial models.[7] Likewise, while analysing the role of Malabar in Asian trade, Ashin Das Gupta, an authority on Indian Ocean trade, comes to the conclusion that the basic causative factor for the disintegration of trading enterprises in eighteenth century Malabar was the invasion and intervention of the Mysore State.[8]

K. Madhavan Nair, the veteran nationalist leader and author of the renowned monograph *Malabar Kalapam*, contended that it was Tipu Sultan's invasion of Malabar and his project of proselytization that became a prominent causative factor leading to the revolt of 1921.[9] According to T. K. Ravindran, the conquests of Hydar Ali and Tipu Sultan still aggravated the ills that bedevilled Malabar.[10] Recent remarks from historian M. G. S. Narayanan and others appear to be unreasonable and far from the methods of scientific historical research. While making evaluation of the national movement in Kerala, M. G. S. Narayanan out rightly condemns the Mysorean presence in Kerala primarily because 'those powers were responsible for the stagnation of process of development in Modern Kerala'.[11] It is quite ridiculous that the way in which we think and act by assimilating and internalising the colonialist views, while arguing for an indigenous model of writing history!

A few of the specialists on the eighteenth century trade and pepper politics do share the same views we discussed above. For a writer such as N. Rajendran, pepper cultivation in Malabar was badly affected by the turmoil following the ravaging reprisals of Tipu Sultan against the Hindu rebels in the area.[12] Instead of making critical analysis of the colonialist presuppositions, the nationalist writers were blindly following the colonial discourses and unfortunately they were echoing the same stereotypical representation of the Mysore rulers' interventions in Malabar. Here, the missing thread of the story is that, the invasion of Hydar Ali and his son Tipu Sultan was staunchly resisted initially by the Muslim rebels without any religious considerations.

An alternative approach to the colonialist and nationalist framework on the Mysorean interventions in Malabar came from another group of historians; who could transgress the nationalist frames. Attempts made by C. K. Kareem, A. P. Ibrahim Kunju and amateur historian P. K. Balakrishnan. primarily focused on raising a defensive stance with regard to the Mysorean rulers.[13] These writes honestly desired to produce a counter narrative in their own way and which could be figured in another discourse on the Mysorean rulers, as for them, both colonial and nationalist writers could not unearth every aspects of the Mysorean intervention and innovative policies of Mysorean administration due to the religious predilections of those writers.

In such a context where the colonialist and the nationalists writers often paid much importance to the religious factor as the main reason for Mysorean invasion of Malabar, a rarely quoted contemporary record leads us to a more logical conclusion and novel insight into the problem.[14] According to Vella's (a brahmin chronicler of eighteenth century) description *Vellayute Charithram*, none other than the native rulers of Malabar were solely responsible for the comeback of Hydar and the subsequent conflicts and depredations. Hydar came through the northern part of Malabar with the aim of extracting the money Zamorin owed to him in connection with the previous battle and its settlement. Several other rulers such as the Raja of Chirakkal also had to pay similar dues to Hydar, states Vella.

As the Zamorin had been regularly paying dues to the British (it is said that Zamorin had mortgaged his ceremonial ornament and borrowed money even from the king of Pandalam at that time) he was not at all resourceful to pay back Hydar's dues. Even though Hydar had extended his date of payment for several times, Zamorin failed to make the payment. Apart from this, the Zamorin's move to seek asylum in Kollam had also infuriated Hydar and as a last resort, thought of attacking the land of the Zamorins. As soon as the cavalry of Mysore landed in Malabar, the Zamorin did commit suicide, setting fire to Ambadi Kovilakom.[15] If we can believe Vella, the Zamorin had already decided to commit suicide. The Zamorin's inability to pay the outstanding dues of the previous years as well as the pressures from his own men led him to resort to the fatal decision. Vella strongly argues that the prime motive of Hydar's assault was nothing but economic than religious. For this he substantiates with his own experience of buying back the stolen Bhagavati idol [which was allegedly stolen by Hydar] of Tirunavaya temple, from one of the markets around Kochi, at a cost of 5000 *panams*. Vella firmly believes that if the motive of the invader was religious, the idol would definitely have been destroyed or desecrated.

If this contemporary chronicle can be taken at its face value, the previous narratives of the colonialists and nationalists will be proved a historical and prejudiced. Of course, Hydar Ali was an ambitious ruler whose prime motive behind invasion of Malabar was purely economic. A ruler who ascended to power mainly with his military credentials, had to prove his mettle as a warrior and had to mobilize resources through raids and invasions. By his conquests and acquisition in in the northern region of Malabar, Hydar Ali could well claim that he was then the sole authority of the territory far larger in size than the original dominions of Mysore that the Raja had reigned.[16] Hydar, like any other autocrats, followed a policy of intimidation not only in Malabar but also in other parts of his territory, where he wanted to establish his influence and mobilize resources. For instance, in Madras between 1780 and 1782, Hydar Ali tried to denude the place called Jagir of its population. Aware that Jagir was a source of food, fodder, labour and even betel leaves for inhabitants of Madras, Hydar burnt villages and either killed or scattered their local populations to intimidate the British.[17] And more importantly, his punitive measures towards the Muslim Nawab of Arcot was harsh, and obviously not in religious terms.

Apart from this, Hydar was moving with an intention of introducing internal restructuring of the state and revenue system of Malabar. His regime represented a combination of existing institution of the Mysore Raj with a blend of Mughal elements. In order to generate much revenue from agriculture, he took the standard Mughal view that the local potentates were zamindars and as such their entitlements were not sacrosanct. His aim was to dispense with their intimidation and imposed the land tax (which was a tax on produce, equivalent to surplus or rent) directly on peasants, realizing through salaried officers.[18] As a matter of fact, such a system of tax imposed upon the land owners according to a survey was quite new and therefore unimaginable for Malabar land lords, say Nambudiris or Nairs. Interestingly, this system was adopted later by Munro and introduced as *Ryotwari* settlement during the British dominance.

Though various factors are attributed as the causative factors for the Mysorean invasion of Malabar, the nuances of pepper politics of the eighteenth century are rarely explained. The expansionist policy of Hydar Ali and Tipu Sultan, in fact, had focused on establishing their monopoly in lucrative pepper trade. They had a long-term vision of controlling the western coast on the backdrop of the British projects of acquisition of spice trade. No other place was strategically so important in the eyes of Mysorean rulers. British had established their presence as early as 1634-35[19] with a view to take control of the spice trade of the region. Colonial documents such as *Tellicherry Consultations* and other records evidently bring out the British role in the extensive spice trade on the coast.

Apart from the Company, the local rulers such as the Zamorin, Vazhunnor of Vatakara and the Arakkal dynasty of Ali Rajas had been the stake holders of overseas spice trade in Malabar. Instances of their involvement in trade can be seen as part of diplomatic relations at the same time, mutual conflicts and intrigues were common throughout the eighteenth century.[20] The most commonly found terms in the Company records such as 'piracy', 'plunder' and 'negotiations' are indicative of the nature of the pepper politics. The Raja of Kolathunad gave permission to the British to construct a factory at Tellicherry in view of the collection of customs duty from the Company. Subsequently, he offered the British to build a fort at Tellicherry in the year 1708, as a fortification against one of his troublesome vassals, the Kurungoth Nayar[21].

The nature of spice trade during eighteenth century can only be understood in the context of the political structure of North Malabar. In the north, 'political cluster' of Kolathunad existed around the dominant household of the Kolathiri who ruled over Chirakkal.[22] The Vazhunnor of Vadakara was in semi-independent position of Kadathnad, that is the territory between Mahe river and Kotta river [Kotta river got its name from the fort of Kunhali Marakkar, who built a fort on banks of the river at Kottakkal. The river is also known presently as Moorad river and Kuttyadi river]. And yet another offshoot was in similar semi-independent ruling family which held possession of the territory lying between the Kavayi and Mahe rivers various portions had come, whether by family alliances of the kind described or by grants, it is difficult to say, into the possession of various chieftains who were more or less dependent on the Kolathiris. Randattara, otherwise called as 'Poyanad' [according to tradition this was the country, *nadu*, from which the Cheraman Perumal went (*poyi*) to Arabia] was under the Acchanmars, that is four houses of the Nambiar caste; Kottayam was under the Puranaat Rajas and Iruvazhinad (including Kurungoth) was ruled over by six houses of the Nayar caste. Iruvazhinaad literally means the country of two rulers. According to tradition, on the division of Keralam by Cheraman Perumal, this part of the country is said to have been vested with the family of two *adiyodis* – a class of Nairs, Tekkadi Adiyodi and Vadakkadi Adiyodi. Lastly, the Mappila Chief of Cannanore (the Ali Raja Azhi Raja or the Raja of the sea) had secured himself a small slice of territory in and around Cannanore. The original Kolathiri dominions were therefore broken up into a large number of petty principalities at the time of the founding of the Tellicherry factory, and the territory which remained under the direct rule of the Kolathiris was of comparatively small in extent[23] (see Map I). *Naduvazhi-Desavazhi-Mukhyasthan* was the way in which the political segmentation was prevailed.

Due to the mutual jealousy and protracted warfare, the political atmosphere was very much conducive for external agressions. By eighteenth century, the Kingdom of Kolathunad was disintegrating. The Raja of Kottayam was by then independent of Kolathiri, the Arakkal of Cannanore was a vassal only in name, and the various princes of the ruling house of Kolathunad were no longer united.[24] Hostility of this sort and tendency to fight against their lords were fanned by the foreign powers from the Portuguese to the British.

The Arakkal of Cannanore was the most arrogant of the Kolathiri's vassals. Its position as a trading dynasty provided the opportunity to amass wealth spent mostly on luxuries and arms. The Dutch at Cannanore were the suppliers of western ammunitions to Arakkal. Both mercantile surplus and fire arms prompted Arakkal dynasty to initiate frequent uprisings against their superiors, the Kolattiri. It was in 1720's one such surprising incident occurred when the then Ali Raja attacked the Prince Regent Cunhi Homo. As he failed to defend the Arakkal insurgency, Cunhi Homo sought the assistance of the British, which was readily provided.[25] This was in tune with the Bombay Establishment's (EEIC's headquarters) policy of supplying arms and ammunitions to the local rulers and to wage wars on their own expense.

When the Raja had ill-feeling with the British, he had approached the Dutch for succour. The positive response from the part of the Dutch again caused the British to fear about the loss of Dharmapatanam [Dharmatom]. In response, they began to take necessary precaution. These developments in the first half of the century gave the Canarese a chance to become interested in the Malabar territories. The British had assisted the prince [Cunhi Homo] with 20,000 *fanams* worth of military stores when Arakkal started to revolt against him. This act quickly silenced Arakkal and by which the British could ascertain their sole dominance over pepper trade in Malabar. However, the emergence of the French as a mercantile power and its claim over Mahe to establish their factory along with the Canarese invasion of 1730's had an influential impact on the British interests in Malabar.

The British from the very beginning had attempted to prevent the French from establishing their stronghold at Mahe and in order to achieve it, the British had influenced the Vazhunnor at Vatakara. As a result, the Vazhunnor had moved against the French but the Nambiars with the Kurungoth and Narangoly sided with the French. The British attributed this to a huge amount as bribes given by the French to the Nambiars. The Canarese invasion was looked upon as a blessing with regard to the commercial aspirations of the French East India Company. By that time, they intensified their plans on Malabar, and accordingly they built the fortress of Peringattur with a view to hinder any access to pepper transporting to Tellicherry from the country of Vazhunnor and Iruvazhinaad.[26] However, they couldn't make a considerable advance in objectives except engaging in their own trade. But at the same time, the British had intensified their policy of intervention in the political affairs of the Rajas, which culminated in gaining the right to collect the custom duties over North Malabar.

The British had gradually extended their sphere of influence by building a series of forts in the island of Dharmatam. There were other forts which were necessary to preserve their commercial interests amidst external as well as internal challenges. The Edakkatt fort which was built in 1737 to prevent "unauthorised" export from the places such as Randattara, the grove island Fort, the Madaccara fort, the Fort of Kutali, the Morocoona [sic]fort, the Millian fort in the Kurungoth Nair's territory etc. were put under the control of the British.[27]

It was at this juncture that the British had to face the most serious challenge to their monopoly of coastal spice trade in Malabar from the state of Mysore. The protracted rivalry between the two powers could be divided into the phases of three Anglo-Mysorean wars of 1768-69, 1780-84 and 1790-92. The commercial operations of the British on the coast had been disrupted due to stringent trade prohibitions imposed by the Mysoreans. In this context, the Bombay Council had even recommended a total withdrawal from Malabar. But it was the determination of the factors of Tellicherry that enabled them to drop such a plan.

Hydar Ali's first invasion on Malabar was in 1757, when he was merely the *foujdar* of Dindigal under the Raja of Mysore. When the Acchan [ruler] of Palakkad appealed to Hydar to rescue him from the harassment of the Zamorin, Hydar positively responded and the Zamorin was compelled to retreat from the boundary of Palakkad. Subsequently, Hydar assumed the power of Mysore in the year 1761 and controlled the administration of Canara in 1763. In 1764 he declared his intention to invade Malabar and appealed the British and other European powers to co-operate with him. While the French gave a definite answer of support, the British contacted the Bombay Council and considering the state of British military resource, Bombay Council advised Tellicherry to remain neutral in this regard. Such a position was taken because of the precaution in the context of the emerging Maratha challenge on the Konkan coast. The Bombay Council had also instructed to appoint some emissaries to discuss the company's commercial plans in Malabar with Hydar. Accordingly, Hydar promised that he would respect the East India Company's interests when he conquered Malabar.[28]

Hydar Ali attacked Malabar with the French assistance and he had assured the neutrality of the Dutch and the British powers. Within a period of five months the Sultan Hydar could conquer whole Malabar. Ali Raja, who had also been appointed by Hydar as High Admiral of the Mysorean navy, played a pivotal role in this conquest by acting as a scout for the Mysorean army which consisted of a cavalry of 4000, and infantry of 8000 soldiers.[29]

Though Hydar Ali left to Coimbatore in June 1766, he was forced to come back to Malabar in the following month due to the resistance staged by the Nairs against the Mysorean suzerainty. Before leaving to Coimbatore, Hydar had announced that he had deprived the recalcitrant Nairs of their second place in the caste hierarchy of Kerala and that he had degraded them to the low status of untouchables. Before he leave the country of Malabar, by a solemn edict, Hydar declared that, "the Nairs deprived of all their privileges and ordained that their caste, which was the first after the *Brahmins*, should there after be lowest of all castes, subjecting them to salute the Parias and others of the lowest castes by ranging themselves before them as the other Mallabars [Sic] had been obliged to do before the Nairs; permitting all the other castes to bear arms and forbidding them to the Nairs, who till then had enjoyed the sole right of carrying them; at the same time allowing and commanding all persons to kill such Nairs as were found bearing arms. By this historic edict, Hydar expected to make all the other castes enemies of the Nairs, and that they would rejoice on the occasion of revenging themselves for the tyrranic oppression this nobility had till then exerted over them".[30] But later on, Hydar himself realized the fact that it was difficult to ensure the submission of Nairs, because they would have thought death preferable than to such a degradation. Then he issued a further edict giving concession to those Nairs who wished to embrace Muhammedan religion.[31] Indeed, such a decree could make impact upon the caste oriented hierarchical power relations of Malabar, by which the sole warrior caste of Nairs became hostile towards the Mysore State.

Though Ali Raja had been requesting Hydar to invade Tellicherry, Hydar wished to maintain a rather cordial relationship with the British, at least its neutrality. Ali Raja had often looked at the Mysorean invasion as an opportunity to expand his commercial and territorial interests. Though he had been appointed as the governor of the former Kolathunad, he felt it was inadequate as some pockets of his territory were controlled by the factors of Tellicherry. By the end of 1766, Ali Raja raised claim on Randattara from where the East India Company obtained a substantial amount of pepper. Then he persuaded Rashad Ali Khan, Hydar's foujdar in Malabar, to stop all commercial transactions between Tellicherry and Kottayam [Cotiote]. He also asked the Mysore governor at Mangalore, Shaikh Ali, to ban the exportation of rice from Canara to Tellicherry, and in that way isolate Tellicherry, and cut off Tellicherry from the major sources of food.[32] The interesting aspect of the policy of Hydar in this phase is his quiet diplomacy, where as the 'mercantile Prince's (Ali Raja) was overt and aggressive.

The first direct act from the part of Mysore towards the control of pepper trade on the coast was in the year 1767, by which the Tellicherry merchants were denied permission by the Mysore powers to buy pepper from the hinterland.[33] As a result, the Tellicherry country merchants refused to sign contracts to supply the English East India Company (hence forth referred to as E.E.I.C.) with pepper as had been the procedure previously. The British commerce on Malabar Coast was dwindling mainly due to these designs of Hydar Ali, especially due to a trade embargo on Tellicherry. Large quantity of pepper was ready in several parts and Mahe, Cannanore, and Badagara merchants were having permission to purchase and export them.[34]

These instances are pointers to understand the very motives of Hydar's conquests of Malabar. Hydar had realized the fact that the commercial success of the Tellicherry factors prior to 1766 in Malabar had been based on three important elements; the factors' financial and, even more so, political potential to buy pepper and behave as politicians; the co-operation of the country merchants in playing the vital role of buying pepper from the interiors of Malabar and transporting it into the Tellicherry warehouse on the coast; and the collaboration of Malabar Rajas, their ministers and some of the Kadathanad landlords.

These elements might have been taken for granted before Hydar's conquest with the establishment of Mysorean administration on the Malabar Coast. However, the elements which had ensured British monopoly of the pepper trade were swept away[35]. Administrative structure and policies in Malabar were entirely undergoing drastic changes during this period of time. Unlike the Malabar rajas, Ali Raja in the north, Maddanna in the south and Ali khan at the apex of power in the Mysorean Malabar administrative hierarchy, felt no particular need to have the British on the coast. The British could no longer use their political influence in protecting their commercial interest any more.

In such a situation, the puzzled Factors of Tellicherry had submitted a request before Hydar to lift the embargo in Malabar and make the honourable Company his friends by giving them all sandalwood and pepper produced in his country. Hydar replied that until and unless the Company stopped its support to the Nair soldiers and helped his soldiers, all the sandalwood and pepper shall not be given to the honourable Company.[36] Hydar was making two points very clearly. First of all, the British can't expect pepper from Malabar, as most of it had been destroyed by the Nairs, to whom the support and refuge was extended by the British. Secondly, the British could get pepper only if they stop protecting the Nair rebels and instead help him to subdue them. Hydar also underscored the fact that without giving military hardware to him, the British couldn't procure pepper from the territory of Malabar.[37]

The British decided neither to supply arms and ammunitions to Hydar nor wage a war with him. Kadathanad Raja and Prince of Chirakkal had demanded the Company's assistance and assured pepper from their country to the Company. In reply to the question of the Tellicherry factors, the Bombay council expressed its opinion against risking direct confrontation with the Mysorean Government.[38] But towards the end of 1767 the British was forced to revise this view and thought of a limited intervention on the issue.[39] This belated decision, however, empowered the Tellicherry factors to supply arms which the Rajas of Malabar were repeatedly asking for.

Implementation of such a policy was mainly aimmed at checking the expansion of Hydar's power in Malabar. This policy found its reflection in the first Anglo-Mysore war in 1768. Though it was a war of short span of time, the British had intensified their policy of extension of arms to the native rulers and they were instructed to begin an open war front against the Mysoreans in their provinces. As a result, the Tellicherry Factory concentrated its attack on Ali Raja of Cannanore with a call upon all local rulers to concentrate on the liberation of their own country. By the end of 1768, Ali Raja had been forced to retreat to Cannanore and Maddanna as well as the new Foujdar Venkata Rao had been compelled to withdraw from Malabar.[40] Except Palakkad, the Mysorean presence in Malabar disappeared near totally. Consequently, the Malabar Rajas who had taken refuge in jungles or Travancore returned and assumed their power and the Company again started to collect pepper freely. The first phase of Anglo-Mysore rivalry was come to an end for a short period of time.

The third article of the Treaty of Madras (1769) reaffirmed the commercial privileges of the British on the coast, while there was no mention about the local powers. The treaty had focused on British non-interference in Mysorean Malabar and forced the Tellicherry factory to shelve their alliance with the Malabar power. The treaty provisioned withdrawal of Company's sepoys from Malabar hinterland. The subsequent development shows that ceasefire was merely temporary.

The second phase of Mysorean occupation started with the expansionist policies of Ali Raja of Cannanore. When the British withdrew their sepoys from the interiors of Malabar according to the Treaty of Madras, Ali Raja had bought the Dutch fort at Cannanore. The Company at that time was observing a second round of neutrality.[41] In 1773 Hydar had sent Srinivasa Rao and Sardar Khan to restore Mysorean administration in Malabar. While Sardar Khan and Srinivas Rao attacked the stronghold of Nair power of Kottayam, Ali Raja incited the Moplahs of Randattara to revolt against the British. Though this revolt had no considerable effect, the military action of Rao and Khan forced the ruling Nair family of Randattara to flee again. Then they moved to South Malabar to crush the suzerainty of the Zamorin of Calicut. As the British turned a blind eye to the request of the Zamorin, he made an agreement with the French for assistance. But when Rao and Khan attacked Calicut, the French remained idle and thus the Zamorin's power collapsed.

A few words about the so called 'Nayar influence' and their political and economic influence on the contemporary society may help us in formulating certain hypotheses on new power structures. Apart from the duty of being protectors, the Nairs were also supervisors or overseers in the case of landed property. The Nairs were originally the overseers or supervisors of the nadu, and they seem to have been employed in this capacity as the collectors of the share of produce of the land originally reserved for government purposes. As compensation for this service and for their additional function as protectors, another share of the produce of the soil seems to have been reserved specially for them.[42] Because of their political authority as the *naduvazhis*, the local landlords and the military authority, [certain families had titles of *Ayyayira Prabhu*, (chief of 5000 men) and *Pathinayira prabhu* Chief of 10,000 men)] the Nairs got a prominent place in the pre-modern Malabar society.[43] These chiefs were also empowered to levy customs duties on imports, exports and transports. The right of usurping the estates of decadent neighbouring chiefs had been vested with them. All types of fines could be levied by them and when a man died without heirs the chieftain took his property.[44]

During the period under discussion, Malabar was ruled over by various *naduvazhis* who were predominantly from Nair *taravadus*. From north to south, the authority was chiefly vested in the local level with the Nairs. Randattara (Achanmar), Iruvazhinaad (Nambiar), Kurungoth (Nair), Payyormala (Nairs), Koothali Pulavayi (Nairs), Kavalappara, etc. were the main ruling Nairs of Malabar.[45] There were also further divisions of Nair *taravadus* in the local level that exercised political, social and judicial powers.

The Rajas like Zamorin and Kolathiri acted like the chief lords of many greater and lesser Nair rulers [other local rulers as well] with complete sovereignty to the Rajas. But in some instances, the subordinates rebelled against their masters when everything was in their favour.[46] Gradually, several Nair chieftains declared themselves independent and the E.E.I.C. concluded their settlements with these chiefs. The case of Nairs of Congad, Manoor and Yerterra should be cited in this regard.[47] According to the Joint Commissioners Report, the Kavalappara Nairs were almost in a position of independent 'state' as this Nayar had never paid revenue to any suzerain authority.[48] This trend was perceptible in the context of Mysorean invasion and subsequent British conquest. The Nairs had sought for succour from the foreign powers as well. After the treaty of 1792, the Company concluded revenue settlement with individual chiefs rather than with the sovereign authority. From these evidences it is possible to come to a conclusion that there existed a strong Nayar power in Malabar. These powers are occasionally referred to in the colonial papers and other reports under the rubric of 'Nayar powers'.

There was a major shift in the political equations during the second coming of Hydar in 1774. While the Raja of Chirakkal and other local potentates were aligned with the British before 1766, the impression had spread that the British was incapable of preserving the security of the Malabar Rajas. Accordingly, one of the hitherto strongest allies of the British, Chirakkal Raja with others changed their side and became the allies of Mysore.[49] In March, the Raja secretly made peace with Hydar and accordingly he was appointed governor of the districts of Cotiote (Kottayam), Waynad, Nambullacottah, Iruvanzhinad and Kurungoth.[50] Several other local rulers dared to come out in similar lines and some had even insulted the Company's flag at that time.[51]

Developments in Malabar after the first Anglo-Mysore war prompted the Bombay council to take a decision of reducing Tellicherry's status from a settlement to a residency. There was a clear indicator to Chirakkal Raja and others that the British were no longer a mighty force in Malabar. As a result, the Raja had sent a force of fighting Nairs to get back Randettara and Ezhimala (Mount Delli) from the British. And he had also tried to cut down the trade links between Tellicherry on the one hand and Chirakkal on the other. Though the British protested, they couldn't succeed. In fact it was a hard time for the Factors' trade motives on the coast.

In this context, though the share of Malabar pepper trade with the E.E.I.C. was dwindling, the demand for pepper increased more than ever before.[52] Realizing this, the Board of Directors instructed the Governor of Bombay to supply with arms and ammunitions in return to pepper and sandalwood. The Company demanded to allow country merchants to collect products in Kottayam district. But it is a fact that even before his invasion of Malabar, Hydar had demanded cash for pepper, sandalwood etc. Since the British refused his request he contacted others and by 1773, the Sultan had been getting a satisfactory amount of these commodities from the French.[53] As it was a belated proposal, Hydar refused to waive the embargo imposed by his officials on Tellicherry. A war between the two on this issue was imminent.

A war broke out between the French and the British in Europe and consequently which had its resonance in the land of Malabar as well. It had begun when the Madras Presidency sent troops to attack Mahe to be joined by the Tellicherry troops. Hydar was enraged and ordered his associates to go to rescue Mahe.[54] Though he had also sent an army from Coorg, the English could occupy Mahe in 1779. Considering the act as a breach of the Madras Treaty (because Mahe was treated as part of *Khudadad Sarkar* by Hydar), Hydar attacked fort St. George in the same year and instructed Sardar Khan to attack Tellicherry simultaneously. Thus started the second Anglo-Mysore war, which was the last stage of the second phase of the British struggle to recover monopoly of pepper trade in Malabar.[55]

Sardar Khan could make great advances in South Malabar, who had closed commercial residency of the British at Calicut and moved on to Kottayam to get prepared for storming of Tellicherry. The Bombay council was unable to assist the Tellicherry Factors because they felt that the most immediate and challenging threat which would determine the existence of the presidency itself was raised by the Maratha forces.

In such a troubled time, Tellicherry tried to get the support of local powers to build defence against Sardar Khan. Anjengo and the Raja of Travancore helped them very much and the Malabar Rajas and Nairs were encouraged to wage war against the Mysorean powers. There emerged an alliance between the Malabar Rajas of Kadathanad, Kottayam and Calicut overwhelmingly that fought and defeated the French in Mahe on 19th March 1779.[56]

The British also asked the local merchants of Tellicherry to contribute liberally towards the defence of the Residency. The response was overwhelming, because the traders found the last "oasis of peace and security and good government" in Malabar, that is, the factory of Tellicherry.[57] The following leading traders such as Paliarandi Macky, Comben Alupy, Chovakkaran Musa, Baile Babajee, Bodocandy Amod, and Banibelli Abdulla, etc. contributed a total of Rs. 14,000/- towards the war effort.[58] Until 1781, the Bombay Council could extend support only in the aftermath of its negotiation for peace with the Marathas.[59] Of course, the Tellicherry could manage with this liberal assistance of Tellicherry traders.

Soon after the arrival of the British troops under the command of Major Abington and Humberstone in Malabar, they could hinder the advancement of Sardar Khan in the North. The Mysorean strongholds in the south were easily submitted to the British. Hearing the news, the local lords who migrated to Travancore, such as the Rajas of Kadathanad, Kottayam and Iruvazhinaad came back to their own countries. Likewise, the Zamorin could also restore his power in Calicut.

Since the clouds of the threat from Mysore had almost vanished, the factors submitted a proposal for annexation of Malabar though which was initially rejected by the Bombay Council. The Tellicherry Factory then thought of making the local lords such as Kadathanad, Kottayam, Zamorin, Iruvazhinaad and their allies and in effect, the tributaries. Each Raja had to sign a treaty of friendship, more importantly for transferring exclusive right of purchasing pepper, cardamom, sandalwood and any other spices.[60] Though similar adjustment was made with almost all local powers, the factors could make out the fact that some of the Rajas could not comply with their assurance of collecting and providing estimated pepper to the Company. In such cases, the factors would admonish the Rajas and issued orders to collect the maximum.

In the course of time, Hydar Ali died in action (1782) and the second Anglo-Mysore war was concluded in 1784, when Tipu Sultan and Madras signed the Treaty of Mangalore.[61] But for Tipu Sultan, it was embarrassing to accept one of the provisions regarding the Malabar Rajas. According to the treaty, the Malabar Rajas were part and parcel of the Company, whereas for Tipu they were indeed inseparable part of the *Khudad Sarkar* and nothing could be decided on the province by the British other than through his own officials.[62] The controversial provision was withdrawn due to the objection raised by Tipu Sultan. Thus the commercial and political motives of the British were once again questioned. Nevertheless, as the Company entered the third and last phase of the struggle for the control of the spice trade, Tellicherry was reinstated to the status of a settlement, largely because of the impressive performance its factors had displayed when resisting Sardar Khan's siege from 1779 to 1782.[63]

The most important task before Tipu was the restoration of power in the province. He launched certain innovations on spice trade with a view to take hold of the British influence and by which to weaken them gradually. He imposed quite severe commercial restrictions on the Tellicherry settlement and Calicut Residency. Consequently, the trade of the English settlement of Tellicherry and the French settlement of Mahe had declined. But while permitting private enterprise, Tipu Sultan became the chief merchant of his country, and established state monopoly over gold, tobacco, sandalwood, precious metals, elephants, coconuts and black pepper. Timber also came under its monopoly, the owners of forest being given three rupees a candy. The income of Tipu from forests in Malabar was calculated as 30,000 pagodas.[64]

From Calicut, one of the major centres of timber trade in Asia, some teak wood was sent to Mangalore, where it was used to build vessels for Tipu, and the rest of which was sold to the Indian, Arab, and European merchants. The collection of timber from Malabar forests was one of the main objectives of Tipu Sultan. Initially, a Moplah was in charge of cutting teak wood trees, but later a brahmin was appointed in his place. In accordance with Tipu Sultan's orders, Raja Ramachandra established state shops in every taluk which did business in gold, silver, cloth and other articles. Apart from this, the Sultan had tried to abolish the local bankers and also to take over the functions of remittance and exchange himself.[65]

The British records speak of Malabar forests of Eranad and Velatre [Vellattiri – the Valluvanad taluk] rich with teak wood, black wood, iron wood, jack wood and bentucka (Ventek) which was being brought from the most remote part of the Eastern mountains. There are also references to the felling of trees by Tipu Sultan, who used to maintain a number of elephants with him for the purpose. This trade of Tipu was transformed into an established one with a number of carpenters, labourers, peons and elephants.[66]

According to Mr. William Gamul Farmer, most of these forests were private property and Tipu had made an allowance to the proprietors according to ancient customs of two *fanams* per tree of ten inches diameter, and that since his assumption of monopoly in 1785, the price of timber had risen at Bombay.[67] The mode of procurement of timber as explained by Farmer is quite interesting. "Before the timber be cut down, it must be barked and allowed to stand two, three or four seasons to dry and consolidate; after which it is generally felled in October and November and drag by elephants (the use of which is indispensable) to the water side, in the month of July and when the rivers being then full, these timbers reach Vipoor [Beypore] in the vicinity of Calicut in September, where a merchant can make all the changes and risks included afford on market places".[68] In this way, about 4000 candies of timber were received by Tipu Sultan from Malabar alone.[69]

It is more sensible to believe that the timber trade along with the spice trade had a determining role in the selection of Feroke (a village formerly called Paramukku) as the capital of Mysorean Malabar. After the treaty of Mangalore, (1784) the British were compelled to give up their claim over the province and the whole Malabar was again moved to the hands of Tipu Sultan. The result was the re-assertion of the Mysorean power over Malabar by appointing Arshad Beg Khan as the Governor. It was in 1788 that Tipu decided to move the old capital at Calicut to a much preferable station between seven or eight miles away from its mouth which was better adapted to become a sea port than any other port, and where he built a fort and city, named as Farookhabad.[70]

This new capital was geographically and strategically more important. As it is situated on the banks of river Chaliyar, it could monitor the conveyance of spices collected from the eastern hinterlands and timber from the hillocks. Similarly, the proximity of Beypore port was also an added benefit. The procured goods could easily be transported from the new city without much risk. The whole trade of Calicut might have been shifted to Feroke within days. According to Buchanan, Tipu had destroyed the commercially flourishing city of Calicut which was the seat of Zamorins.[71] It was because of this flourishing river borne timber trade, the British later constructed a saw mill under the initiative of Mackonochie at Beypore, which was a failure.[72] It was along with the establishment of the mill that the British proposed a survey of the forest resources of Malabar. During the time of the British, the timber was also coming from Kuttyadi forest area to Calicut.[73] Apart from that, Baliapatam (Valapatanam) in the North was another centre of extensive timber trade.[74]

The Mysorean administrators, especially Tipu Sultan, had established a wide network of roads in order to expand their commercial as well as political ambitions. Another notable measure by Tipu in order to restrict the British influence on Malabar was to intimidate the local potentates as well as local traders. He realized the fact that the success of British commerce in Malabar was primarily because of the subordination of the local merchants to the E.E.I.C. through the practice of credit system. Similar to his father, Tipu also had realized that the merchants of Tellicherry were lucrative source of revenue. The need to retain the merchants under the *Khudadad Sarkar* was therefore considered important. He thought that the best way to eliminate the Company from the spice trade in Malabar was to ensure that the Moplah merchants should be forced to withdraw from Tellicherry.

Tipu Sultan found Arakkal Beebi as the most appropriate person to implement such an important plan and accordingly she was assigned one in January 1786. Firstly, she sent this message secretly to Chovakaran Moosa, one of the principal merchants of Tellicherry and other five merchants to leave from "the British territory" and she offered assylum either in her own district or in those of the Nawab. Hearing this news, the scared merchants fled to Tellicherry factors seeking asylum and then decided not to leave Tellicherry.

By the beginning of the eighteenth century, Tellicherry had been emerged as one of the prominent trading centres of Malabar. The British flourished in Tellicherry as they conferred contracts to local merchants for collection of spices from hinterlands of Malabar. *Diaries* and *Consultations* of Tellicherry Factory refer to a number of merchants names like Batilapaqui, Baurribetti Cunhippy, Comben Allipy, Chato of Agar, Cacart Tupy, Cunhiseu of Cotiote, Ticandy Cunially, Ekoda Moosa, and Madicarrem Calandera etc., though we are of the exact names.[75] Of course, they were the feeding agents of the British who helped them in flourishing their trading enterprises. By that time, Tellicherry had developed to a modern township and later on became one of the major trading centres on the western coast, where there was even a branch of Madras Bank and branches of three European banks in the beginning of the twentieth century.[76]

Flourishing spice trade, especially in pepper, made Tellicherry to such a prominent commercial centre in Malabar. The mode of procurement of pepper from the farmers of Malabar according to Buchanan was as follows: "In the southern division of Malabar, the traders go to the cultivators of pepper in June, July or August, and advance them money, on condition that in January or February the cultivators shall deliver their pepper at a given price. The money advanced was according to the needs of the cultivator. If he pressed for money, not above two thirds of the value will be given. In other cases, where the cultivator is not so needy, the money advanced was nearer the true value of the pepper. If the cultivator does not deliver the stipulated quantity of pepper, he must pay for the deficiency at the Calicut price, which is considerably greater than the common rate of the interior part of the province. The advance was frequently made in cloth or other goods; but most commonly in old *fanams*, worthy of quarter a rupee. There were many Moplah merchants who were prudent enough to wait for their money until the produce of their gardens is ready for delivery".[77]

Compared to the farmers of southern districts, the farmers in the north were almost under control of the great monopolist Chovvakkaran Moosa, observes Buchanan. The major centres of pepper cultivation in Malabar were Randattara, Irikkur, Kottayam, Kuttyadi, Mananthavadi, Pulpalli, Thamarassery, Kodenchery, Eranad, Valluvanad and Nilambur. Buchanan adds that "farmers of prudence and substance, such as the Mappilas mostly received no advances; but, when their pepper was fit for market sold it to the best advantage, and delivered it at the sea-port towns from 24 to 25 old *Viraraya Fanams* per a *Tolam*, or at from 120 to 125 Rupees a *Canti* of 640 Ib. The case, however, is different for most of the Hindus, who in Malabar are as remarkable for a thoughtless profusion, as in other province they are notoriously penurious".[78]

During Tipu Sultan's reign he had established regional warehouses [*Pandyalas*] in various places in Malabar.[79] In the year 1789, when he declared a monopoly of trade in Malabar, the Sultan established the principal factory at Badagara [Kadathanad], others were in different parts of the coast such as Mahe, Koyilandy, Calicut etc. In any of these factories, the goods were received at a fixed rate, and paid by the government, and were afterwards sold by the factors, on its account, to any person who chose to export them. The price fixed on the goods at delivery was lower, the produce of the country was chiefly exported in vessels coming from Muscat, Cutch, Surat, Bombay, Goa and Mangalore.[80]

The British Factors understood the fact that the local rajas had an influential role in the control of pepper in Malabar. Being the land owners, the Rajas received pepper from the cultivators on payment of rent and in return advanced money to them to provide food and necessities of life. They wielded their power and influence to purchase at low prices the greater part of the balance of pepper. Hence, the Rajas worked closely with the merchants of the province, who bought pepper from them and disposed it to foreign traders, such as Arabs and merchants from Gujarat and the North. The merchants also collected supplies in small parcels from individual cultivators to whom they advanced money and they were not under the direct influence of the rajas.[81] The rajas and the merchants of Malabar, most of them were Mappilas, maintained the pepper trade in a tight grip between them. When there was a competition between the French and the British on trade in Mahe, the rajas and the traders made large profits. Another policy followed by Mr. Farmer was bribing the ministers of the rajas like Shamnauth, the minister of the Zamorin, for easy access of pepper. This strategy was found to be effective as he offered to deliver pepper from the southern part of the territory by using the Zamorin's officers to collect at the vines.[82]

Soon after the Company gained supremacy over Malabar, for the first time the company could claim a total monopoly. Pepper, which was not bound for the Company's warehouses, was declared contraband, and any merchant found carrying it would be expelled from the province.[83] This plan of monopolising pepper was supported by Lord Cornwallis and he expressed his wish that the revenues of the province might be received in pepper as far as possible. The Commissioners were also ordered to turn their attention to Travancore and to secure for the Company a large share of that country's pepper trade as was possible. The Commissioners had soon begun to realize that their policy was a reckless one because pepper was being smuggled at the price of Rs. 200/- per *kanti*[84] [one *kanti* is a unit of measure for weight approximately between 500lb and 560 lb]. Almost all of the Company's pepper was moved to the hands of private merchants.

In 1793, when the British were contemplating on establishing their administration in Malabar, they made no attempt for renewal of the pepper monopoly. The Company demanded half of the pepper produce of the northern districts in payment of revenue.[85] Many of Tipu Sultan's old revenue officers were re-appointed by the Commissioners to undertake the duty of collection of revenue. However, the smuggling done by some Company officials such as Murdoch Brown, traders like Chovakaran Moosa and the Rajas remained unbridled. The fall of Mahe had not put an end to the foreign demands for pepper, because Arab and Gujarati merchants still traded on the coast. It is believed that half of the pepper produce of northern Malabar was smuggled.[86] In fact, by May 1796, four years after the end of the war, the Company had little success to its name in Malabar. It had failed to establish its authority in the northern part of the province, where the revenue was largely unrealised, and its commercial position was little better than that was enjoyed under Tipu. Thus, the company failed to materialize their major objective in the establishment of the monopoly over pepper.[87]

One of the most influential merchants, who emerged in the context of British trade, was Chovvakkaran Moosa of Tellicherry[88]. Moosa's name was firstly found mentioned by the Tellicherry Board in 1779, about eight years after the death of Ezekiel Rahabi, the Jew merchant of Calicut. Buchanan's reference to Moosa as the great monopolist of Tellicherry proves that during the days of Buchanan's journey (1800) Moosa was at the crescendo of his glory.[89] The British accounts from the year 1783 to 1793 speak of the quantity, value and price of pepper supplied by Moosa to the Company. By 1790's Moosa had grown to send his own ships to Mocha and to persuade the king of Kochi to let these vessels unharmed. His trump card in all difficulties was the E.E.I.C., whom he would amiably describe as 'our own Company'.[90]

With the unwavering support of the factory officials, Chovvakaran Moosa created an expanding sphere of influence that steadily swallowed up large chunk of the Arakkal domain. By the 1770's Chovvakarans had become the richest and the most powerful lessees of Randattara district. The English factory considered Ali Rajas as the strong supporters of Hydar Ali on the coast of Malabar. Inorder to hinder the rising influence of the Arakkal house, the Company formulated following measures. Firstly, it could systematically ruin their economic base in the hinterland. Secondly, it patronized the Mappilas who defected from their camp, in the wake of their declining influence in Dharmapattanam as a deliberate strategy to undermine the community support for the Arakkal House.[91]

Moosa's power, prestige and influence were unparalleled and he cannot be portrayed merely as a merchant of Tellicherry. He was entrusted with the task of revenue collection for the local Rajas of Chirakkal, Kadathanad, Kutaku [Coorg] and Arakkal to make payment to the Company.[92] And on several occasions he had extended financial support to the local rulers as well as the Company as their 'banker'.[93] He had also lent large amount of money to the British Company, when it was in great misfortunes. For instance, according to a reference, an amount of 20,000/- *sicca* rupees were borrowed by the Company from Moosa, which denotes to the economic affluence of Moosa.

By becoming revenue farmers and extending loans to states and rulers, the merchants were having leverage over the states. Transforming to be the revenue farmers, merchants were also thought to have achieved direct access to the state power.[94] Instances of payment of cash in lieu of revenue collection, issue of loans to the rulers and the Company etc. shed light to the multi-faceted role of Moosa, a business tycoon of the time. At least three of the qualities of a 'portfolio capitalist' can be attributed to Moosa.[95] To be precise, the indigenous traders, with the association of colonial powers had attained a capacity to accumulate capital in Malabar, though it had not flourished. However, Moosa and other traders adorned a towering presence towards the end of eighteenth century and early decades of the nineteenth century.

As mentioned, Tipu Sultan's aim was to prevent these influential traders from procuring pepper and other articles and transporting them from hinterlands to Tellicherry. However, the Mappila Merchants didn't respond favourably to the call by the Bibee of Cannanore to move from Tellicherry to the *Khudadad Sarkar* for fear of the fact that they would be dispossessed of their wealth.[96] Because they found Tellicherry as the "only oasis of peace and security and good government" in Malabar; their property was not assured of security anywhere else along the coast of Malabar.[97] But they stood aloof from the trade contracts with Tellicherry. The British were deprived of the chance to secure even small quantity of pepper that they had obtained in 1785 for the Company's official trade. [98]

In south Malabar, Arshed Beg Khan was reported to have taken stringent measures against British export and import at the Calicut port. He had issued a series of orders restricting all sorts of freedom of the company trade in Calicut. Mr.Firth, the Calicut Resident resigned because of this 'tyranny and oppression'. Subsequently, Mr. Gribble was appointed as the new Resident and very soon he also realised that he could not get on with freedom. He reported that he had not been permitted even to bring a few necessaries (such as whisky and gin) from Tellicherry. Thereafter Mr. Gribble also resigned and subsequently Arshad Beg Khan was forced to close the Residency of Calicut.

The trade embargo imposed by Tipu Sultan had a far reaching impact on the British trade on the coast of Malabar. Their attempt to lift the embargo was quite futile. They realized that as long as they were reluctant to supply the fire arms to the Mysore Government they would not be permitted to engage in trade in Malabar. It was because of this that in order to beat the Mysorean embargo, the Bombay council deemed Travancore as the major source of pepper. The political condition was favourable for the British as the Raja was anxious to get British assistance against Tipu Sultan.[99] As expected, Tipu made an attack in December 1789, and the British (Bombay Council) considered this attack as a grave threat to the last reliable source of pepper. The Governor General looked at this war as a matter of great importance and initiated a Tripartite Alliance against Mysore. So in 1790, with the support of Hyderabad Nizam and Peshwa of Poona, Cornwallis declared war against Tipu Sultan. [100]

The merchants stayed at Tellicherry until the end of the third Anglo-Mysore war of 1790-92, by which Malabar was annexed by the British.[101] The Governor of Bombay, Abercrombie, viewed the seizure of Malabar as a chance to further the commercial interests of the Company. The Mappila merchants looked upon it as the occasion to further their commercial activities in the interiors of Malabar which had been hindered due to Tipu Sultan's hostilities. Abercrombie, on the other hand, was very much concerned about the necessity to "protect the Moplas who were a very useful merchant class" for their own benefit and that of the Company. Thus the Mappila merchants continued to be one of the principal commercial allies of the Company.

The British had seriously thought of making an alliance with the Malabar rulers and the Governor General Council wrote on the 8th of April and 31st of May 1790 to the Government of Bombay to "encourage the Nayars and native Rajas in Malabar to shake off all dependence on Tippoo...." The Company instructed the Nayars and chiefs to be their dependent subjects and the "Company will pay them a moderate tribute, provided they will give the Company advantageous privileges for carrying on commerce in the valuable productions of their country".[102] To materialise these schemes the British found the Raja of Travancore as "a faithful ally and best friend in India" [103]

Cornwallis had done further to attract the rebels and Rajas to assist in the war. A paper of protection was published inviting the rebels to come under the Company's shelter and support them in their attempt to oust Tipu Sultan from Malabar Coast. It reads: "In the name of honourable company, I, Robert Taylor chief for transacting affairs of the English Nation at Tellicherry, who hereby assure you (here enter the Raja's name) that provided you will enter heartily [sic] into war against Tipu Sultan and act vigorously against him, the E. E. I. C. will assist and protect you and do everything in their power to render you independent of Tipu Sultan . . . . I do hereby further assure you that in any future treaty that you may take place between the Company and Tipu Sultan you shall be included and considered as an ally of the Honourable Company". [104]

In response to this, the local rulers such as Chirakkal Raja, Kadathanad and Kottayam Raja signed treaty of alliance with the English.[105] Similarly, a treaty of friendship was sighed between the Raja of Cochin and the English.[106] The Zamorin of Calicut also signed a treaty to "exert his authority and influence in embodying Nayars of that country and in directing their operations against the common enemy either separately or in conjunction with the British forces.[107] Though the Beebi of Cannanore was one of the allies of Tipu Sultan, she was compelled to sign a treaty with the British.[108] Thus the British brought local potentates under their control and planned to wage a war with their support.

Soon after the attack of the British forces from Madras, Tipu Sultan was forced to withdraw from the Malabar Coast. The British succeeded in making the dissenting Rajas of Malabar as their allies except Beebi of Cannanore. In December 1790, when Abercrombie arrived on the coast, there were only two places, Feroke and Cannanore having the nominal presence of the Mysoreans. The Mysore force had to face the great fall at Srirangapatanam as a result of the joint attack led by the British, the Marathas and the Nizam of Hyderabad. By every means, this battle opened the way for establishment of the British dominance in Malabar.

With the declaration of the takeover of Malabar, the Company decided to constitute a Commission, popularly known as the Joint Commission, to enquire into the affairs of Malabar. The first measure of the United Commission was to announce to the inhabitants a general freedom of trade in all articles except pepper, which was under the restricted privileges of the Company[109]. Though the introduction of the free trade was declared, in other words, it indicated the Company's monopoly in spice trade over the province of Malabar.

Conclusion

As we have seen, the Mysorean state had made a conspicuous presence in the latter half of the eighteenth century in Malabar around a quarter of a century. It is evident from the sources that the most sensible reasons for Mysorean invasion of Malabar were, indeed, economic as well as strategic factors. Lucrative spice trade on the coast, expensive timber, apart from strategic significance of Malabar prompted Hydar and Tipu Sultan to attack and conquer Malabar[110]. For example, the income from revenue until the Treaty of Srirangapatanam was 68, 89, 892 pagodas (over two crores of rupees) including the tribute of 66,666 pagodas from Kurnool. Apart from land revenue, the Mysore state had a huge income from the trade monopoly as well. Of course, this huge sum of income was the main attraction for Mysoreans and later by the British to conquer Malabar.

Hydar Ali and Tipu Sultan desired to control the rich trade of the coast, as much to further commercial links with Muslim West Asia to break down dangerous dependency on the Europeans.[111] Tipu had realised that the decline of Muslim-controlled trade in the Arabian Sea and the rise of the Company's pepper interests on the West coast presented an insidious threat to all the Indian States of the region. Accordingly, he tried to stimulate trade with Arabia and Persia by setting up state trading institutions in the port towns. Tipu seems to have realized the political weakness when confronting the surrogate of a powerful European nation state. Still, he had made an attempt to face the challenges raised by the British mercantilist power with great vigour along with the state monopoly in trade and an aggressive ideology of expansion.[112] He was the only Indian ruler to die in the battle field after a fierce resistance against the British. In such a situation, it is bizarre to add a religious tint to the whole business of statecraft. If religious sentiments can be attributed in the case of the Mysoreans, why don't we consider religion in the case of the Nayaka invasion in Travancore? How far can we argue that all the conquests other than the Mysoreans' are purely expansionist (political) and only the Mysorean invasion religious?

There is no doubt that religion has played a determining role in the case of Mysorean state and bureaucracy. Unlike the Mughals or other Muslim rulers, both Hydar and Tipu were personally pious and were strict practitioners of the religion of Islam and had tried to synchronize the state affairs with Islamic principles. But at the same time they gave ample space for persons belonging to other faiths and, the personnel in their service were appointed without any religious considerations and significant posts were held by non-Muslim bureaucrats. It was on similar grounds that these rulers made liberal grants of land, gold, or money to the temples or religious heads in their own and conquered territories. At the same time, the references to conversions or the cases of religious persecutions are not negligible, though such stories are not fully substantiated so far. Cases of conversions and religious persecutions may be better understood as a strategy of punishment against those who challenged the Mysorean power or state. When some questioned their authority, they retaliated at their best, especially the people of a conquered land. The conquered land, for the army and ruler, is always a conquered one, so the conquerors treated the people of the conquered land as the enemies. In pre-modern times, religious conversions such other atrocities formed modes of punishment either to embarrass the local rulers/ people or the British. When Tipu invaded Jagir near Madras, the territory of Muhamed Ali, the same policy was followed without religious considerations. In the eyes of Hydar, Muhammed Ali was not a co-religionist, but simply an alien ruler.[113] Likewise Tipu had taken staunch punitive measures to a certain sect of Muslims for their bad behaviour. At the same time, there are instances of umpteen number of donations and land grants to the temples and religious institutions of other faith made by the Mysorean state not only in Mysore but also in Kerala[114]. Until and unless we are able to depend upon the indigenous records, it is not possible to get rid of from the British fabricated stories of the conversions and religious persecutions.

The argument based on the religious identity becomes a mockery when we come across the fact that the ever staunchest resistance against Hydar and Tipu Sultan in Malabar was from Gurukkals of Manjeri and Hydros Kutty of Chavakkad, the Mappila rebel leaders. Likewise, the Mappila merchants' attitude against the Mysoreans also, as we have seen, was hostile. They were actually scared of the Mysorean invasion and found it as a severe blow to their 'fortunes' in the context of flourishing British trade. They neither left the place nor sought asylum in Beebi's territory in order to escape from the wrath of the Mysoreans. Rather, they opted for associating with the British, and those who had even financially assisted the British.

To be precise, as could be seen elsewhere, the economic motives played a predominant role in the whole affairs of the state and warfare in Malabar during the Mysore administration. Religion never served as the uniting factor in the case of Muslim rulers in the eighteenth century South Indian rulers. The most obvious example is that of Nizam of Hyderabad, who stood aligned with the British against Tipu Sultan. Every ruler in those times acted according to their political prospects, or immediate gains and religion was never a factor of unity. Religion, for the state or the ruling class was simply an instrument that would make use of the religious sentiments for their political motives, according to the needs of the time. Of course, pepper and other spices determined the whole course of politics commonly termed as 'pepper politics', in the eighteenth century Malabar. And this process was made possible as mentioned earlier, with the assistance and support by the Mappila traders, Rajas and the Nairs of Malabar. Precisely, considering the role of pepper and other spices, the influential role businessmen in state affairs, the rulers' love for spice trade etc. there are abundant corroborative evidences to portray the eighteenth century Malabar state as a 'pepper state'. And for conquest of this pepper state was the sole political engagements evolved.

Notes

1. For a detailed survey of colonial administrator's and nationalist writers predical representations, see, M.P. Mujeebu Rehiman, *The Other side of the Story: Tipu Sultan,Colonialism and Resistance in Malabar,* Kottayam, 2016.

2. Meadows Taylor, *Tipoo Sultan, A Tale of Mysore War*, Madras, 2001 (Reprint), p. 267.
3. Edward Thompson and G. T. Garrett, *History of British Rule in India*, Vol. 1, New Delhi, 1999, p. 206.
4. Francis Buchanan, *A Journey From Madras through the countries of Mysore, Canara and Malabar*, Vol.2, Delhi, 1988 (reprint), p. 350.
5. William Logan, *Malabar*, Vol. 1, Madras, 1951, p. 499.
6. Theodore Gabriel, *Hindu Muslim Relations in North Malabar, 1498-1947*, New York, 1996, p. 203.
7. K. V. Krishna Ayyar, *The Zamorins of Calicut*, Calicut University, 1999 (Reprint), p. 232.
8. Ashin Das Gupta, *Malabar in Asian Trade*, Cambridge, 1967, pages 103 and 113.
9. K. Madhavan Nair, *Malabar Kalaapam* (Mal.) [Malabar Rebellion], Kozhikode, 1993, pp. 13-14.
10. T. K. Ravindran, *Malabar under Bombay Presidency*, 1969, p.1.
11. M. G. S. Narayanan, in P. G. Haridas ed., *Keralavum Swaathantrya Samaravum* (Mal) [Kerala and Freedom Movement], Trivandrum, 2000, pp.21-22.
12. N. Rajendran, 'Shifting Balance of Pepper Trade in the late Eighteenth century', in *Eighteenth Century India, Papers in Honour of Prof. A. P. Ibrahim Kunju,* Calicut, 1981, p.175.
13. C. K. Kareem, *Kerala Under Haider Ali and Tipu Sultan*, Ernakulam, 1973; A. P. Ibrahim Kunju, *Kerala-Mysore Relations*, Trivanrum,1975; P. K. Balakrishnan, *Tipu Sultan*, Calicut, 1959.
14. Dr. N. M. Nambuthiri, ed., *Vellayude Charitram*, (Mal.) [History of Vella], Sukapuram, 1998; See also M.P. Mujeebu Rehiman, 'Bigotry Historiography and Ideology : Gleanings from an 18th Century Chronicle' , *Calicut University Research Journal,* Vol.5 Aug 2005, pp.96-103.
15. N. M. Namputiri, 'A Malayalam Chronicle on Hydar's Invasion of Kerala' *Indian History Congress,* Bombay, 1980.
16. Irfan Habib ed., *Resistance and Modernisation under Haidar Ali and Tipu Sultan*, New Delhi, 1999, Introduction, p. xxi.
17. Eugene F. Irschick, *Dialogue and History*, Delhi, 1994, p. 14.
18. Irfan Habib, *op.cit.*
19. Logan, *op.cit*, p.338; The Kolathiri gave the British an old fort 'Cotacunna' on the banks of river Baliapatanam in 1669. But Logan states that the factory was established in 1694-95; Logan, *Malabar*, p. 343.
20. For example, See, *Tellicherry Consultations*, 15th Dec, 1726, p.55; 2nd Jan 1727, p.61; 6th Jun 1727, p. 112.
21. Logan, *Treaties*, p. 2.
22. Bonaventure Swai, 'Trade and Politics in eighteenth century Malabar', Unpublished Ph.D. thesis, mimeo, University of Dar-es- Salam, Tanzania, 1979.
23. See, William Logan, *Malabar*, *op. cit.,* pp. 343-44. Traditionally, it is believed that Iruvazhinaad and Kottayam were under the suzerainty of Kolathiri. But in

practice we see that some of these principalities independently concluded the treaties with the British.

24. Swai, *op.cit.*, p. 44.
25. *Tellicherry Diaries* (henceforth referred to as T. D.), 1434, p. 21.
26. William Logan, *Treaties*, No. CVII, pp. 97-98.
27. *Ibid.*, No. XXXI, p. 28.
28. B. Swai, *op. cit.*, pp. 96-97.
29. Logan, *Malabar*, p. 405.
30. *Ibid.*, p. 413.
31. *Ibid.*
32. Swai, *op.cit.*, pp. 99-100.
33. T. D. (Tellicherry Diaries), No. 1467, 22 Jan 1767, p. 103.
34. T. D. No.1476, 22nd Mar, 1767.
35. Swai, *op.cit.*, p. 101.
36. T. D.,No. 1478 A, 5th August, 1767.
37. T. D., No. 1476, 22nd March, 1767.
38. Logan, *Malabar*, p. 410.
39. T. D., 1478 A, 30th September 1767.
40. B. Swai, *Op.cit.*, p. 106.
41. T. D., No. 1591, 26th Feb. 1771.
42. Logan, *Malabar*, p. 133.
43. T. K. Gopala Panikar, *Malabar and Its Folks: A Systematic Description of the Social Customs and Institutions of Malabar,* Delhi, 1983 [1900], p. 111.
44. *Ibid.,* p. 112.
45. Logan, *Malabar*, pp. 627-662.
46. *Report of a Joint Commission* [henceforth referred to as *R. J. C.*], Kerala State Regional Archives, Kozhikode, Para 23, p. 23.
47. *Ibid.,* Para 109, p. 134.
48. *Ibid.*, Para 179-80, p. 203-04.
49. B. Swai, *op.cit.*, p. 108.
50. *Ibid.*
51. *Secret and Political Department Diary* [S.P.D.D], No. 21, 1779, Maharashtra Srtate Archives, Mumbai, pp. 654-2.
52. N. Rajendran, 'Shifting Balance of Pepper Trade in the late eighteenth century India,' in *Papers in Honour of Prof. A.P. Ibrahim Kunju*, Calicut, 1981, p. 175.
53. T. D., 11th December, 1773.
54. S.P.D.D., 19A, 13th September, 1778 and *R. J. C.*, Para 27, p. 32.
55. B. Swai, *op. cit.*, p. 114.
56. *R. J. C.*, Para 28, p. 33.
57. T. D , 1514, 3rd April 1794, p. 125.
58. B. Swai, *op. cit.*, p. 117.

59. S. P. D. D., No. 26, Para 37, 1782.
60. For more details of proposals and provisions of treaties, see, S. P. D. D., No. 27.
61. Logan, *Treaties*, p. 83.
62. B. Swai, *op. cit.*, p. 124.
63. *Ibid.*
64. Mohibul Hassan, *History of Tipu Sultan*, Delhi, 2006 (1951), p. 347.
65. *Ibid.*
66. *R. J. C.*, Para 445, pp. 452-53.
67. *Ibid.,* Para 447, p. 454.
68. *Ibid.*
69. *Ibid.,* p. 455.
70. *R. J. C.,* Para 54, p. 62; Buchanan, *Journey from Madras through the Countries of Mysore Canara and Malabar*, Vol. 2, 1800, p. 474.
71. Buchanan, *op.cit.*, p. 474.
72. Pamela Nightingale, *op.cit.,* pp. 100-01; for more details, see also S. P. D. D., Nos. 106, and 109, 1801.
73. Logan, *Malabar*, p. 41.
74. P. Nightingale, *op. cit.*, p. 101.
75. *Tellicherry Consultations*, 1743-44, p.144; pp.26-7.
76. C. A. Innes, *Malabar Gazetteers*, Trivandrum, 1997 (2nd Reprint), p. 455.
77. Buchanan, *op .cit.,* p. 455.
78. *Ibid.,* p. 467.
79. Joseph Scaria ed., *Thalasseri Rekhakal,* Kottayam, 1996, p. 27.
80. Buchanan, *op. cit.*, pp. 515-16.
81. P. Nightingale, *op.cit*., p. 84.
82. *Ibid.,* pp. 85-86.
83. *Ibid.*, p. 87.
84. *Ibid.,* pp. 90-91.
85. *Ibid.,* p. 92; *R. J. C.*, Para 257, p. 294.
86. P. Nightingale, *op. cit*., fn. 3, p.106.
87. *R. J. C.*, Para 210, p. 243.
88. For a detailed study of Chovvakkaran Moosa's engagement with colonialism, See, M. P. Mujeebu Rehiman,'Merchants Colonialism and Indigenous Capital : The case of Chovakkaran Moosa and the East India Company' *, Arts and Ideas* Vol.3, Nos. 1&2, Thrissur, June, 2007, pp. 129-139.
89. Buchanan, *op. cit.*, p. 456.
90. Ashindas Gupta, *op. cit*., p. 128.
91. Ruchira Banerjea, 'A Wedding Feast or Political Arena? Commercial Rivalry between the Ali Raja and the English factory in North Malabar in the eighteenth century', in Rudrangshu Mukherjea and Lakshmi Subramaniam, eds., *Politics and Trade in the Indian Ocean World*, New Delhi, 2003, p. 99.

92. Joseph Scaria, *op. cit.*, p.3, pp.213-14, 399, 540.
93. A. P. Ummer Kutty, *Keyimarute Charitram* (Mal.) [History of the Keyis], Tellicherry, 1995 (1916), p.194; *R. J. C.*, Para 137, p. 164.
94. Prasannan Parthasarathi, 'Merchants and the Rise of colonialism' in Seema Alavi, ed., *Eighteenth Century India*, New Delhi, 2002, p. 201.
95. A 'portfolio capitalist' is an entrepreneur who farmed revenue, engaged in local agricultural trade, commanded military resources, as well as on more than the odd occasion had a flutter in the Great Game of Indian Ocean commerce. For a discussion on portfolio capitalist, see Sanjay Subramaniam and C. A. Bayly, 'Portfolio Capitalists and the Political Economy of Early Modern India', in Sanjay Subramaniam, ed., *Merchants, Markets and State in Early Modern India*, New Delhi, 1990, pp. 242-265.
96. B. Swai, *op. cit.*, p. 135.
97. *Ibid.*
98. *T. D.*, No. 1500, 8th Jan 1787.
99. S. P. D. D., No.32, 25th November 1786.
100. S. P. D. D., No. 40, 28th January 1790; 25th Feb. 1790.
101. S. P. D. D., No. 43.
102. *R. J. C.,* Para 68, p. 79.
103. T. K. Velu Pillai, *Travancore State Manual*, Vol. II, Trivandrum, 1940, p. 354.
104. *R. J. C.*, Para 69, p.80; C. K. Kareem, *op. cit.*, pp.113-14.
105. Logan, *Treaties*, i. XCV, pp.85-86.
106. *Treaties*, i. XCIX, p. 89.
107. *Treaties*, i. XCVII, p. 87.
108. *Treaties*, i. XVI, p. 86.
109 *R. J. C.,* Para 155, pp.181-82.
110. See M. P. Mujeebu Rehiman,'Pepper Timber and the Ports: Towards an Economic Interpretation of Mysore's Engagements in Malabar' , *Journal of the Institute for Research in Social Sciences and Humanities,* Vol 9, Nos 1&2,January-Dec 2014, pp. 39-60.
111. C. A. Bayly, *Indian Society and Making of the British Empire*, Delhi, 1987, p. 62.
112. *Ibid.*, p. 97.
113. Eugine F. Irshick, *op. cit.*, p. 14.
114. For a detailed reference of Tipu Sultan's land grants to temples and Brahmins in Malabar, see Inam Regiset, in C. K. Kareem, *Op. Cit.*

Chapter III

The British Power in Malabar: Genesis of Transition to a Colonial Structure

The formative phase of colonial endeavours in India has gained considerable scholarly attention by historians and social scientists. Those who have attempted to unravel the intricacies of the process of transition of India to a colonial state and economy have also tried to unearth the forces behind those changes. Substantial volume of literature has been appeared as a result of microscopic studies concentrating on the economic and political transformation that occurred in various regions of India. Makeover of the English East India Company (E.E.I.C) from a trading corporation to the administrative establishment in the regions like Bengal, Coromandel, South India, Awadh, Western India etc. has been subjected to serious investigations by the scholars.[1] Interestingly, Kerala is the only region having the least number of studies highlighting the nuances of the changes that occurred in eighteenth century.

The present chapter actually will look into pertinent aspects of the formative phase of the incipient British state and nature of its administration in Malabar. The way in which the historians perceived the early phase of the establishment of the British dominance over Malabar is quite interesting. Most of them, by and large, regarded the Treaty of Srirangapatanam (1792) as a point of reference and a land mark in the transitional phase of the pre-colonial to a colonial society and they are of the view that immediately after the signing of the treaty, there heralded a new era of colonial state in the province. For instance, Pamela Nightingale, who has meticulously explored the nature of trade and politics of imperialism on the whole west coast, observes that gradual transformation of trade into administration occurred between April and December 1792, when the province of Malabar was under the *exclusive* [emphasis added] control of the Bombay Presidency. She underscores the fact that it was for the first time that the roots of imperialism began to appear.[2] N. Rajendran also considers the *acquisition* [emphasis added] of the territory of Malabar in 1792 as a by-product of the commercial rivalry of the European Traders[3]. Likewise, K. K. N. Kurup observes that, 'now [by 1792] their long cherished ambition of Britain was fulfilled and they became the *real masters* [emphasis added] of the coast of Malabar'[4]. Margret Frenz is highly enthusiastic to popularise the stereotypical assumption of 'conquest' than to study the process of transition seriously.[5]

However, the authors mentioned above never attempted to address the questions regarding the process of British 'acquisition' of the territory of Malabar. One has to enquire into the real motives of the British in the period mentioned, by probing whether the British had been successful in pursuing their commercial projects rather than contemplating on the immediate take over of Malabar for direct administration. The early responses from the Joint Commissioners and their correspondence between the Company authorities and the policies taken by the British government induce us to pose some questions regarding the early phase of the British projects in Malabar. The existing theories of 'conquest', and 'intrusion' should be subjected to serious scrutiny against the backdrop of the British revenue settlements and retaliatory steps taken by the indigenous population against the British.

As observed in the previous chapter, the British commercial interests culminated in the protracted warfare and the subsequent treaty of Srirangapatanam in the year 1792 (March 8th). By this historic treaty, two of Tipu Sultan's provinces, say, Calicut (63 taluks) and Palagatcherry [Palakkad] were ceded to the British[6]. Thus, the Malabar rajas expected that they would be got rid off the yoke of Mysore dominance as well as menace of the British, immediately after the victory of war. However, contrary to the agreement of 1790, the Governor General Cornwallis had decided not to grant independence to the rajas of Malabar, but to place them under the direct administration of the British[7]. Actually, the British had no legal status to do this, because, prior to the Mysorean dominance over Malabar, the indigenous rulers exercised the customary right to rule the land, and they hoped that the British would reinstate them after the Mysoreans were defeated. On the contrary, the British officials claimed legitimate authority over Malabar. They followed the same strategy throughout India without any legal or moral basis. This move is interpreted by some as a strategy to achieve economic monopoly over the products of Malabar with the aid of political control.[8] For the local rulers, 1792 was indeed a thunderbolt of dominance that fell upon them by a stronger alien force.

However, there was no easy way out for the British to execute their ambitious projects. Resistance by the local population, decline of agriculture and challenges from other European competitors prompted them to formulate a policy on extraction of spices and related resources from Malabar. They saw the direct agreements with the local rajas as the only solution to the problem. But as there was no effective state monopoly over the pepper trade as prevailed in Malabar (compared to the State of Travancore), the British assumed that such agreements would not be effective. As a result, the Company embarked on reversal of the earlier policy of considering the Malabar Rajas as independent princes paying tribute to the Company but to reduce them to the status of 'Bengal Zamindars'. This is argued to be the most significant factor in the process of the establishment of British power in Malabar.[9]

Cornwallis, the Governor General, was anxious to introduce and establish a feasible system for their future government that shall be calculated to prevent internal dissensions amongst the chiefs and to procure under a regular administration of justice, all advantages to the Company, which their situation and productions are capable of affording both in revenue and in commerce.[10]

For this purpose, Cornwallis directed Abercromby to establish peace and order in Malabar to sign temporary settlements with the Rajas for the payment of one year's revenue in cash or kind. He promised to draw up a plan for managing the commerce and revenues of the newly acquired territories and for the administration of justice.[11] Cornwallis had also instructed Abercromby, the governor of Bombay, to enquire into the present state of the country and to establish a system for the future government. He also promised to offer two civil servants from Bengal in addition to the Bombay officials to investigate the resources and produce of the province and to report the best means of governing it.[12] Apart from this, the Commissioners had to enquire whether the illicit trade, which had long been carried on at Mahe, was so detrimental to the Company's interests. The Bombay establishment revealed its apprehension regarding the ports of Malabar by probing that whether the Company possessed all the Malabar ports, and Tipu could be effectively isolated from the French supplies and military stores.[13]

Apart from this, the following instructions of Abercromby to the newly appointed Commissioners William Gamul Farmer and Maj. Dow reflect the Company's commercial interests in the region of Malabar. One of these instructions was to use mild language with the chiefs and to claim tribute in return for protection. He reminded them that the Company had one powerful arrangement on their side. The Rajas could not very well insist on a literal interpretation of the treaties when they had broken the most essential article – 'the exclusive trade of the country'. Abercromby concluded his instructions by pointing out that it would be more advantageous to the Company if the tribute were paid in pepper, sandalwood and cardamom[14].

It was a huge task for the Commissioners to establish the British state since the local rulers and their lords were in anticipation of the restoration of their powers and titles. That is why General Abercromby instructed the commissioners to adopt a rather cautious dealing with the Malabar Rajas. He had even directed them to use a mild language while dealing with the local chiefs. But this 'policy of mild language' lasted only for a few months. From September 1792, a policy of intervention was favoured, in order to assure E.E.I.C of a monopoly of pepper.[15] Directions to use mild language and five months of uncertainty in the affairs of Malabar Rajas are obvious proof of the Company's lack of confidence to pursue a colonial policy in Malabar.

According to some authors, certain developments in Britain were actually responsible for the Company's delay in annexation of Malabar Rajas prior to 1792. Because the calculations of the British Government and the Directors in London were antithetical to the calculations of the Company officials in India. The loss of American colonies and the ongoing substantial national debt had made the British government in need of revenues but was wary of costly military enterprises. The British cabinet thus wanted its share of the resources from the conquered territories without the burden of administration. On its part, the dominant factions within the Court of Directors continued to envisage the Company as having primarily a commercial, rather than political role in India although many of the Directors also coveted the land revenues of Bengal[16]. But what is not clear is that, why the British couldn't surpass their hurdles in their way to the complete dominance over Malabar after 1792.

When the Bombay Commissioners met at Tellicherry on 22nd April 1792 to discuss their tasks, they had at least three objectives to achieve in the matters of administration of the province. Cornwallis instructed that the company had to make temporary agreements with the Rajas to deliver one year's revenue and was to consider the means of transferring all judicial powers in the province in to the hands of the Company servants. In addition, the Commissioners were to discover how best to enforce a monopoly of pepper trade in the province, which as far as possible was to include the Travancore produce[17].

Though the British establishment acted as masters of the land, there remains the question, why didn't they engage in the permanent treaties? It is argued that, since the Malabar rajas had to play little role in the treaty of Srirangapatanam, the British annexation was no longer conceded by them. It was because of the collapse of the cordial relation between the British and local rulers. In the seventeenth and eighteenth centuries, the Malabar rulers and the British had largely accepted one another as trading partners, but the increasing commercial and administrative motives of the British culminated in the conflicts. The British had formed alliances with the local rulers against Tipu Sultan until 1792. In return, they promised the rajas their independence. After the treaty of Srirangapattanam, the Rajas were reduced to the posts of tax collectors and administrators of the British government and their sovereignty was neglected[18]. The British had no legal right to the rulers of Malabar, and their claim of sovereignty in Malabar can be attributed partly to the view that they were a 'better' superior civilization. To them, it was their moral obligation to liberate the Indian people from the rule of 'despots'. This self image gave the British the idea that their law was superior to other systems and that it was quite unnecessary to take notice of the existing law of a conquered country. The Orientalist perceptions of the British were able to justify their claim to rule, and its associated sovereignty, by preserving the difference between the colonizers and the colonized[19]. The fact is that the British had no actual right to rule over the land of Malabar.

Amazingly, Farmer and Dow, the Commissioners, had firmly raised their objection against expansionist policies of the British and they had also registered their reservations against the policies of Governor General in the first official meeting itself. Another observation of the Commission was that there were even no records to rely on, as Tipu had destroyed all materials. The British presented certain prejudicial statements as if they were facts; for example, to the British, there prevailed no systematic revenue system as the records regarding details of land revenue system in pre-modern Malabar were absent. The same reason was alleged by Mackenzie, that the sources of history of Malabar were destroyed by the Mysoreans[20]. It is to note that, there is no corroborative evidence with regard to these sorts of allegations having the overtones of colonial stereotypes.

In the mean time, the Rajas had returned back to their countries to reassert their previous authority and the British thought that it was unlikely that they would willingly give the commissioners the information needed. There was a possibility of obstructing the Commissioners' enquiries and the rajas would falsify their revenue returns so that their tribute to the

Company should be meagre. It was in this context that Mr. Farmer and Dow insisted the Company to let the Rajas the power of the country in their hands and leave the administration accordingly[21].

The nature of the revenue collected by the British can be better understood as a form of protection money. All Malabar Rajas were reminded of the erstwhile depredations made by Tipu Sultan and their panic was exploited by the British. The rulers such as Zamorin and the Nair chiefs believed that the country might go back to Tipu, and instead of living in peace under the shadow of the Company, all their troubles and vexations might return and they might be driven back into the Travancore country[22]. The Joint Commissioners believed that Tipu had taxed Malabar too heavily, particularly its northern half, and that he had monopolized the internal trade. Logan and others argued that the Mysorean policy towards Malabar was characterized by tax increases which placed a heavy burden on the farmers[23]. The British justification for revenue policy in Malabar was the over-taxation of Tipu Sultan[24]. The revenue records refer to the term *negady* for tax[25]. Thus, by creating a sharp division between the taxation of the 'despots' [read the Mysoreans] and that of the British, they could justify the introduction of a lesser heavy tax.

As mentioned, the Commissioners had earlier criticized the Company's system of government in India. They argued that the Rajas would rule the province far more effectively than the English could do. The Commissioners were conscious of the fact that the British alone could not police the country side in Malabar and the administration can only be made possible through the mediation of the local rajas. The proposals echoed the so-called Cornwallis system, which had underscored the need to compromise with the landlords and other local potentates[26]. The Company followed this policy not only because it was short of trained administrators but also it was lacking a thorough knowledge about the province.

The Commissioners also had proposed to give up the Company's plans of monopolising pepper trade and to put an end to consider pepper in a commercial light. The attempt of monopoly had failed and would continue to fail because the private traders at Mahe had offered higher prices for pepper far in advance than of those given by the Company. Farmer and Dow had realized the fact that when the Malabaris could sell their pepper at Rs. 175/- per *kanti* at Mahe, no threats or coercion could make them sell it to the Company at Rs. 130/-. They had directed the Company to give up its policy of enforcing monopoly by coercion and instead prompted to pay higher prices to their product[27].

This proposal, however, shows an obvious departure from the official colonial policy in Malabar. The Commissioners contested the deliberations of the Court of Directors, and the Governor General had put forward their position before their attempt to carry out their instructions. It is worthwhile to mention Murdock Brown's opinion on the shift in commercial policy of the company soon after its takeover. Brown maintained that "when the Company became sovereign, their interests demanded a total change of the principles hither to adopted in their mercantile transactions in the article of pepper. It was not their interest to reduce, but to raise the price as much as possible so long as there were foreign competitors to purchase it". The Company, he insisted, should have looked into the revenues of the province to reimburse them for the higher prices they had to pay for pepper, and by these means defeated the competition of foreign merchants[28]. It is believed that the commissioners began to change their earlier opinion about the administration of Malabar, shortly after these suggestions were submitted by Brown.

The Commissioners were directed to formulate a temporary scheme of internal administration which might continue until the Governor General had sufficient knowledge of the country to authorize the introduction of a permanent administrative system. As they noted on 22nd April 1792, the local rulers had been retrieved of their previous principalities, the Commissioners were in favour of maintaining the power of the rajas and leaving the administration of the country into their hands[29]. Accordingly, they decided to enter into annual agreements with the local chiefs.

Politically speaking, Malabar was segmented, and in fact the commissioners failed to understand the parcelled nature of power, the mode of appropriation of surplus and status, they were haunted by the problem of determining the real rajas in Malabar[30]. The Bombay Commissioners began at Tellicherry to effect settlements with the northern Rajas of Chirakkal, Kottayam and Kadathanad, who were in cordial relations with the British[31]. In the first set of treaties with the northern rajas, Dow and Farmer had to consider them only as allies of the British. The British granted the Rajas territorial sovereignty over their lands only on the condition that the right of the revenue ultimately will remain in the hands of the British. The Commissioners were highly thoughtful of the fact that if the lesser rajas refused to collect the land revenue, military aid should be given to the different rajas to enforce this right[32]. The raja of Kadathanad was "to remain in the exercise of all his rights on the condition of the Company, deriving from it an adequate revenue, and exercising at the same time a just perception about the inhabitants, their subjects and security for themselves exclusively its valuable products"[33].

Gradually, the British endeavoured to invalidate the legitimacy or the traditional rights of the local potentates by issuing several new orders. For instance, the custom of the rajas and the landlords accepting gifts from the people on the occasion of *Onam* and *Vishu* (annual festivals) was banned by a declaration[34]. In response, there echoed some voices of dissent, especially by the raja of Kadathanad who had refused to forfeit his right to *chunkam* to the company, since this constituted one of the most important sovereign rights of the Malabar rajas[35]. The lack of resources and men was a hindrance towards pursuing resistance movement, and so that the Raja of Kadathanad was forced to succumb to the conditions of the treaty with the Company[36], followed by the Rajas of Chirakkal, Kottayam[37], Iruvazhinad, Randattara and Beebi of Kannur[38]. The treaties and engagements provide ample evidence to suggest that the British had not as yet established absolute power, influence or autonomy over the rajas or the land of Malabar. The immaturity of the Company's policies in the initial phase shows that there were little traces of a coercive rule/state over Malabar at that time.

After eight months of appointment of Bombay Commissioners, the E.E.I.C. appointed the Bengal Commissioners Mr. Jonathan Duncan and Charles Boddam, who joined the former on 12th December 1792. There is no evidence to believe that William Gamul Farmer and Alexander Dow, the two Bombay Commissioners, were inefficient or inept in administrative affairs. Major Alexander Dow had been the military commander at Tellicherry since 1789, and Farmer, though he had no experience of Malabar, had a thirty years career with the Company in various capacities. Then the question arises, why did the British decide to appoint the Bengal Commissioners to work along with the Bombay Commissioners? The possible explanation offered by Holden Furber on the matter is that, in the initial phase of extension of British trading interests, Bombay was looked up on by the Company's authority as less attractive than Madras, or Calcutta primarily because of its unsettled conditions in the Malabar Coast[39]. It was in the light of the confusions and uncertainties that the British decided to appoint two Commissioners from Bengal in the province of Malabar.

Duncan, one of the Bengal Commissioners, started his career as company official in Bengal and Benares and proved that he was one of the first able and upright administrators of British India.[40] He was a man of science, social reform, a philanthropist, cultured, learned, an able economist and a fine revenue administrator[41]. This judgment on him receives powerful support from the opinions of Lord Cornwallis, who looked on Duncan with high favour and pressed the Court of Directors to give him a seat in the Bengal council. It was this impression by the Governor General that caused the appointment of Duncan, firstly as the commissioner in Malabar and then the Governor of Bombay from 1796 to 1811.

Cornwallis had already given general instruction and had explained the scope of the Joint Commissioners. According to which, "they had to enter into full investigation with as much accuracy as possible in the general and particular situation of this ceded country, in respect to its former as its late and present governments and to enquire into judicial administration[42]. The land holders and cultivators were directed to improve the condition of their respective districts and increase productiveness of pepper vines[43]. Both these plans may be deemed as a part of laying foundation to the commercialization of agriculture in early modern Kerala. Agriculture was now exclusively transformed to the production for the market, which was a major shift.

Proclamation of general freedom of trade in articles except pepper[44] (20th December 1792) and prohibition of slave trade and establishment of two special courts of enquiry of justice etc. were the other measures introduced by the Commission. The new Commission was not satisfied with the way in which the treaties were concluded by the previous commissioners and had criticized Mr. Farmer's improper concessions given to the Northern Rajas[45]. They had to undertake a further serious and minute enquiry into the situation of the country about the former and future administration and revenue so as to make commercial advantages in pepper[46]. Accordingly, the commission began to execute its plans by dividing the country provisionally its revenue divisions or collectorships and jurisdictions, civil, criminal and commercial agencies etc[47].

Abercromby transferred the headquarters of the Company from Tellichery to Calicut in the year 1793 by a circular.[48] The establishment of two separate courts of enquiry and justice at Calicut[49] was considered not only as "a channel for authentic information as to the manner and degree in which justice had hither to been administered there in but impress the natives in the enjoyment of their several rights, lives and properties".[50] This establishment was proposed to strictly control the existing system of dispensation of criminal justice based on traditional rules. Neither death sentence nor mutilation of any part of the body was suspended thereafter[51]. The British found judiciary as the appropriate instrument of dominance over the people of Malabar without exerting any form of coercion.

On 8th February 1793, the Commissioners subsequently declared a general amnesty for encouraging reconciliation among the people of Malabar[52]. Such a favourable ambience was very much preferred for pursuing the Company's commercial interests in the region. William Gamul Farmer was appointed the first supervisor and Chief Magistrate, under him two superintendents were to be served for northern and southern districts at Tellicherry and Cherpulasseri respectively[53]. Abolition of extraction of *purushantharam* from Mappila families by the local rulers also was there by come into effect[54]. By introducing such an act, the British might have thought of either the appeasement of rebellious Mappilas or to make the local potentates less awesome to them. On the first anniversary of the treaty of Srirangapatanam (18th March, 1793), the governor handed over a letter to Mr. Farmer, containing instructions and orders from the government[55]. It hints that the Company establishment was suspicious about the effectiveness of the imperial administration in Malabar within one year.

By June, the Company prepared and passed a civil code and the superintendents were directed to function as judges apart from their existing powers. After one month, the rules for revenue administration and for the conduct of the supervisor and superintendents were drafted and passed by Duncan, William Page and Boddam. The initiative to the system to record collection of the country is worth mentioning[56]. As the annual agreements completed their tenure, new agreements were signed with the rulers such as Iruvazhinad Nambiars[57], Kurumbranad Raja[58] (as the legal heir of Kottayam), Kadathanad[59], Chirakkal[60], Randattara etc. A belated agreement was signed with the Beebi of Arakkal for the first time in the year 1795 and she had to pay arrears for the years 1791 and 1792, also had signed another accord regarding Lakshadwip[61]. The case of exemptions given to the Beebi of Kannur stands as the evidence to the absence of an imperial character of the Company.

In the meantime, the British had prepared regulations for the customs house collections, and also prohibited the export and slave trade and trade in gun powder, war like weapons and stores. They also had "declared trade in timber to be free[62], and abolished the levy of profits on black pepper, coconuts etc. as impolitic and instructed the supravisor to levy a modern tax in the shape of license on the retail tobacco trade"[63].

The Company adopted certain further reforms in revenue collection and pepper trade in the second year of its annexation. The most important of which was its decision to relinquish the pepper monopoly and by which it would claim in future only half of the produce by right of its sovereignty[64]. This system, according to the Company, was applicable only to the northern districts, where the cultivators of the southern districts were left free to sell their pepper. In January 1795, Philip reported that the Company had to pay between Rs. 180/- and 205/- for each *kanti* of pepper while private merchants paid only Rs. 150/-[65].

According to another plan, the Company had claimed four-fifths of the revenue for its own use and this was to be collected by its own agents. The former revenue collectors of Tipu were appointed for the posts and theoretically, the power of the Rajas was curtailed[66]. Major Dow urged the government to adopt Tipu Sultan's Plan, according to which, *Moopans* (headmen) were to be appointed to various districts with a proportion of armed Mappilas to assist them[67]. In the case of some local rulers like Chirakkal Raja, the Company had made agreement for a joint administration[68]. This was in one sense a reversal of the existing policy and acceptance of the position of the earlier Commissioners who suggested making the power of the Raja pivotal instead of introducing the Bengal system. The British justification for those recommendations was to meet the overburden of maintenance of army and the lack of sufficient Company personnel.[69]

As mentioned elsewhere, the intervention of the British into the domain of revenue and customary rights such as *janmam* and *kaanam* is a matter of great significance. The Commissioners viewed the status of *Janmi* as being equivalent in all respects to that of Roman *dominus*[70] and by its proclamation in 1793, formally recognized the *Janmi*s as owners of the soil[71]. With the help of the newly established courts of justice the British could legitimize all their reforms regarding the ownership of land. The motive behind this reform, in fact, was the creation of a landed aristocracy as a class of collaborators with the British similar to the case of Bengal. As E. M. S. Nambutirippad rightly observed in one of his earlier writings, by reinstating the landlords and local rulers to collect the revenue, the British were trying to create a 'rent receiving parasitic class'.[72]

The new revenue settlements and reforms were highly detrimental to the existing system of customary rights or *avakasoms*, [the intricacies of which have been previously discussed] so that the beneficiaries of which, the local rulers and regional *Kaanakkaars* aspired to make a concerted effort to get rid of the menace of the colonial rule. The Zamorin was the first Raja to express his opposition to control land revenue under the terms imposed by the Malabar Commissioners[73]. Similar voices of dissent were raised by the ruler of Palakkad, Kunji Achan and his people and many other local chiefs[74]. Apart from which, W. Fawcet had requested the Company to deduct some of the *Jama*[75], and there were also complaints of Kurumbranad Raja and his subjects about the heavy revenue burden.

Likewise, the Southern Superintendent, in one of his letters submitted his inability to collect revenue[76], and also complaints of some 3000 Nairs of Kadathanad[77] were sent to the Company about the anomalies of the revenue collection of the Company. All these point to the fact that the British revenue policy was proved totally ineffective from the initial phase itself.

The immediate and striking manifestation of such a feeling was that of uprisings led by Pazhassi Kerala Varma Raja along with some local chiefs like Kannoth Nambiar, Kaitheri Ambu, Kumaran Emman, Elambilaya Kunchan, Rairu, Menakoran, Paithalottu Nair, Moylan Kannachan Nambiar etc.[78] Parappanad Raja, Unni Mootha Mooppan and Athan Gurukkal were leading figures in the south to pose such challenges against the British. The details of the nature and course of resistance will be discussed in a separate chapter. Interestingly, it was at the same time that the Commissioners recommended shutting down of the Tellicherry Factory alleging increase in expenditure[79]. Added to this were the problems with regard to the treaties with Tipu Sultan, who had intermittently raised his claim over Wyanad[80]. According to the Sultan, Wyanad was not to come under the purview of the Treaty of Srirangapatanam, so that it really belonged to him.

Stevens, the Supervisor, had formulated certain ideas on commercial reforms to be followed by the Company. First, the Company would encourage production of pepper if they levied a tax in cash on the vines in the north, instead of taking half of the produce in kind. Secondly, guards were to be stationed in each pepper garden to see the Company gained its share of pepper.[81] He defended his policy and insisted that it was not practical to purchase pepper directly from the cultivator. He emphasized the great hold of Rajas and merchants on the pepper supplies and repeated Robert Taylor's proposal that the Company should pay the merchants in cash for the pepper they delivered and levy high penalties for any failure to carry out contracts[82]. According to Nightingale, the unbroken hold of the rajas and pepper merchants on the spice trade, the activities of Murdock Brown, and the private interests of the Company's servants in Malabar, in several ways combined to deprive the Company of the commercial advantages envisaged in the acquisition of the province[83].

The power and influence of Murdock Brown within the Company was enormous. Mr. Brown, a French merchant of Mahe joined the Company's service in 1793. Born a Scot, he became successively a Dane, an Austrian and later a Frenchman, and wherever smuggling or illicit trade was carried out, he was sure to be involved. Even his detractors had admitted his intelligence and unparallel knowledge of Malabar and if anyone had the influence or initiative necessary to overcome Tipu Sultan's prohibition, it was he alone. Brown had been described not only as a shrewd merchant but also as a man of close contact with the higher bureaucrats of the E. E. I. C., especially the Governor Jonathan Duncan.

Walter Ewer, one of the directors of the Company and William Gamul Farmer etc. had high impression regarding Brown. As Brown spent most of his time in Malabar, he had a good command over Hindu laws, culture, and the vernacular language, that is, Malayalam. Since Duncan was one of the founding members of the Asiatic Society of Bengal, he was keenly interested in these matters and had appreciated the work of Brown. Most of the British officials disliked the dubious activities of Mr. Brown[84]. However, Duncan's ignorance of commercial knowledge gave Brown a great deal of influence over him. Duncan never questioned the commercial advice of Brown and he used his influence to defend Brown's appointment as the Deputy Commissioner of Police, despite the fact that it was opposed by the Bombay government[85].

The Report of the Joint Commissioners was submitted in October in the year 1793. The Supravisor Farmer had been directed to suppress the insurgency of the local rulers especially in the high range of Wayanad. The rebels were Pazhassi Kerala Varma Raja[86] and local Chiefs such as Kannoth Nambiar, Kaitheri Ambu, Kumaran, Emman, Elambilaya Kunchan Rairu, Mena Koran, Paithalottu Nair etc.[87] Being a failure in suppressing the uprising, Farmer was forced to resign and Stevens was appointed to take up the task. Though he had some particular proposals in tune with the British mercantilist ambitions, an allegation of bribery was raised against him and accordingly he was succeeded by Mr. Handley. Even when strategies of war were designed, and compromise formulae were repeatedly chalked out, the Company officials failed to gather the spices.

Besides, out of total revenue of more than Rs. 140,000/- due for the years ending September 1795, no less than six lakhs of rupees remained unrealized on 31st October 1795. Prior to Mr. Duncan's arrival at Calicut on 21st November, the Supervisor had, however, collected Rs. 1, 67, 704/- of the arrears, but a balance of nearly 4.5 lakhs of rupees remained unaccounted. It is clear that the system of settlement adopted by the Joint Commissioners was unsuited for the circumstances of the country[88].

Thus, by May 1796, four years after the end of the war, the Company had little success to its credit in Malabar. It had failed to establish its authority in the northern part of the province, where the revenue was largely unrealized and its commercial position was little better than it had enjoyed under Tipu[89].

In this situation, Duncan created a new Malabar Commission by appointing Thomas Wilkinson, Alexander Dow, Augustus William Handley and Robert Rickards on 19th May 1796. The new Commission brought Murdoch Brown back to prominence and influence and removed his enemies from power. But some of his clandestine activities were subsequently identified and one of the Company officials thought that Murdoch Brown was the Chief incendiary of the country. And it was realised that, in the correspondence with the local Rajas, Brown was not paying proper respect and it is believed that, it was a serious matter 'as contempt of the rajas, has always been one of the first seeds of revolt'.[90]

Though the Commissioners sent troops to suppress the revolt of Pazhassi Raja In January 1797, because of the Pazhassi's mode of jungle warfare, it is said that the Company had lost more men than had Cornwallis at the siege of Srirangapattanam[91]. The Company had requested for peace and accordingly Pazhassi stood aloof from further retaliation against them. However, the peace agreement did not last long, as Wellesley was appointed as the Governor General with larger imperial motives. His pursuit of an unrivalled mastery over the province was occasioned by the death of Tipu Sultan (1799).

For William Thackeray, who prepared a report on the revenue affairs of Malabar and Canara, the civil war had dissipated the revenue collection in the province. The table produced by him shows that only 3, 85, 223 pagodas were collected against the settlement amount of 37, 92, 856 pagodas. An exorbitant rate of 60 percent of land tax, he states, was unbearable for the rulers[92]. The British were collecting revenue from the local potentates and they were extracting the same from the farmers[93]. It was in this context that the Company appointed a new Malabar Commission to make arrangement for exaction of revenue under John Smee and naturally it caused fresh incidents of conflicts and as a result, the atmosphere of peace was got clouded again.

From 1784 onwards, the Company upheld the view that Tellicherry as a settlement was useless to the Company. The intermittent wars, Tipu Sultan's embargo on Malabar Coast etc. had forced them to think as 'nothing is to gain on Malabar side'.[94] Even in 1789, when Tipu attacked the territory of the Raja of Travancore, Lord Cornwallis was of the opinion that the Bombay Presidency be dissolved[95]. The experiences after the establishment of the Company administration in Malabar prove that no considerable advancement was made possible during that time. Inability of the British officials to collect the estimated revenue demand and persistence of non-payment of revenue and uprisings led by the local chiefs proved that it was very difficult to establish colonial administration in Malabar. Consequently, the province was transferred to the jurisprudence of the Madras Presidency in May 1800 with a view to fight the rebels expeditiously[96]. It was followed by abolition of the two superintendent ships and dismissal of the Malabar Commission. The generally stated instant reason (also the official version) was the convenience of administration, and prosperity of the people, "as it is the object of the British Government to promote and ensure." [97] This, however, cannot be taken at its face value, though the actual reason for the transfer was the above mentioned climate of rebellions.

The new regime of Fort St. George (Madras) introduced certain important measures. First, it was the dismissal of the second Malabar Commission and the appointment of William Mc. Leod as the principal collector. Secondly, Mc. Leod's orders to disarm Malabar (Arms Act) in 1802[98], which was followed by new tax policy and governor's declaration of martial law of 1803[99]. These measures gave a fillip to the rebels and they raised an unprecedented resistance, culminating in the storming of Calicut prison. Accepting the moral responsibility of deterioration of law and order in the province, Mc. Leod resigned and Rickards was appointed as the new principal collector. As an immediate response to the troubled situation, Rickards introduced new measures of reduction of rate of revenue.

Nevertheless, Richards also could not surmount the waves of popular discontent, manifested in the form of revolts at Kalliat and Anjarakandy, which finally led to his own expulsion from the seat of district administrator. Thomas Warden, the new collector could make some advances in 1804 November by assigning *Malikhana* to the former rulers with a view to mollify them and to get their support in the future. The only ruler who stood defiant was none other than Pazhassi Raja. It was only after a protracted and bloody encounter that the Company could capture Pazhassi Raja in the year 1805[100]. As their age-old enemy in Malabar was being made part of history, it culminated in the beginning of the colonial rule in the province.

Most of the studies that analyze the character and impact of early phase of colonialism in India lead us to certain generalizations. The most notable and debated among them is the concept of "partnership" between the British and the Indians. Holden Furber was the first scholar to formulate the idea of "dialogic" character of British colonialism. He used to call the period between 1500 and 1750 as the "age of partnership". This aspect of dialogic process was later elaborated by Eugine F. Irshick in his elaborate study on colonialism in Madras (Jaghir)[101]. He observes that for the process of interaction, the British used to refurbish or establish the religious centres [temples] and had followed the custom of beating 'tumukku', a drum to announce the state policy, with a view to get respect and obedience to the government[102]. In the case of Malabar, there were also directions to the company officials from Governor General on the need for knowing Malayalam, which can also be considered as a technique for making the people of the land closer to colonial administration[103]. There were also some directives to use force and make changes in culture in order to dominate the indigenous people culturally.

Similar kind of an example was also seen in 1775 in Benares, where the British obtained sovereignty over the land and became the protector of that great Hindu pilgrim centre[104]. More or less the same practice was followed by the British in Malabar that, three *thangals* or *Sayyids* (highly revered Muslim spiritual leaders whose pedigree is related to the prophet) of Malabar, namely, Putiyangadi thangal, Koyilandi thangal and Kondotty Thangal, by making a grant exempting their lands from payment of the revenue, as had been the custom during Tipu Sultan's time, on the condition that their people would stand loyal to the British.[105] Issuing of *Malikhana* also may be considered as a step towards this direction.

In fact, the actual loyalty or direct support was extended from the merchants and newly created class of Zamindars, bankers etc. To Bayly, the British colonial establishment was instituted and extended upon a strong base of partnership with Indian merchant class. The influence of Jagath Seth and Omi Chand in Bengal and Delhi is cited as examples[106]. Both had benefited from each other in their business where the "Indians remained therefore active agents and bystanders and victims in the creation of colonial India". By this process, India was made tributary to the capitalist world system[107]. But, Indians were merely passive agents, and really the unfortunate losers. Scholars such as Prof. A. K. Bagchi, in one of his recent works, challenge the collaboration position of Bayly and other Cambridge historians[108].

However, the argument that commercialization on Malabar coast had gone further than Bengal and Madras[109] is not corroborated by substantial evidences. One thing is certain that though the state was parcelled, the economy of Malabar was not a static one, as the production, especially agriculture, was aimed at the 'national' or international markets. Nightingale is of the view that both in India in general and Malabar in particular, merchants found it necessary to exert political power in order to safeguard and extend their trading interests[110]. But scholars like P. J. Marshall maintain that Wellesley's larger political motives were the causative factor for expansion of India[111]. (The most crucial thing we lose in this sort of discussion is the real culprit, that is, colonialism and its policy, instead of revolving around a few individual administrators). Similar to Aukrur Dutta of Bengal[112], the British had made some influential merchants such as Chovvakaran Moosa in North Malabar, their allies, with whose association they could collect the spices with lesser strain.

Nevertheless, the Company failed in establishing a powerful colonial state during the initial years of its acquisition. For example, in theory, the settlement of 1765 had established a British Bengal, though Orissa remained unconquered until 1803[113]. And in the case of Benares, though the British had obtained administrative powers in the year 1775 in Benares, they couldn't exercise any direct political authority for quite some time. From 1788 to 1795 it was a brief transition period for Benares. In Madras also the British could make a break though only by 1821 with the introduction of *Ryotwari* settlement, although it had acquired the right of direct administration in 1782[114]. In the period from 1792 to 1805, one cannot claim the existence of any sort of a powerful state/government. Rather it can be termed merely as a transitional period of colonial economy and polity. Obviously, the imperial state during this time had failed to consolidate as an integrated state or an administrative structure.

As a matter of fact, the British introduced Permanent Settlement in order to make the elite class its allies. In the new system petty kings, the revenue and military entrepreneurs, the great bankers and warrior peasant lords represented the forms of indigenous capitalism[115]. The British created a market in land by making permanent land revenue settlement in 1795, "by giving title to land to those the British considered *zamindars*; by using land sales to realize delinquent tax payments; and by failing to settle land rights within lineages which were recognized as zamindars"[116]. They had also introduced signing of revenue settlement in Malabar with the local chiefs and landed aristocracy. And it was their method to look at *janmis* as the owners of land like that of European system (It will be discussed in detail in the next chapter). Apart from this, permanent registration of land was also introduced in 1794.[117] In order to create private property in land, the British started to occupy and control the waste land and whose 'owner' would be required to pay the revenue to them.[118]

According to the Cambridge historians, the Indians had always been collaborated with the British in their political expansion in India. According to them, the British administrators had realized the fact that, in order to assign routine business of the Company, the Indian civil servants were better option. In places like Benares, the British district officials were faced with the immediate task of recruiting a large number of clerks, scribes and peons, who also had to employ some Indians in responsible positions as *amils* or *tahsildars* (local tax collectors) and low officers[119].

In Malabar also the British had experimented recruiting indigenous people in to the emerging British bureaucracy. For instance, officers called *Moopans* or chiefs, who were formerly the local revenue collectors, were appointed by Mysorean rulers and now their rights were reinstated. The *Menons* and other upper caste Nairs had opportunity to get appointed to the clerical and other coveted posts under the British. As the British revenue system introduced in Malabar was simply the adaptation of the Mysorean revenue administration[120], a large number *paradeshi* (foreign) brahmins who were previously the civil servants of Mysore were also reinstated. However, these instances are sufficiently frail to argue that the British had considered Indians as equal partners; indeed, the equal partnership in a state craft, where white superiority ruled roost, was quite intolerable.

Bernard S. Cohn argues that even the country-born Europeans, the *dubashis* (bi-lignuist), many of whom engaged in small-scale trading activities, were looked upon with suspicion and they were treated as untrustworthy[121] by the colonial state. He goes on to argue that by the opening up of the colonial project of 'knowledge', which includes translation, surveys, studies etc., a great number of Indian scholars, teachers, scribes, priests, lawyers, officials, merchants and bankers, whose knowledge as well as they themselves were to be converted into instruments of colonial rule. And more importantly, they were subjected to the scrutiny and supervision of the white *sahibs* who ran the everyday affairs of the Raj[122]. In fact, the British wanted to make use of Indian service, which does not mean it was an association of partners with equal power and political clout. Indians always were a subject class under the colonial masters. So it can be categorically argued that the "partnership" theory of the Revisionist historians is a "motivated" and absurd one.

In the formative years of the British colonial rule in Malabar, the British had made some attempts to bring the land under their control by survey of resources, preparation of maps etc. Since 1790's the British had started to conduct exclusive surveys in India. They began a systematic survey of India as early as 1765, when James Rennel was appointed to undertake a general survey of the newly acquired Bengal territories[123]. Much of the information that enabled the British to control and tax their Indian possessions was gathered by army and naval officers and resulted from the growing military character of the Company after Cornwallis. Officers accompanying residents on their postings extended the techniques of the great cartographer James Rennel to the Indian interior and drew the maps which were later filled out by the revenue surveys of 1814-35[124].

Malabar also was not an exception to this nationwide project. In Malabar, the Vettattunad estates were surveyed by Capt. Moncreif, along with Col. Sartorious. He had surveyed the rivers of the country and Lieutenant Monier Williams drew up the first map of Malabar under Moncrief's supervision.[125] Investigations of Indian resources, particularly on the west coast were driven by the need to find suitable varieties of timber for the Bombay Marine[126]. As the rivers were the main channels of conveyance of products, especially spices and timber, this kind of surveys or inspection invites special attention.

These projects of surveys and preparation of cartography must be seen as part of a larger colonial project, which were associated with the preparation of a series of reports and travelogues with specific objectives. For instance, The Report of a Joint Commission (1792-93), The Revenue Report of William Thackeray (1807) etc. were closely associated with the larger frame work of colonial dominance. The Joint Commissioners' Report can be seen as a typical example of the colonial 'gaze' upon the people, their customs as well as resources. It had attempted to survey almost all details with regard to the state and economy. It is argued that the work of Buchanan is the best example of what Cohn has called as 'survey modality', one of the early colonial strategies of creation of knowledge of the colonized people.

The description of Malabar landscape presented by Buchanan goes beyond a simple report of a traveller or surveyor but its assumptions of a plantation owner interested in transforming the landscape for furthering his investment opportunities[127]. His journey must be seen as part of colonial knowledge production, similar kind of which were undertaken in many other regions of the country. Like Buchanan, Thackeray, in the year 1807, describes the natural resources, especially of rivers and the possibility of widening and connecting them for convenience[128]. The establishment of plantations of cinnamon, coffee, pepper, nutmeg, spices, cotton etc. can be understood as part of the continuous process of colonial extension. The plantation at Anjarakandy in Kannur under Mr. Murdock Brown's supervision was a very palpable development[129].

The British had posed serious danger to the ecology of this region in the very early phase of colonial intervention in Malabar. Protracted warfare in the hilly regions along with the introduction of plantation and monoculture had badly affected the environment as well. The teak plantations of Eranad and Valluvanad taluks were the commercial destinations, the reported deforestation, felling of teak by the British etc. had contributed to the reduction of water level in the area[130]. Besides, Arthur Wellesley played a prominent role towards this, when he drove roads through forests of Malabar by clearing trees to a mile on either side in his campaigns against Pazhassi Raja (1800-02)[131].

The new regime was established in societies which were undergoing ecological, cultural, social and economic transformation. According to the New Cambridge school of historians, the process of change had begun long before 1765. Taking the case of Bengal, P. J. Marshall maintains his position that, the phenomena such as commercialization of some parts of agriculture, a brisk circulation of right to collect revenue and stratification of cultivators into rich and poor that are sometimes attributed to the British, were clearly present in the Bengal under the Nawabs as well.[132] The motive behind this kind of position is to popularize the view that colonialism had done nothing detrimental to the colonies except pursuing their civilizing mission. According to them, the adverse effects attributed to colonialism, were of course present long before in the pre-colonial society-though which has been challenged by historians. (However, the coming chapters will pay attention to those arguments in the context of Malabar, and examine the validity of such arguments.)

Conclusion

In fact, the existing understandings on the British annexation of Malabar demand serious re-consideration. The analysis of the positions of scholars like Pamela Nightingale, K.K.N. Kurup, N. Rajendran, Margret Frenz and others, tempt us to argue that Malabar was neither conquered nor consolidated by the British in the year 1792. Instead, until the death of Tipu Sultan (1799), they failed to materialise any breakthrough in state formation, but could only make some arrangements for the fulfilment of the spice trade. A close examination of the annual treaties and permanent treaties with the local potentates of Malabar, leads us to the conclusion that the treaty of Srirangapatanam had no legitimacy and the rulers of Malabar paid no serious attention to it. Secondly, instead of introducing a genuine revenue policy of their own, the British in the initial phase imitated the *Jamabandy* system of the Mysore State. Thirdly, the nullification of once declared pepper monopoly in Malabar is a clear indication of the lack of confidence of the British establishment. Fourthly, the British were puzzled as they failed to tackle with the claims of Tipu over Waynad and intermittent challenges posed by Pazhassi Raja and other rebels. This had greatly hindered the British appropriation of revenue and spices throughout the region of Malabar. Since the insurrections along with the resignation/ dismissal of the collectors or officials became order of the day, the British were demoralized to pursue their administrative ambitions. As they were unsuccessful in attaining its goal of absolute control over Malabar province, the British were forced to declare transfer of Malabar to Madras Presidency in 1800, but still the problems remained unchanged.

To be precise, the dilemma of the British in Malabar continued up to the annihilation of Pazhassi Raja in the year 1805, and only after which they had embarked on preparing the new revenue settlement and sought for new collaborators. This was accompanied by conducting surveys and preparation of cartography in Malabar. And in most of the regions in India, the British were not able to establish their predominance and sovereign power soon after their 'annexation'. But they had to wait for a favourable environment which was to be made possible by the collaboration of native 'partners'. The practices of accepting some cultural motifs and paying reverence to religious leaders, refurbishing or establishment of temples, supporting temple festivals, exemption from taxes to religious leaders or giving directives to learn local languages were in fact experiments towards getting support of influential sections of the Malabar society. Nonetheless, with the limited power they attained, the British could succeed in creating a rupture in the pre-colonial economy and society. Indeed, it is worthless to apply a stereotypical model of British acquisition of Malabar and establishment of colonial state without going deep in to the details of state craft.

Notes

1. P. J. Marshall, *East India Fortunes: The British in Bengal*, New Delhi, 1976; *Bengal; the British Bridge head, Eastern India, 1740-1828*, New Delhi, 1990; C. A. Bayly, *Indian Society and Making of British Empire*, New Delhi,1987; *Rulers, Townsmen and Bazars, North Indian Society in the Age of British expansion*; New Delhi, 1992; Bernard S. Cohn, *An Anthropologist Among Historians and other Essays*, Delhi, 1990, Holden Furber, *John Company at work, A Study of European Expansion in India in the eighteenth Century*, 1948; Eugine F. Irshick, *Dialogue and History, Constructing South India*, New Delhi, 1994.
2. Pamela Nightingale, *Trade and Empire in Western India, 1784-1806*, New Delhi, 1970.

3. N. Rajendran, *Establishment of British Power in Malabar (1664 to 1799)*, Allahabad, 1979.
4. K. K. N. Kurup, *History of Tellicherry Factory, (1683 -1794)*, Calicut University, 1985, p. 212.
5. M. Frenz, *From Contact to Conquest, Transition to British Rule in Malabar 1792-1805*, New Delhi, 2003.
6. William Logan, *A Collection of Treaties Engagements and other papers of importance Relating to the British Affairs in Malabar* (here after *Treaties*), ii, No. II, 18th March, 1792.
7. Correspondence between Cornwallis and Henry Dundas exposes the underpinnings see, P. Nightingale, *op. cit.*
8. M. Frenz, *op. cit.*, p. 76.
9. N. Rajendran, *op. cit.*, p. 236.
10. Letter from Cornwallis to Abercromby, 23rd March 1792, cited in P. Nightingale, *op. cit.,* p. 69.
11. *Ibid.*
12. W. Logan, *Malabar*, vol. 1, Madras, 1951, p. 475.
13. Bombay to Charles Mallet, 21st March 1792, cited in Nightingale, *op. cit.*, p. 70.
14. Letter from Abercromby to Maj. Alexander Dow, cited in P. Nightingale, *op. cit.,* pp. 74-75.
15. M. Frenz, *op. cit.*, p. 99.
16. Michael H. Fisher ed., *The Politics of the British Annexation of India, 1757-1857*, Introduction, Delhi, 1993, p. 13.
17. P. Nightingale, *op cit.,* p. 74.
18. M. Frenz, *op. cit.,* p. 152.
19. *Ibid.*
20. Mahalingam ed., *Mackenzie Manuscripts,* cited in M. Frenz, *op. cit.,* p. 175, 177.
21. Minute of the Joint Commissioners, Farmer and Dow, 22nd April, 1792, Tellicherry, cited in P. Nightingale, *op. cit.,* p. 75.
22. Logan, *Malabar*, p. 506.
23. *Ibid.,* p. 638.
24. R.J.C., 1792-93, para 459-61. pp. 465-468.
25. R.D.D., No. 14, 1795, p. 126.
26. B. Swai, 'Notes on Colonial state with special reference to Malabar in eighteenth and 19th Centuries', *Social Scientist*, Vol. 6, July 1978, p. 52.
27. Minutes of the Joint Commissioners, 22nd April, 1792; cited in P. Nightingale, *op. cit.*, p. 75.
28. Letter from M. Brown to Malabar Commissioners, 1st September, 1792. The role of private merchants like M. Brown in the shaping of Company Policy has not been properly studied.

29. Minutes of Joint Commissioners, 22nd April 1792, cited in P. Nightingale, *op. cit.,* p. 75. For a detailed discussion of the political structure of pre-modern Malabar and the question of land revenue, see chapter I.
30. B. Swai, *op. cit.,* p.55.
31. K. K. N. Kurup, *op. cit.,*, p. 214; Logan, *Malabar*, p. 475; Secret and Political Department Diary (here after S. P. D. D.) No. 44, 1792, pp. 921-26.
32. B. Swai, *op. cit.*, p. 56.
33. *R. J. C.*, Para 83, p. 109.
34. *R. D. D.,* No. 14, 1795, p.126; *R. J. C,* Para 257 and 262; Logan, *Treaties*, No. ii. xxxv, 19th Jan. 1793. Though the treaty was actually signed with the Zamorin, it was applicable to the Rajas of Chirakkal, Kottayam, Kadathanad, Beypore, Kurumbranad, Parappanad, Vettattunad, Vellattiri, Palaghat, Kavalappara etc.
35. *R. J. C.*, Para 308, p. 344.
36. Logan, *Treaties*, No. ii. IV; *R. J. C.*, Para 83, p. 109.
37. Logan, *Treaties*, No. ii. V and VI; *R. J. C.*, Para 83, p. 109.
38. *R. J. C.*, Para, 83, 84, 85 and 86, pp. 109-113.
39. Holden Furber, *Bombay Presidency in the Mid Eighteenth Century*, Bombay, 1965, p. 3.
40. See, Narain V. A., *Jonathan Duncan in Varansi*, 1959.
41. P. Nightingale, *op. cit.*, p. 94.
42. Logan, *Malabar*, pp. 481-82.
43. *Ibid.,* p. 482
44. *R. J. C.*, Para 155, p. 181; Logan, *Malabar*, p. 484; Logan, *Treaties*, No. ii. XXXIII.
45. *Jonathan Duncan's Report on Revenue Settlement of Malabar*, 1794, p. 1.
46. *R. J. C.*, Para: 154, p. 180.
47. *Ibid.*
48. Circular letter of 30th March 1793, by general Abercromby to Principal rajas and all rajas, cited in T. K. Ravindran, *Malabar Under Bombay Presidency*, Calicut, 1969, pp. 72-74.
49. Logan, *Treaties*, pp. 171-72.
50. *R. J. C.*, Para 156; Logan, *Treaties*, No. ii. XXIV.
51. *R. J. C.*, Para, 190; Logan, *Malabar*, p. 485.
52. Logan, *Treaties*, No. ii. XXIX, 8th February, 1793
53. *Ibid.*, No. ii. XXXII, 30th March 1793
54. *R. J. C.*, Para 185; Logan, *Treaties*, No. ii. LXIII, *Purushantharam* levied by the Zamorin and other Rajas of Malabar on the effects of deceased Mappilas varying from 5% to 20%.
55. K. K. N. Kurup, *op. cit.,* p. 273.
56. *Ibid.*, p. 224.
57. Logan, *Treaties*, No. ii. XLI; *R. J. C.*, Para 265-68, pp. 305-09.
58. *Treaties*, No.ii. XLII; *R. J. C.*, Para 314, p. 351.

59. *Treaties*, No. ii. XLV; *R. J. C.*, Para 264, pp. 304-05.
60. *Treaties*, No. ii. LV; *R. J. C.*, Para 26, p. 27.
61. Logan, *Treaties*, No. ii, XXXIV, XXXV; *R. J. C.*, Para 246, pp. 282-83.
62. Free trade in the case of timber means that both the English and natives can engage in freely; in the case of pepper, British found the monopoly was in failure and cultivators were declared free to sell their products to their wishes (on April 15, 1793). See Nightingale, *op. cit.*, p. 91.
63. Logan, *Malabar*, p. 496.
64. Nightingale, *op. cit.,* p. 91.
65. *Ibid.*, p. 104.
66. *Ibid.*
67. Spencer, Smee and others, *Report on the Administration of Malabar*, cited in T. K. Ravindran, *op. cit.,* p. 7.
68. Logan, *Treaties*, No. ii. LV, 5th July 1793.
69. S. P. D. D., No. 43; pp. 445-512.
70. Logan, *Malabar*, p. 495.
71. B. H. Baden Powel, *The Land system of British India*, Vol. III, 1990 (1892).
72. E. M. S. Nambutiripad, *Kerala Yesterday Today and Tomorrow,* Calcutta, 1968 [1967], p. 93.
73. B. Swai, *op. cit.*, p. 56.
74. R. D. D., Vol. 2, No. 14, 1795, pp. 88-89.
75. *Ibid.,* p. 348.
76. *Ibid.*, p. 94.
77. *Ibid.*, p. 263.
78. K. K. N. Kurup, *Pazhassi Rekhakal* (Mal.) [Pazhassi Records], Calicut, 2004, p. 49.
79. *R. J. C.*, Para 509, pp.518-19; Logan, *Malabar*, p. 500.
80. *S. P. D. D.*, No. 55 (1797); No. 57, 1797.
81. Michael H. Fisher ed., *op. cit.,* p. 156.
82. *Ibid.*, pp. 156-57.
83. *Ibid.*, pp. 157.
84. P. Nightingale, *op. cit.,* pages38, 56 and 97.
85. Letter from Law Deptt., 18 Dec.1796,Malabar Collectorate Records, Vol.1694,pp.108-113, cited in P. Mohandas, 'A study of the Colonial Investments in Malabar and the Nilgris in the 19th century', unpublished Ph.D. thesis, University of Calicut, 2005, p. 61.
86. M. Frenz, *op. cit.*, pp. 105-106; W. Logan, *Malabar*, p. 638.
87. K. K. N. Kurup, *op. cit.,* 2004, p. 49
88. Logan, *Malabar*, p. 505.
89. Michael H. Fisher, *op. cit.,* p. 158.
90. P. Nightingale, *op. cit.,* p. 116.
91. Michael Fisher, *op. cit.*, pp. 164-65.

92. William Thackeray, *Report on the Revenue Affairs of Malabar and Canara, 1807*, Madras, 1911, pp. 9-10.
93. P. Nightingale, *op. cit.*, pp. 87-88; M. Frenz, *op. cit.*, pp. 105-106.
94. P. Nightingale, *op. cit.,* p. 47.
95. *Ibid.,* p.56
96. Logan, *Malabar,* p. 528; Notification to the Rajas and chiefs of the transfer of Malabar, Cochin and Coorg from the Bombay to Madras Presidency, 2nd July, 1800, cited in T. K Ravindran, *op cit.,* p. 81.
97. Logan, *Treaties*, ii. CCXII; Logan, *Malabar*, pp. 528-29.
98. Proclamation by Mc.Leod, dated. 30th January 1802, cited in M. Frenz, *op.cit.*, fn. 219, p. 122.
99. Logan, *Treaties*, No. ii. CCXXXIV.
100. Logan, *Malabar*, pp. 528-43
101. Eugine F. Irshick, *Dialogue and History, Constructing South India, 1795-1895*, Delhi, 1994.
102. *Ibid.*, pages 20, 22.
103. Letter from Governor General in Council, R.D.D., No. 13, (1794), p. 205.
104. C. A. Bayly, *Rulers, Townsmen and Bazaars, North Indian Society in the Age of British Expansion, 1770-1870*, Delhi, 1992, p.1.
105. Logan, *Malabar*, Vol. 1, pages 494, 498, 527.
106. C. A. Bayly, *Indian Society and Making of the British Empire*, Delhi, 1987, p. 49.
107. *Ibid.*, pp. 4-5.
108. A. K. Bagchi, 'Merchants and Colonialism', in idem *Capital and Labour Redefined: India and the third world*, Delhi, 2002, p. 36.
109. C. A. Bayly, *Indian Society*, p. 61.
110. Nightingale, *op. cit.*, p. 239.
111. P. J. Marshall, 'Economy and Political Expansion, the case of Oudh', in M. Fisher, *op. cit.*, p. 201.
112. Subhra Chakrabarty, 'The English East Indian Company and the Indigenous sloop Merchants of Bengal: Akrur Dutta and his family, 1775-1857', *Studies in History*, 20, 1ns, 2004.
113. P. J. Marshall, *Bengal the British Bridge head, Eastern India, 1740-1828*, Delhi, 1990, p. 141.
114. Eugine Irshick, *op. cit.*, p. 127.
115. C. A. Bayly, *Indian Society*, p. 47.
116. B. S. Cohn, *An Anthropologist*, p. 335.
117. *R. D. D.*, No. 14, 1795, pp. 126.
118. C. A. Bayly, *Indian Society*, pp. 107-108.
119. B. S. Cohn, *An Anthropologist*, p. 329.
120. C. A. Bayly, *Indian Society*, p. 86
121. B. S. Cohn, *Colonialism and its forms of Knowledge*, Delhi, 1997, pp. 20.

122. *Ibid.*, p. 21.
123. *Ibid.*, p. 7.
124. C. A. Bayly, *op. cit.,* p. 87.
125. Logan, *Malabar*, p. 522.
126. C. A. Bayly, *op. cit.,* p. 87.
127. K. N. Ganesh, 'European Perceptions of Kerala landscape: From Barbosa to Buchanan', in Kesavan Veluthat, P. P Sudhakaran eds., *Advances in History, Essays in Memory of Prof. M. P. Sreedharan*, Calicut, 2003, pp. 180-197.
128. William Thackeray, *A Report on Revenue Affairs in Malabar and Canara*, 1807, p.1.
129. Logan, *Malabar*, p. 522.
130. C. A. Bayly, *Indian Society*, *op. cit.,* p. 140.
131. *Ibid.*, p. 139.
132. P. J. Marshall, *Bengal*, p. 137.

Chapter IV

Land Rights and Relations in Malabar: Problematizing British Perceptions

The earliest phase of colonial intervention on the coast of Malabar was essentially a period of surveillance and the subjective understanding of indigenous society resulted in forming the British perception on the region of Malabar. Once the Company established its dominance over Malabar, several fundamental reforms were introduced in developing a systematic and organised form of state power in the region. Initially, the British introduced a land settlement throughout the province along with a judicial and revenue system that led to the process of commercialisation of agriculture and transformation that occurred in almost every sphere of the political economy.

Among other reforms introduced in Malabar, the most significant was the enactment of proprietary rights in land, according to the British administrators, which was non-existent in Kerala. In fact, there prevailed a form of property right in land in Kerala, which was not recognized by the British. The basis of the property in pre-colonial Kerala such as *swam* was in the nature of right; or *avakasam* held by the household, which was only transferable according to the customary laws or practices. The owner of the land was generally known as *janmi* and his power was a graded one though the power of the *janmi* was shared by many other sections of people as well. However, once the British introduced a property right in the British sense in Malabar, the *janmi* or traditional landlord became the single person having the ownership in land. The British were only concerned about the tax payers of land; as a result, the customary rights or *avakasams* came to an end. The British actually could not comprehend the nature and intricacies of land ownership and land controlling class that existed in a traditional society such as Kerala.

By 1780's, following the passing of Pitt's India Act in 1784, the Company was largely transformed into a governing establishment and thereafter its servants were declared to be no longer traders but magistrates and judges. In 1784, the Company's directors retained control of patronage and day today administration in India. But the Board of control, subordinate to the parliament, was constituted in London. This Board of Control, whose president was in effect an India Secretary, supervised all activities of the company and had to approve in advance all activities of the company and despatches sent to India. Similarly, the Governor General of India was appointed by the company, but subject to recall by the crown.[1]

When the British started to study the land tenurial system in India, they initially tried to find out who actually "owned" the land, so that that the person could be made responsible for payment of revenue. In theory, it seemed simple but in practice, it was fraught with difficulties.[2] An understanding of various theoretical underpinnings that influenced the British may help us to get a picture of the background of colonial policies introduced in various parts of India.

As has already been pointed out, the British introduced a system of property right in India, in tune with the western theories on land ownership. As rightly observed by, Anslee T. Embree, the land settlements of the eighteenth and nineteenth centuries should be understood as exercises in application of theory but at the same time to ignore the extensive examination of the nature of property that went on in England from about the third decade of the seventeenth century, until the beginning of the nineteenth century is surely to miss the significance of much that happened in India.[3]

According to James Grant, who wrote "Political survey of the Northern Circars", in Eastern Societies, the proprietary right of the soil was constitutional and solely vested in the sovereign. Thomas Hobbes' argument on property right also is more or less the same. He suggests that "no private man can claim a property in any land, or other goods, from any title from any man but the king of them that have the sovereign power. But the thoughts offered by John Locke were dominant in the eighteenth century British society. For Locke, private ownership was a law of nature, while the earth was given in common to all men, nevertheless, "every man has property in his position", and no one else had any claim on this property but himself. Locke was probably insisting on the right of the individual against the state but his argument was used to exalt private property as an inalienable human right.

One's human rights included, along with liberty, that of owning and disposing of the property that one had gained by mixing one's labour with the land.[4] The belief that property was a natural right was one of the ideas that the Company's servants took with them into rural Bengal in the 1770's and 1780's as they faced difficulty of translating political power into administrative control. Lockean concept of private property found restatement in the very end of the 19th century in the works of B. H. Baden Powell.[5]

According to Neeladri Bhattacharya, prior to the publication of the work of Eric stokes,[6] the British land revenue settlements were often seen as the outcome of a series of experiments, of trial and error that had little relation to the ideas internalised by officials from the European heritage of the time. Eric Stokes' work was the first of its kind to analyse the ideological influence of Europe on the British policies.[7] The ideas of utilitarianism, liberalism and the doctrine of rent developed by Malthus, James Mill and Ricardo shaped the British legislation in the 19th century.

For Ricardo, rent was the surplus produced on fertile soils: the poorest land yielding the normal rate of profit but no rent. Since this rent which was appropriated by the landlords it did not help the process of productive accumulation, and since the landlords were the unproductive class, it was necessary for the state to appropriate this rent and abolish the intermediaries between the state and producers. For Mill, even further the rent in fact belonged to the state because the state was the actual owner of all lands. And the collection of this rent did not constitute taxation as long as normal profit and production were not affected.

The doctrine of rent, according to Stokes, provided the rationale for a high revenue demand and its periodical revisions to prevent the appearance of an inappropriate rent-fund with landlords. Hence, there was a rejection of the Permanent Settlement and a shift to *ryotwari* or *mahalwari* settlements.[8] According to Ranajit Guha, the complex interaction of mercantilist and physiocratic ideas and faith in the doctrine of private property defined the outlook of those who conceived of the Permanent Settlement. The central theme of this policy 'assessment for ever' had already been vaguely anticipated by some of the junior officials in the E.E.I.C's service during the period separating the assumption of Warren Hastings to the governorship of Bengal. It was originally formulated as a policy recommendation by Alexander Dow in 1770,[9] who shared a mercantilist concern with trade, that agriculture was auxiliary to commerce. British rule in Bengal, he felt, had led to a drain of wealth, scarcity of money, decline in production, rise in prices and collapse of internal trade and industry.[10]

Dow, Pattullo, Philip Francis, Thomas Law and Cornwallis were the leading champions of Permanent Settlement in the eighteenth century. In spite of their differences, they had between them some common area of agreement in two respects: first in conceiving of the Permanent Settlement as a clear break with what was the basic agrarian policy of the Company's Government in Bengal up to 1785; and secondly, in justifying their alternative as an indispensable measure to ensure the right of private property in land.[11]

One section of the advocates of Permanent Settlement was more influenced by the Physiocrats, who saw agriculture as the source of all wealth; and for them, trade was important only as an outlet for agriculture goods. For the production of a surplus within agriculture they felt that a Permanent Settlement was essential.[12]

The Physiocrats treated land as the chief source of wealth and their works were written in the interest of the landed classes, containing arguments in favour of high prices for grain.[13] Only agriculture, they maintained, including mining, fishing and other extractive industries, is able to increase the wealth of a nation.[14] The only branch of production on which taxes could rightly be levied was that which created value - i.e., the agriculture. According to Physiocrats, to tax industry was only to tax the land in a roundabout and, therefore, uneconomical way.[15]

According to the philosophers of this genre, 'natural order' was the chief concept of that theory. Human society, according to the Physiocrats, has been ruled by natural laws which could never be altered by the positive laws of state crafts. For Quesnay, the natural laws should be taught with the 'tableau' [means table] forming presumably an important part of the instruction. The essential aspect of the *natural order* was the right to enjoy benefits of property, to exercise one's labour, and to have such freedom as was consistent with the freedom of others to follow their self-interest.[16] There is an almost feudal savour about the Physiocratic attitude to land, indeed which is reinforced by their passionate defence of landed property.

The basic idea of Permanent Settlement came from France, from the writings of Physiocrats. It was sponsored in England in the 1770's and 1780's by several persons but most particularly by the highly controversial Sir Philip Francis. What was hoped and intended was that the Permanent Settlement would have the effect of promoting the development in Bengal of a prosperous capitalist type of agriculture of the kind that had just grown up in England. Land, according to Physiocrats, was the source of all wealth.[17]

Towards developing an argument in support of *zamindari* rights, Francis had to contend with a stream of interpretation of Indian history. In the seventeenth and early eighteenth centuries several European travellers had come to believe that, in India all land belonged to the king. Foreign chroniclers such as Francois Bernier had made very definite statement to that effect, and his authority was often quoted in support of the view that under the Mughals there was no private property in land.[18] Here again Francis drew largely upon the French Philosophers. The security of private property was according to them, an essential characteristic of good society. They had also been writing about the oriental governments particularly of India and China.[19]

According to Francis, the structure of rural society in Bengal before the English conquest was similar to that of England in the eighteenth century. But there was a gentle farmer at the centre in English agrarian scene, who was the agent of all improvements- it was his capital that made it productive, and often his inventiveness that provided it with new techniques. Francis's new *zamindar* was conceived after this image.[20]

Therefore, it was the role of the *zamindar* to promote improvements in the productivity of land. For that he would require capital, and there were two ways in which Francis thought this might be availed. First, he thought of the permanent settlement to revive the collaboration between the landed and moneyed property. Secondly, the sale of lands, he was sure, would further facilitate the flow of capital. He conceded on the one hand that 'investments in land must turn it into a commodity; but on the other hand, he was not quite prepared to face the consequences except that the laws of demand and supply must inevitably tend to eliminate an effete aristocracy and replace it by moneyed interests' having no hereditary connection with the land and often described by Francis as 'strangers' and 'adventurers'.[21] Francis, a Physiocrat, saw in landed property, and the figure of the gentleman-entrepreneur, the source of English prosperity; and he consequently cast the Bengal *zamindar* in this same image. Cornwallis too sought to 'restore' the principal land holders' to what he conceived of as their previous position of prosperity and influence.[22]

Under a Permanent Settlement, Cornwallis thought that landed property unknown in Hindustan with the result that 'the large capitals possessed by the natives' now employed in usury, will be applied the 'more useful purposes of purchasing and improving lands'. Guided by this ideal of 'improvement', Cornwallis thus launched what was meant to be an agrarian revolution in Bengal.[23]

The particular emphasis on the relationship between private property secured by the civil government and the general peace and prosperity of society is the assumption that underlies much of the discussion in the late 1780's over the Permanent Settlement in Bengal and is especially evident in Cornwallis' minutes.[24] Though he had realised the possibility of injustice in the proposed settlement, he emphasised the fact that only when property was defined and ownership known and respected, could the foundation be laid for a peaceful and prosperous state.[25]

Once the right of personal ownership of property was upheld, of necessity require a system of law and courts to safeguard it. The law courts that the British inherited in Bengal did have as one of their functions, the settling of disputes between landlords and tenants but they did not survive for long. New concepts and definitions of property and new courts were required to adjudicate them. It was the context in which new courts were introduced by the British all over India.

The reforms done by the British in land, as Holt Mackenzie observed, was a 'melancholy revolution'. It destroyed the age old land control system and established an absolute, heritable and saleable right in land on the part of the person. Under the British, men who had been tax farmers and traders obtained control of the land, first at acquisition of the rights of delinquent revenue payers and later through money lending activities.[26] With the emergence of this new class of landlords, the cultivators and smaller intermediaries became economically and politically less significant. Many cultivators lost their hereditary rights to cultivate particular lands, and the number of tenants -at - will increased.[27]

As Nicholas B. Dirks comments, by implementing the Permanent Settlement, it was meant to regularise Company revenue through a steady tax rather than by extortion to normalise administration by setting high public standards for the service of the Company officers and to create a loyal elite based on landed property rather than military alliance, by restoring to the putatively traditional landholders their rightful position. The Company authority, including Court of Directors, and the Board of Commissioners for the control of India which represented the Parliament, and its representatives in India, believed that the Bengal system (Cornwallis System) of administration should be extended to other areas of India also. The Permanent Settlement was seen by many as a measure 'which was effected to naturalise the landed institutions of England among the natives of Bengal; without pretence that such institutions were already there awaiting recognition.[28] Similarly, both Henry Dundas, the President of Board of Control, and Wellesley in India were realised that the Bengal methods should be extended to every region under the Company's authority and in 1798 Wellesley sent instructions to Madras towards introduction of revenue and judicial arrangements in tune with those reforms of Bengal.[29]

Madras Board of Revenue came to the conclusion that no *zamindari* land holding was existed in Madras. Therefore, the Board proposed to group the villages in order to form the estates of convenient size and to be sold by auctions to the highest bidders. [But it is a fact that, though similar type of *zamindari* was non-existent in the south, it doesn't mean that there was no big landlords]. As a result, an assessment on these lines was begun in the districts of Baramahal, Dindigal and the Northern Circars. In 1802, a judicial system was introduced in those districts that had been permanently settled and by 1806, the courts had been established even outside the permanently settled areas.[30]

In the meanwhile, however, the opinion of the Home authorities of England, both in the Board of Control and the Court of Directors, had been undergoing a stark change. This change, according to official explanation, was due to some, 'practical inconveniences', 'mistakes', 'injustices' and evils of the Bengal Permanent Settlement which were experienced or discovered within the few years of its conclusion.[31] The defects of the Permanent Settlement were described as 'grave', 'serious' and 'enormous' and extended to all branches of the British administration viz., the revenue, the judicial and the police.[32]

Interestingly, the single voice of dissent raised against the policy of Permanent Settlement in its hours of triumph was by John Shore. He had hailed the appointment of Cornwallis with great enthusiasm, but after three years of collaboration he emerged as Cornwallis' most formidable critic.[33] He had also urged the Company to take a rather more cautious stance.

In London, there had emerged a group of critics with strong discontent against the Cornwallis system and they held that it was not fine for Bengal. There were strong critics like the great economists and thinkers such as Adam Smith and Edmund Burke against the Company administration in India, though whose concerns were not responded properly.[34] All the criticisms levelled against the British government was on the basis of its failure to achieve the objectives of the Cornwallis System viz., a regular and steady flow of revenue, by security and protection of the rights of all agricultural classes, and the permanency of the demands of land proprietory rights etc.[35]

In 1802, Henry Dundas left the Board of Revenue and the Court in a despatch had ordered that in those districts, where the settlement had not been made its conclusion should be suspended until the Madras Government was able to find out whether all possible information had been obtained on the real value of their resources, and until this had been specifically reported to the court with the relevant information. In Madras also there was a growing opinion that the Cornwallis system was not suited to those territories.

Within a short period, it was exposed that many of the claims made by the prophets of Permanent Settlement were absolutely false. The Permanent Settlement failed to demonstrate that *zamindars* were by and large interested in promoting cultivation on their estates by investing their capital.[36] As a result, the British authority firmly believed that it was the paramount duty of the government to give protection to the occupant proprietors from the *zamindar's* oppression, exactions, and maintaining them in their tenures. And this was a paternalistic view of the utilitarians of the time. The utilitarian legacy in India was different from its influences in England. What triumphed in India were its underlying conservatism, latent authoritarianism and paternalism.[37] When the ceded territory in Madras Presidency were (including Baramahal and Salem) handed over to the British, Capt. Read the Superintendent and collector was appointed to survey, assess and to formulate a settlement in the period between 1792 and 1799, and he was to be assisted by Munro, Graham and Macleod. The same theory was actually applied, by Thomas Munro during his administration of ceded districts from 1801 to 1807.

The British Government was reforming or modifying the existing form of revenue settlement. In his extensive survey, Read had identified various causes due to the deplorable state of administration in the regions under his purview: the lack of exertion and ability to collect a fair share of government due, the corruption prevailed among all classes from *amildar* to the ploughmen, the insecurity of husbandman with regard to his property or the enjoyment of the fruits of his labour.[38] The evils which characterised Tipu Sultan's land revenue administration, as alleged by the British, were heavy taxation, inadequate revenue to the state, administrative inefficiency, departmental corruption and the misery of the ryots.[39] Read had acquainted manifold sectors, when he was working formerly in Kolar and Haskote districts. He was well informed about the fact that the *ryots* were brutally oppressed by the renters. Considering all aspects, Read and his assistants were expected to restore the sense of security. On the whole, they were supposed to build up a simple but effective revenue organisation which would not be burdensome for the government and at the same time acceptable to the people.

The ultimate objective of Read was to avoid the existing evils by an individual settlement- to be precise, elimination of the class of intermediaries. It had neither a preconceived plan of a *ryotwari* settlement, nor was this the result of a sudden brain wave. As his aim was to build up an efficient administrative system beneficial to the *ryots*, and also advantageous to the government, the *ryotwari* system, although it was hardly mentioned as such in the voluminous Baramahal records, was forced upon Read by the logic of acts. Primary objective of Read's survey was the equalization of rents, so that he didn't forget to come to close contact with the *ryots*. Mr. Read had visited even small villages and walked in the fields without any attendants, and he concluded a triennial or quinquinial settlement at an earlier date.

Interestingly, Thomas Munro, one of the assistants of Read, initially raised severe criticism against his superior, though later on he became the most ardent champion of the *ryotwari* settlement. In the course of his surveys from 1802 to 1806, Munro identified the *patels* and the principal cultivators as the landowning class and they were not to be expected to promote improvement by assisting the poorer classes with advances or allowing them to participate in the remissions granted by the government.[40]

Munro preferred *ryotwari* to Permanent Settlement due to its advantages: He thought that the *ryotwari* would provide the *ryots* more independence as proprietors holding directly from the Company while at the same time diffusing more widely than any other system the benefit of private property in land. He expected that the produce of the country under *ryotwari* system can be optimized and the chances of revenue defect would be minimal. He also believed that the authority of government and of the court of justice would be more respected under *ryotwari* than under any other system. Besides, the minutes of William Bentick and the report of Thackeray were against the introduction of Permanent Settlement in Madras.

As a prelude to the introduction of the settlement, Read undertook a project of survey to get an idea of the physical features of the territory. It led to the preparation of maps and sketches giving all necessary geographical information. It was followed by a demographic and economic survey of the region affording information about the inhabitants, their peculiar ways of life, the products and tenures, the state of cultivation and other facts of the agrarian economy. The objective of which declaredly was the good of the *ryots* as well as the advantage of revenue.

As Dirks observes, Munro, entrusted with the task of settling the Baramahal, Canara and the Ceded Districts, found himself often followed in Tipu Sultan's footsteps. Indeed, in these assignments he often contained Tipu Sultan's efforts to suppress the power of *Paliyakkars* (Poligars) and to introduce in its stead regularised bureaucratic procedures designed for civil administration and revenue collection.[41] According to Nilmani Mukherjee, the *ryotwari* system originally resulted in the destruction of private property. Conditioned as it was by the system of Tipu Sultan and other princes who took steps to destroy all privileged tenures, the *ryotwari* system in many instances completed the process.[42] But when the *ryotwari* settlement was re-introduced in a revised form to rectify its errors, the private property was reconsidered.[43] The nature of the land revenue was transformed in many cases when *varrum* or share of the produce was forcibly changed into *teeruva* or money assessment.

The benefits of the *ryotwari* settlement, as emphasized by the historians, are as follows. Firstly, the benefits of remissions went to primary producers, who were the principal payers of revenue to the state and were most enthusiastic to increase their production and wealth. These independent farmers with greater wealth and food production would add to the sparse population of the ceded districts. Other benefits were also specified; Primarily, with the principle of variable taxation under the *ryotwari* system, the great number of revenue payers would assure that failures of individual farmers would not affect the income of the state. Secondly, as the general wealth of the *ryots* increased, their cultivation would become restricted to irrigated lands, assuring fewer revenue failures and increased well being. Finally, under *ryotwari* system, government retained possession of all waste land and thus, as wealth and population increased so would revenue proceeds without adding to the burdens of cultivators.[44] Thus, the *ryotwari* settlement was hailed by the British as the most suited settlement for South India in general and Ceded District in particular.

Against the backdrop of these debates and discussions the new challenges in land were introduced throughout India as a whole and a part of which in Malabar as well. The British plan of making a propertied class was basically in accordance with the Physiocratic doctrines. For the British, the Physiocratic perception on propertied class in land was a pre-requisite for peace and prosperity of the people. In the light of which the British in Malabar, as in many other regions in India, had decided to introduce new land ownership rights by very early phase of its subjugation,. As mentioned, in order to understand the complexities and relations and structures of an agrarian economy, the British had appointed a series of commissions with an objective of transforming traditional concepts of land.[45] As a matter of fact, the British pre-occupations with regard to the land ownership were seriously more or less approved by the ideological foundation of the predominant class in Kerala, the Brahmins[46]. It was quite natural that the British project of comprehending various aspects of land was basically depending upon the Sanskrit texts such as *Keralolpathi* and *Vyavaharamala*,[47] and in its light they came to the overall conclusion that, the Brahmins were the real proprietors of the whole land. Apart from that, they also established that, since the *Brahmins* had been traditionally exempted from land revenue, there existed no systematic land revenue in Malabar prior to the establishment of Mysore State.

Before we go to the validity of these types of arguments, an examination of the interpretations made by various British commissions with regard to ownership or property is worthwhile. Starting from the very beginning, the first report of William Gamul Farmer (who was one among the Joint Commissioners) had accepted the brahminic tradition of land ownership and tenures in Kerala. He found that there were two types of possessions of land in Malabar; firstly *jenm-kars* or free holders who hold their land either by purchase or by hereditary descent. And the second group, he notes, known as the *kaanam-kars* or mortgagees, to whom an actual delivery of the land appeared to be made, although the money taken upon it was not at all proportioned to the value of the land.[48]

The earlier British position was reinforced by subsequent officials such as Major Walker. He stated that the *jenm-karan* [*janmi*] possessed the entire right to the soil and no earthly authority can with justice deprive him of it. But his right was confined to the property, and he possesses neither judicial nor political authority.[49] Almost whole land in Malabar, according to William Thackeray, 'was held by *jenm* right, having full absolute propriety right in the soil'.[50] They had enjoyed a landlord's rent, which they borrowed on the security of the land, and it has been taken as good security. The *jenm* right, according to Thackeray, conveys full absolute property right in land.[51] Mr. Warden (1815) also reiterated that the British official position that the '*jenm* right of Malabar vests in the holder an absolute property right in the soil'.[52]

The policy of considering the *janmis* as the sole owners of the whole landed property in Malabar was accepted by Warden's time itself and the British administrators unconditionally had taken steps to implement it. At the same time, Munro argued that the intermediaries were not necessary for the purpose of securing revenue which is essential to the attainment of the higher objectives of good government and the future improvement of the people.

Almost a century after the introduction of *ryotwari* system, William Logan, the collector of Malabar, shared his views that the idea of property in the soil, the Western or British perception of land ownership, was evidently not the idea uppermost in the minds of the person who executed the *janmam* deed. He observed that the Malayali was "looking chiefly *to the people* located, on the contrary to the European view of looking *to the soil"*.[53] Logan underscored that the essential difference between a Roman *dominus* and a Malayali *janmi* was unfortunately never taken seriously by the British at any ocassions of its administration.[54]

By the intervention of the British state, such as the installation of civil courts, the *janmi* had been elevated to the position of a *dominus*. Actually, this legally superior position of *janmi* as *dominus* indeed was a matter of convenience. Initially, the British actually had settled with the local Rajas, until they found that it was a great mistake and subsequently they made settlements with the *janmis*. It was disastrous as far as the people of Malabar/ Kerala was concerned. In 1805-06, Mr. Warden carried out a [preliminary to new] settlement which was called as the *janmi pymash*, according to which the position of *janmis* as the proprietors of land was re-affirmed.[55]

William Logan's concluding remarks which is often termed as 'remarkable' and 'profound' warns that 'it is erroneous to assure that the *jenmi* was the *dominus*, it is equally inaccurate on the other hand, to say of the *Kanakkar* or supervisors that they were the real proprietors of the soil'.[56] The close examination of this perception offers nothing new. For, it actually was the replication of the Mysore State's settlement that previously introduced in Malabar. A few historians made mistakes by highlighting Logan as the champion of the intermediary landholders. Indeed, Logan was the champion of land holders and never was the champion of primary producers. By the introduction of the western notions of proprietorship in Malabar, there created a wide gulf between the cultivators and the proprietors. Contrary to the familiar notions, one who was capable of paying the land tax was considered to be the owner of land. Apart from the primary producing class of *atiyar,* there were *paattakkaaran* and *verumpaattakkaaran,* who constituted the producing class. Majority of the *verumpaattakkaar* were belonged to the lower strata of caste society and others were the Muslims. The *kaanakkaaran* did not participate directly in production, but was elevated. Eventually, Logan's recommendations directed the British government to empower the tenants by rendering them the right of ownership of land. The recommendations, however, were unacceptable to the Company. More importantly, the British found that the *kaanakkaars* were the most ambitious group of people and whose greed and dreams of expansion have prompted them to be 'cautious'.

The British policy in India was to consider the state as the superior landlord; hence they didn't accept the allodial right claimed by the *janmis,* which ruled out (through the Parasurama legend) the recognition of any superior power over them.[57] The British government went a little further than the case of the zamindars of Bengal in accepting even the whole of waste lands of the region as the private property of the *janmam* and recognising every inch of land in Malabar as *janmam* land.

But on the basis of the scheme introduced in 1805, the Company was not able to assess the waste lands that were gradually put under cultivation by the *ryots*. In order to solve this problem and to make revenue collection easier, a variant of Sir Thomas Munro's Madras *ryotwari* was extended to Malabar, which was by then had been a district under Madras Province.[58] According to the Madras *ryotwari* settlement, the state's share was fixed as the half of the net produce of the land after deducting the expenses of cultivation, the actual cultivator would, in turn, be assured of the other half of the net produce. Munro's recommendations, favouring the reduction of expenses on army and the government, and by which he thought to increase the share of the actual cultivator, however was not favoured by the company. The Malabar *ryotwari* settlement was something different from that of the Madras settlement, according to which the *janmis* were considered as the sole legal proprietors of the whole land.

As we have seen, the customary rights and practices in Malabar were absolutely misunderstood or misrepresented by the earlier British civil servants. In order to comprehend the interventions of British in land, a few words about the features of land ownership and land revenue system in the pre-British and pre-Mysorean period would be worthwhile. The landownership in pre-modern Kerala is always considered as a distinctive one, which was inextricably bound with the age-old customs and traditions. It was popularly known as *janmi-kudiyan sampradayam* or *janmam-kaanam-maryadai.*[59]

As it is discussed in the first chapter, the landlord in pre-modern Kerala, the *janmi*, whose right was based upon *janmam*, the hereditary right or birth right. The land was occupied by the descent from his predecessor.

Hence his ownership of land doesn't imply any services or dues that he has to pay to an overlord for maintaining his right. In this sense, his right over the land was autonomous. The *janmi* loses his right only if he transfers or sells his land and the new owner has to pay rent or dues because he does not come to own the land as a birth right.[60] This birth right, as already mentioned, was legitimized by the *brahmins* with the support of their sanskritic, legal and genealogical texts.

The dominant view regarding the existence of land revenue in Kerala is that there was no systematic land tax prior to the establishment of the Mysorean administration. While some historians prefer to reject the possibility of existence of land revenue in pre-modern Kerala, Prof. Elamkulam has emphatically argued that there was an organised form of land tax in Kerala till 13th century C.E.[61] Baden Powell also shares almost similar view on the matter. He maintains that so long as there was a king or overlord, he levied the grain share as land revenue; and when the rule of the supreme overlord broke up and the country was divided into a number of smaller chieftains, we cease to hear of the revenue shares.[62] It was in such a premise that the medieval chronicler Sheikh Zainuddin categorically stated that the medieval state in Kerala had never extracted any kind of land revenue from the cultivators.[63] Francis Buchanan also is of the view that there was no land tax under the local rulers of Kerala. But the recent explorations have succeeded in shedding much light on this issue. Such studies demonstrate that the medieval court records like *Grandhavaris* reinforce the view that there was a system of land revenue in medieval Kerala, especially in Malabar.[64] The paragraphs below discuss the various forms of revenue prevailed in the course of Medieval times in Kerala and which underscore the fact that there was a revenue system even though not well structured.

Actually, there existed more than one form of surplus extraction prevailed in the pre-modern societies. In Kerala, as mentioned elsewhere, both the overlords and overseers had rights to collect various dues from the producers. Those dues were collected either by the temple custodians or by the royal coffers. *Kavalpalam* or *Rakshabhogam* was the dues to be paid to the temple servants (*Changatams*) who were in charge of the protection of land. Some rulers of Kerala had also collected *Rajakaram* during the early eighteenth century.

Paattam, the share of produce to the land holder by the *paattam* holders was normally a fixed amount and the amount was to be fixed on the basis of sowing capacity of the land. *Paattam* as a mode of payment has similarity to *vaaram*, generally known as the overlord's share. The terms such as *Melvaaram, Melpaathi, Melodi*, etc. signified the collection of a fraction of produce of land usually collected by the rulers, the temples or chieftains. *Melvaaram, Melpaathi,* etc. were considered the owners' share of produce but generally enjoyed by the ruling family or the temples. Considering the dual nature, these dues are better identified as rent- tax by K.N. Ganesh.[65]

The mode of extraction of surplus produce in pre-Modern society, as it is identified as 'tax- rent', showed the features of both rent and tax. It was like tax, which was collected in the Malayalam month of *kanni* after the harvest. Rent was extracted to meet the needs of the state, and it was exempted by tolls and customs. Rent was collected normally in kind and rarely in cash. The rent received in kind was often redistributed in the form of daily *oottu* (serving of food to the destitutes or Brahmins), but the British, who were not at all bothered about the customs, strictly demanded the money rent. Previously, there was no uniform form of rent and traditionally, the relationship remained untouched for centuries. When the British intervened in the practices of a graded society, the relations of production was subjected to change.

Melvaaram and *Paattam*, the two forms of rent, were generally collected twice a year (in the Malayalam months of Kanni and Kumbham) in the case of double crop lands, and once in the case of single crop lands. In the case of *Melvaaram*, the realisation differed from half of the total yield to one fifth to one-sixth of the total yield. Lands yielding *Melpaathi* or *pathivaaram* might have been held on a share-cropping basis. Collection of a fixed amount per crop was more common than the collection of a fraction of the produce. Apart from the land revenue, there were also other sorts of dues like *chungams*, *kuthira panthi* and some other dues for maintenance of the ports. Accordingly the general perception of the absence of land revenue in pre-colonial Malabar is proved to be a myth.

Baden Powell had attempted to offer a sensible answer to the baffling nature of the revenue system in Malabar. He observes that 'when the chiefs were overthrown by the Mysore conquest, and afterwards regained their place as a sort of local zamindars, those who retained lands or acquired them as 'landlords from time immemorial', having paid no revenue under their former organisation, so that they naturally claimed that, until the Mysorean conquest, they had not paid land revenue. Hence, the belief that at any point of time land revenue did not exist in Malabar, gained acceptance'.[66]

The general perception regarding the land revenue should be subjected to further enquiries; according to which, the Mysorean state was first to introduce an organised land revenue system in Malabar. But one thing is obvious that the Mysorean revenue system known as *jamabandy* was the first revenue system organised and implemented along with a sophisticated bureaucracy.[67] Accordingly, the Mysoreans surveyed the land and imposed a fixed amount of *jama* on the intermediaries after examining the value of property by each holder.[68] It had thus happened because the Mysoreans misunderstood the Nairs and other intermediary classes as the actual owners of land. As a result, the Nair chiefs were reduced to the position of local revenue contractors of the Mysore state. According to the settlement of Arshad Beg Khan, one *para* of seed sown will on a medium produce in each year, whether from one or more harvest, 10 *parahs*; where of 5 ½ will go to the cultivator, and 4 ½ remain to be divided between the *janmkar* or land holder and government; on which 4 ½ remaining *para* of produce, 1 *fanam* was fixed as the payable *jama* or money value per *para*, 1 ½ of which went to the *janmkar,* and three to government[69].

There are differences of opinions with regard to the Mysorean settlements in Malabar. According to one of these versions, when the Mysoreans came, the *janmis* mostly fled, or refused to appear so that the revenue settlements were made with the *Kaanakkaars* and others in managing or cultivating possession.[70] It is important to note that there is no clear evidence testifying to these migrations. The Mysorean collections were arbitrary, and varied from time to time, from place to place. The Mysore rulers, according to some reports, took nearly all the produce and the cultivators' profit and subsistence and the costs of cultivation and wages of farm servants. They converted the state grain-share into money at certain rates. And also with the garden produce: they valued the fruits of different kinds, the arecanut, the coconut and the jack fruit etc.

The Mysoreans introduced *hobali* as the administrative unit of revenue. When the British felt it unsuitable for further purposes, they adopted a sort of 'parish' grouping called, *amisham* (*amshom*) for each of which there was a headman (*adhikari)* and an accountant called *Menon*. Under the Mysoreans, the village headmen called *Moopans* performed the functions later did by *adhikari*s. The Mysore administrators surveyed the land and fixed the land tax on the basis of the produce where such a practice was exotic and unfamiliar to the people of Malabar.[71] As mentioned, they made settlements not with the landlords but with the intermediary *kaanakkaars*. A certain portion of *paattom* or rent collected from the husbandmen by the *janmis* was extracted by the government as revenue. With the introduction of this new revenue system, they thought that the intermediaries between the cultivators and the landholders were eliminated.

They surveyed the land, the government's share was fixed on the actual produce, and above all, the government made direct relations with the tenants. This system of *huzur niguti*, as the Mysoreans called it, was collected on the *janmi's* share of rent. This was the period from which direct intervention of the state into production and its assessment in Malabar had been begun. And more importantly, since Hydar's time the right of *janmkars* had been taken or absorbed by the government and the Mappila *kaanakkaars* were started to disregard the authority of the *janmis*.[72]

What the British did in this domain, in some respect was quite different and in many others were imitation of the existing Mysorean measures. The 'observational modalities'[73] of the colonial state was found functioning when the Joint Commissioners appointed the native inspectors (to monitor), under the name of *Seristadars*, who were sent to all districts "with an instruction to the rate or proportion of the collection on Arshad Beg's *Jama*, as well how it was rated on the different articles of produce, as also to prepare the lists of *janmkars* or landholders, and a statement of the collections of the preceding years, together with all such other information as might tend to enable us to form a just estimate of the true state of the country".[74]

Chacterisation of the *janmis* as the owners of the soil and the *kaanakkaaran* as the owners' lessee by the Joint Commissioners[75] was followed by the later debates and disputes regarding land rights. The reason behind this, according to Logan, was not only the proclamation but also the newly appointed chiefs as a sort of 'temporary zamindars' (Logan's term) avidity to amass wealth more as the scourgers and plunders but as the protectors of their respective little states.[76]

The pre-colonial land deeds are substantial sources to state that the nature of ownership of land in Kerala was customary and no absolute proprietary right was ever exercised; but only the right to use the land. Some of the typical deeds are mentioned to get a picture:

> "*Attipettolakkaranam*, executed in Karkadaka Nyar (solar month) of the year (which has) advanced to 800 [A.D. 1625]. The blessed name of Nallattat Uralan of Kuruvalleri *Ur* (village). The *Uralan* of the God paid the current market value, joined the interested Anantiravas for the time being, paid the full value in gold, settled the price obtained *attipper* and water of the Kurumani house belonging to Perunkillat Pilarat Chattu Nambiar. In this way, the boundaries south as far as the fields, west and far as Katakandam, north as far as Aviyaram kandi (eastern boundary not given); thorns, good and bad stones, the stump of *Nux vomica*, and cobras included in the circle of the above

boundaries, are granted on *attiper* and water, after fixing the price. The witness on behalf of the grantor and grantee is...written by Valli".[77]

Another example of *attipper ola karanam* of the closing of solar month of the *Chingam* of the year 951(A. D. 1776) is given below:

"Pilaparambil Kelan Koman and heirs having received the current market *attipper* value as found at the time by four people granted (wrote and gave) the *attipper* with pouring of water of the plot lying east to west on the northern slope of the hill in the western *odi* (*odi* = division or range of fields) of Karaka Akathutta belonging to them in Kutuvur *desam* so as to extinguish the (right in) mango tree, the (right in) sand the right in water and to convey the right of ceremony without any dispute respecting this and touching that. In this way Iluvan Tharayolil Kalavan Maman and heirs obtained the *attipper* with pouring of water of the plot lying east to west on the northern slope of the western hill and belonging to Kelan Koman and heirs, in a manner to extinguish the (right in) mango tree; (the right in) sand and the (right in) water and to convey the right of ceremony and without any dispute respecting this and touching that. Thus the witness who knows this is Otaparambatt Kuttan Nair written by Poringellil Chennan".[78]

The above mentioned deeds are potential evidences which may direct us to the conclusion that the ownership right transferred in pre modern times was never considered to be a commodity at all. The current value of the land (which is corrupted by Logan's translation as market price) was decided by a panel of four men and according to which the land was written and given away with libation of water. The Malayalam term, which is recurrently found in deeds, "*annu perum artham*" doesn't mean the price of the land but only the value measured according to the value of the yields or seeds.[79] The price of land (vila) was understood as a negotiated form.

By the new system introduced by the British, the transfer of land from one owner to another was considered to be transfer of *janmam* as *janmam theeru*, according to which, the sole properietorship on land was actually transferred along with the transfer of land. No redeemable right to the *janmi* existed and every fruit was to be enjoyed without any objection. While the pre-colonial land right was giving right only for using the land, the British introduced absolute right - saleable, transferable and mortageable right on land.

The newly established administration of the Joint Commissioners launched a plan of two sets of codes, the civil code of 12th June 1793 with its supplementary articles of 9th July 1793 with a separate code of *Foujdari* Regulations.[80] However, since it was found unviable, several reforms were being suggested and came in to effect in this administrative machinery before it was finally supplemented by the Cornwallis System (reforms in judiciary) in 1802. The Cornwallis System featured the separation of the revenue and judicial functions of the district collector and it also inaugurated a regular system of appeals from the lower to the higher tribunals. It was on the basis of understanding that there is a chain to tyrannise the people by the officer in charge of revenue and justice administration. Only a strict administration of justice by officers wholly unconnected with revenue collection could check abuses and violations of the rulers. Cornwallis was aware of the fact that "the prosperity of the people" was largely depended upon the effectiveness with which the law protected the rights of property.[81] In the words of Thomas Munro, who later improved the system, a greater degree of protection and security in their persons and property would be extended than they had enjoyed before. The basis of such a judicial system was the emerging sense of property rights evolved in Europe and protection of which was also considered as a pre-requisite for transforming the proprietary rights into a capitalist one. Obviously, everywhere the British made the local aristocracies as the "natural proprietors" of land in India. Based entirely on contemporary Whig doctrines about land and society of Britain, that assumption was soon to be dressed up as a fact of Indian history and used as an argument in favour of a zamindari settlement.[82]

By the introduction of the colonial legality, the courts were empowered to take cognizance of all suits and complaints respecting succession or right to real or personal property, land rents, revenues, debts, accounts, contracts, partnerships, marriages, claims to damage for injuries and generally to all suits and complaints. With the accumulated experience of several years of operation, in unison with the western ideas of justice and property, this organisation contributed abundantly sufficient to the advancement of legal system.[83] Thus the primary objective of colonial legality was establishment and sustenance of the newly emerged landed aristocracy whom the British depended largely though the latter also cherished the fruits of this alliance. Nevertheless, in a long-term basis, a large section of the landed class also had suffered due to various pressures of the time.

As mentioned, soon after the British became the overlord of the territory of Malabar, they had appointed commissioners and observers in order to understand the features of land, resources and its people. Apart from the Commissioner's reports, the travelogue of Francis Buchanan has a great significance with regard to its colonialist perceptions and valuable suggestions towards the establishment of the colonial administration. Such interventions in the field of land can be considered as an exemplary model for what Bernard Cohn has termed the 'survey modality'. For more than one reasons, Buchanan's observations and suggestions were seen as a hand book of the colonial administrators.

Buchanan had attempted to quantify whatever he sees or gathers from other sources. His observations were intentional and aimed at the transformation of traditional practices and systems. For example, Buchanan states that there existed no land measurement at Palakkad.[84] Along with this statement, he had suggested certain changes in the measurement of land as well. Actually, there prevailed a traditional land measurement in Palakkad as well as the rest of Malabar known as *parai-kandam*, based upon the sowing capacity of land.[85] The land cultivated to the prescribed number of *para*-s of paddy seeds will have to be calculated on the basis of acres, for which he calculates that land sowing one *para* of seed will generally measure to 7622 square feet. Buchanan himself had understood the variations in the extension of *parai-kandam* in places such as in Chelakkara comes to 5825 sq. ft. and near Calicut on an average comes to 5113 sq. feet.[86]

Apart from that, there were some significant developments. In the pre-colonial times, the procedure of measurement of land was depended on the type of land, that is, the paddy fields were measured based on their sowing capacity, *parambas* and *purayidams* on the areas of tree planted or *kuzhi* and the areas of forests on the basis of the forest trees or *kutti*. This classification was replaced by the measurement by feet, square feet, acres and hectares, which made the measurement procedures uniform.

This uniformity of measurement enabled the British to quantify the landscape and bring all the lands into a common system of classification. Thus lands classified as *nilam, purayidam, parambu, kaadu, medu* and so on under the traditional classification were now brought under a simple, uniform criterion, in the form of square feet, acres or hectares of paddy field, garden lands and homesteads. It is argued that while the earlier classification was based on land use, the British classification was based on the physical extent of the land alone, while land use terms merely specified its use for the present. A *nilam* or *vayal* [paddy field] cannot be made a *parambu* as they signified two different landscape patterns, while under the British classification such transformations were possible, for the change would be only in the type of seed planted, and not in the nature of the land itself.[87]

The suggestion of Buchanan on the transformation of natural forests into teak plantations is also interesting. Buchanan had become very much conscious of the prospects of timber trade in Malabar. The conversion of forests, according to him, was very profitable to the proprietor and the government, Buchanan laments that 'these people are so ignorant that without compulsion, it could not be expected that any such, plans would be carried in to effect'. Buchanan's plan was conversion of forest into a monoculture plantation, and felling of all trees that are not remunerative. Buchanan notes that forests were considered as private property, and people interested in cutting down timber had to obtain a *kuttikkaanam* from the landlords. "The forests spread all over Malabar", states Buchanan, "were valuable in terms of various forest produce."[88] Nowhere in his description he does refer to the capacity of the forests and trees to sustain the livelihood of a population but he considers their value in terms of the saleability or commercial values. In fact, the British had treated the suggestions of Buchanan at its face value. That was reflected in the establishment of a colonial state in Malabar.

In brief, when the British East India Company was transformed in to an administrative establishment, the Enlightenment paradigm of 'civilizing mission' and the Orientalist perception of the West played a predominant role in understanding India. The administrator historians such as Alexander Dow have contributed much to portray the Indian state as 'despotic', and thereby society as static. Contrary to the general understanding of the British government and bureaucracy, it could not set a strong foundation in a short span of time. Instead, the British administrative body had no ideal plan of government in India. And even if they had developed in a crude form, it was absolutely not feasible throughout India.

In order to extract revenue completely and administer the land and people in an 'effective' manner, the British had to know the land, culture and custom of this vast land. Much of the new knowledge served instrumental functions of the capitalist, military and administrative expansions by the company. It will be a great mistake to argue that the most important thing for the company was to create the orientalist knowledge about India rather than to collect the revenue. The knowledge also was important for the British. Actually, the British created a knowledge system primarily on the basis of their experiences with regard to the collection of revenue, in order to sustain the emerging colonial state. Then the learning of indigenous language also became very important. The result of this accumulated knowledge was preparation of travel reports, surveys, enumeration, etc.

It was after the capture of Srirangapattanam that the Company embarked on a systematic effort to explore and document India's past. It culminated in the preparation of maps and travel reports. Those activities functioned as the foundation of their future administration and served as an instrument of knowing the region closely and clearly. The ideological debates on the property rights in Europe basically were influenced by Hobbes, Locke, Physiocrats, and mercantilists and which had been leading to the establishment of a rule of property in India. The basic ideological foundations of the British land reforms were borrowed from Physiocrats, who found agriculture as the source of all wealth. The prime objective behind the introduction of rights of property was to promote the development of a prosperous capitalist way of agriculture. Declaration of the right of property to zamindar was a gesture towards the capitalization of land-relations.

As the Permanent Settlement was found to be an error, Read and Munro developed the *ryotwari* system applicable to South India which was primarily aimed at exclusion of intermediaries. It is believed that the ryotwari system introduced in in original form was having similarity with the settlement introduced previously by Tipu Sultan in Malabar, who always tried to eliminate the intermediaries. However, the British in Malabar introduced a variant of their own policies. The British understanding of the intricacies of land ownership and its relations was essentially colonial, which misguided them to identify *janmis* as the sole owners of land in Kerala. In order to create the landed aristocracy as the supporters of the British administration, they made settlements with the class of landlords, the *janmis*. In such a way, the British converted the *janmi* to the position of European *dominus*, which was for the British, "a matter of convenience". Thus, when the *ryotwari* system was introduced in Malabar, the British state was not making settlement with the actual cultivator, but with the land owning class. According to the customary practice, there was no absolute right over land but only customary right to use the land. The new concept of ownership and relations of land were guaranteed by the introduction of a strong judiciary of British origin. As the British government established courts of inferior and superior powers, the ownership right in land was defined and understood as having a value and to be maintained and retained on the basis of this new legality.

The colonial understanding of the land revenue, that there was no land revenue in pre-Mysorean period in Malabar or Kerala as a whole, is now proved to be false. There existed, of course a land revenue system in pre-modern Kerala, nonetheless, which was not in conformity with the modern concept of taxation. The tax system that existed in pre-modern Malabar can be aptly termed as 'tax-rent', which was a share of rent divided between the landlord and the state. But when the Mysoreans came, they surveyed, assessed and introduced a system of revenue under the title of *jamabandy* settlement. Indeed, there were drastic changes in the whole concept of right of land and taxation when the British, in later times, introduced the modern system of revenue though some features of the Mysorean system was replicated. And to be precise, most of the agrarian revolts and anti- colonial struggles in Malabar in nineteenth century and early twentieth century were the after effects of such interventions by the colonial state.

Notes

1. Thomas R. Metcalf, *Ideologies of the Raj*, New Delhi, 2005(1998), p. 17.
2. *Ibid.,* p. 59.
3. Anslee T. Embrie, 'Land holding in India and British Institutions', in R. E. Frykenberg ed., *Land Control and Social Structure in Indian History*, Delhi, 1979 (1969), p. 38.
4. *Ibid.*, p. 39.
5. See, B. H. Baden Powell, *The Origin and Growth of Village Communities in India*, London, 1899; *The Indian Village Community*, London, 1896.
6. Eric Stokes, *Utilitarians in India*, New Delhi, 1959.
7. Neeladri Bhattacharya, 'Colonial State and Agrarian Society', in Burton Stein ed., *The Making of Agrarian Policy in British India, 1770 - 1990*, Delhi, 1992, p. 113.
8. *Ibid.*, p. 114.
9. R. Guha, *op. cit.*, pp. 11-12.
10. Neeladri Bhattacharya, *op. cit.*, p. 114.
11. R. Guha, *op. cit.*, p. 12.
12. Neeladri Bhattacharya, *op. cit.*, p. 114.
13. Lewis H. Haney, *History of Economic Thought*, 1949, p. 173.
14. *Ibid.*, p. 182.
15. Eric Roll, *A History of Economic Thought*, Calcutta, 1980 (1938), p. 135.
16. *Ibid.*, p. 135.
17. R. Guha, *op. cit.*, p 97.
18. *Ibid.*, p. 99.
19. *Ibid.*
20. *Ibid.*
21. *Ibid.*, pp. 106-107.
22. Thomas R. Metcalf, *op. cit.*, p. 21.
23. *Ibid.*
24. Anslie T. Embree, *op. cit.*, p. 41.
25. *Ibid.*, p. 42.
26. Bernard S. Cohn, 'Structural Change in Indian Rural Society 1596 – 1885', in R. E. Frykenberg ed., *op. cit.*, p. 55.

27. *Ibid.*
28. T. H. Beaglehole, *Thomas Munro and the Development of Administrative Policy in Madras, 1792-1818*, Cambridge, 1966, p. 3.
29. *Ibid.,* p. 6.
30. *Ibid.*, p. 7.
31. Sulekha Chandra Gupta, 'Retreat from Permanent Settlement and Shift towards a new Land Revenue Policy', in Burton Stein ed., *The Making of Agrarian Policy in British India, 1770 - 1900*, Delhi, 1992, p. 66.
32. *Ibid.*
33. R. Guha, *op. cit.*, p. 187.
34. Burton Stein, *Thomas Munro, the Origins of the Colonial State and His Vision of Empire*, Delhi, 1989, p. 2.
35. Sulekha Chandra Gupta, *op. cit.*, p. 66.
36. *Ibid.*, p. 82.
37. Eric Stokes, *Utilitarians in India*, Delhi, 1959, p. xvi.
38. Nilmani Mukherjee, *The Ryotwari System in Madras, 1792-1827*, Calcutta, 1962, p. 6.
39. *Ibid.*, p. 7.
40. *Ibid.*, p. 26.
41. Nicholas B. Dirks, *op. cit.*, p. 113.
42. Nilmani Mukherjee, *op. cit.*, p. 199.
43. *Ibid.*, p. 216.
44. B. Stein, *op. cit.*, p. 133.
45. See, for example, *Report of a Joint Commission*, 1793; *Jonathan Duncan's Report*, 1793; *Major Walker's Report, 1800;* Francis Buchanan *A Journey from Madras through the countries of Mysore Canara and Malabar*, 1800-01, William Thackeray, *Report on Revenue Affairs Malabar and Canara*, 1807, etc. are of historical significance.
46. For a discussion on the proble, see, M.P. Mujeebu Rehiman, 'Colonial perception of Land Ownership in Kerala: The Case of Janmam', *Calicut University Research Journal*, Vol.4, No.2, June, 2004, pp. 30-39.
47. We had attetailed discussion on this aspect in Chapter I.
48. Cited in C. A. Innes, *Malabar District Gazetteer* (reprint), Trivandrum, 1997 (1908), p. 306; R. Mahadeva Iyer, *Land Revenue History*, 1915, pp. 33-34.
49. Major Walker, *Report on the Land Tenure of Malabar*, 1801.
50. William Thackeray, *Report on the Revenue Affairs of Malabar and Canara*, 1807, pp. 3-4.
51. *Ibid.*
52. Cited in C.A. Innes, *op. cit.*, pp. 307-08.
53. William Logan, *Malabar Manual*, Vol. I, Madras, 1951, p. 603.
54. *Ibid.*, p. 604.
55. C. A. Innes, *op. cit.*, p. 331.

56. Logan, *Malabar*, p. 603.
57. T. C. Varghese, *Agrarian Changes and Economic Consequence, Land Tenures in Kerala, 1850-1960*, Bombay, 1970, p. 25.
58. *Ibid.*, p. 27.
59. K. N. Ganesh, 'Ownership and Control of Land in Medieval Kerala: *Janmam* and *Kanam* Relations during the 16th – 18th centuries', *IESHR*, 28, 31, 1991.
60. *Ibid.*
61. Elamkulam, *op. cit.*, p. 343.
62. B. H. Baden Powell, *The Land System of British India*, Vol. 3, New Delhi, 1988, p. 159.
63. Sheikh Zeinuddin, *op.cit.,* p. 46.
64. N. M. Nambutiri, *Maamaankam Rekhakal*, *op.cit.*; *Malabar Patanangal: Samutiri Nadu*, [Malabar Studies: The Land of Zamorin], Trivandrum, 2008.
65. K. N. Ganesh, "Agrarian Relations and Political authority in Medieval Travancore, (AD 1300-1750)", Unpublished Ph. D. Thesis, Jawaharlal Nehru University, New Delhi, 1987, pp. 130-31.
66. Baden Powell, *op. cit.*, pp. 159-60.
67. It is a known fact that the beneficiary of the *jamabandy* system was the British, as they subsequently founded upon their own systems.
68. *R. J. C.*, p. 153.
69. *R. J. C.,* Para 195, p. 222.
70. Baden Powell, *op. cit.*
71. John W. Wye, *A Report on the Southern Division of Malabar*, p. 8, cited in C. K. Kareem, *Kerala Under Haidar Ali and Tipu Sultan*, Trivandrum, 1973, fn. 24, p. 147.
72. Details on the basis of interaction between J. Duncan and influential Mappilas; reproduced in Logan, *op. cit.*, p. 611.
73. B. S. Cohn, *op. cit.*
74. *R. J. C.*, Para 198, pp. 225-26.
75. Logan, *Treaties*, part II, No. LXVIII.
76. Logan, *Malabar*, p. 616.
77. This deed is translated version of the years A.D. 1625; reproduced in William Logan, *Malabar*, Vol. II, Appendix XII, Collection of Deeds, No. 16, p. cxxiii.
78. *Ibid.,* Appendix No. 43, p. ci.
79. See another *Attipettolakkaranam* which states, "*Nirattipper* of two pieces of land sowing 20 para and lying above Vakappatat Aryakka Chira lands sowing 45 paras down from Eluvat Potta in Kalayam Kolumbu and above Ankarat Nilam, others sowing 20 *paras* above Talatte teru Niram, and others sowing 20 paras above Karakkatan Chira in Kosavan Kuli, making a total of land sowing 105 pars, and parambas on the side, together with upper and lower produce ..." cited in Logan, *Malabar*, Vol. II, Appendix, XII, No. 18 p. cxxxiv.
80. T. K. Ravindran, *Cornwallis System in Malabar*, Calicut, n. d. p. ii.
81. Aspinwal, *Cornwallis in Bengal*, p. 240, cited in *Ibid.,* pp 4-5.

82. Ranajit Guha, *Dominance without Hegemony*, Delhi, 1998, pp. 1-7.
83. T. K. Ravindran, *op. cit.*, p. 20.
84. Buchanan, *op. cit.*, vol. 2, New Delhi, 1988, p. 355.
85. K. N. Ganesh, 'European Perception of Kerala Landscape: From Barbosa to Buchanan', in Kesavan Veluthatt and P.P. Sudhakaran, ed., *Advances in History*, Calicut, 2003, pp. 180-197.
86. *Ibid.*, see also Buchanan, *op. cit.,* pp. 395-96, 478.
87. K. N. Ganesh, *op. cit.*
88. *Ibid.*, pp. 189-190.

Chapter V

Anti-colonial Resistance and Consolidation of British Power

In fact, shortly after the province of Malabar was captured by the British from Tipu Sultan, the British had equipped to introduce new revenue and judicial reforms. As discussed in the previous chapter, the newly introduced policies were conflicting with the hitherto existing customs and practices of Malabar, which forced the Rajas and their associates to fight against the British. Taking the observation of Kanakalatha Mukund in to account, the establishment of judicial courts marked the separation of judiciary from administration and bureaucracy, and the entire indigenous population came under its jurisdiction.[1] It is true that the last decades of the eighteenth century and the first of the nineteenth century witnessed a series of protest against the colonial regime, the causes according to the local rulers' version, was the colonial state was established without any justification or legal validity. The present chapter primarily zero in to explore the nature of responses of the local rulers and their associates with regard to the British. A series of powerful and prolonged fight waged against the British by one of the local rulers of North Malabar, Keralavarma Pazhassi Raja of Kottayam and also by various Mappila chiefs of South Malabar and their associates could be seen.

The dominant historiographical position on these early uprisings proves to be ambiguous to a certain extent. Right from the very beginning, the British writings, especially the Joint Commissioners' Report, characterised the operations of Kerala Varma Pazhassi Raja and the Mappila chiefs in derogative language. The Commissioners epitomized Pazhassi Raja as the most intractable and unreasonable of the rajas.[2] It was his disagreement with the newly imposed revenue settlement that compelled him to take arms against the British.[3]

The British looked at such expression of resistance with utmost disgust and contempt. The Company records refer to the rebels especially the Mappila rebels as 'bandits' and 'robbers'[4]. The Joint commissioners considered the Mappilas of south Malabar in racial terms as 'Jungle Mappilas' and 'robbing Mappilas', 'who never would voluntarily or quietly submit to pay the revenue.[5] Lt. Munn was of the view that, "they should by some means or other be brought over as otherwise the country near the mountains will be continually subject to their incursions".[6] All these revolts by the local lords, Nairs and Mappilas were termed by the British with a general nature as "disturbances".[7]

Contrary to the British writings, the indigenous/nationalist historians and amateur writers have followed a style of eulogizing Pazhassi and his associates. The most explicit example for which is the historical novel, *Kerala Simham* (Lion of Kerala) by the renowned Nationalist historian, K.M. Panikkar.[8] In an attempt to characterise the south Indian rebellion as the first war of Independence, Prof. Rajayyan traces the roots of nationalism in the Pazhassi revolts as in the case of other south Indian revolts.[9]

One of the pioneering historians on the theme, Prof. K.K.N. Kurup, is enthusiastic to portray Pazhassi Raja a 'Hindu-peasant nationalist' throughout his works on Pazhassi insurrections.[10] Most of his writings are part of a general perception that Pazhassi Raja's struggles articulated the nationalist consciousness. The missing aspect of the story is that, earlier, Pazhassi Raja had joined with the British against Tipu Sultan with the expectation that, he will be reinstated as the ruler of Kottayam after Tipu Sultan's defeat. However, the British violated the agreement and by which deceived the Raja by assuming control over the whole province of Malabar. Indeed, only then onwards the Raja becomes a rebel, so that his own power was his prominent concern.

Afterwards, Pazhassi Raja signed the one year settlement under the British pressure as most of the Malabar Rajas did.[11] But when the British started to over-burden him, he raised his protest though after a discussion on the issue the Raja again signed an agreement with the British.[12] However, until the British challenged his authority as a ruler, Pazhassi Raja remained as the close ally of the British. Kathleen Gough, while characterising various revolts in India, regarded the revolts led by Pazhassi Raja, as "restorative revolts".[13] The objective behind these rebellions, according to Gough, was "to drive out the British and restore earlier rulers and social relations."

It is interesting to explore the role of the peasants, other than petty rulers or revenue agents, and how far did those section of people could accept rebellion as their own, before adjudicating it a peasant rebellion. It can be argued that Pazhassi Raja fought for the agrarian cause, though which is not substantiated by reliable evidence.[14] It is clear that the nobility of Kottayam had submitted their complaints with regard to the increase of the rate of taxation.[15] So the 'popular support', as argued by Prof. Kurup, to the Pazhassi revolts is actually misunderstood as agrarian revolt. And more importantly, Macleod's *paimash* of 1803 had been played as a catalyst for the vigorous participation of the landlords. In fact, most of the leaders of the Pazhassi Revolts were erstwhile local landlords who lost their powers and privileges under the British. The same was the cause of Mappila landlords as well as the chiefs that made them rebels. When they lost the right of the collection of revenue, conferred up on them by Tipu Sultan, they rose in revolt. For example, in the case of Athan Gurukkal of Manjeri, who raised protest when he lost right to collect dues over Manjeri and Areacode *Angadi*s (markets). It is a fact that the leading figures of the rebellions were basically the local lords rather than the common people/ peasants, contrary to Prof. Kurup's argument.

Yet another genre of literature attempts to appropriate the history and career of Pazhassi Raja from a communal perspective. Predominantly, this historiographical approach, is dedicated to the spread of religious/mythical versions of historical events in a populist way, and gives more stress on religious sentiments than corroborative source materials. For instance, in one of such recent works, there is a description that the Porkali Bhagavati, the family deity of Pazhassi Raja had herself joined with the side of the Raja and had defeated the enemies.[16] Such a tendency of substituting legends in the place of history, by any paradigm, is anti-historical. Though the religious idioms such as temple, deity or oracles etc. were made use of by a ruler like Pazhassi Raja, it cannot be treated purely in religious or communal terms. Actually, by all means, it was absolutely a political act. Equally important is the recent trends of adding of religious colour to the support base of the Pazhassi revolts by stating that only the Hindus were the compatriots of Pazhassi Raja and the Mappilas during the period were not in favour of such anti-British uprisings. Indeed, this is against the historical facts. In order to get these problems clarified, and to delineate the features of the British conquest, a description of the nature of revolts led by Pazhassi Raja in the northern Malabar and the Mappila rebels in the south is worth while.

As mentioned, when the British signed new revenue settlements with the Malabar Rajas, Pazhassi Raja Kerala Varma signed in one-year settlement with the designation of Kottayam Raja.[17] Pazhassi family was one of the closest allies of the British in the second half of the eighteenth century. When the French Governor General came to Malabar to uproot the British from the coast, the Pazhassi family had sent 6000 Nair troops, and as a result, the British could capture many French settlements. Similarly, when the Mysore rulers conquered Pazhassi Raja's territory, the British promised to restore the area to him after the Mysore warriors were defeated, on the condition of his assistance to the latter. Accordingly, Kerala Varma rendered assistance to the British.[18] However, once they became victorious over Mysore, the British became the sole authority over Malabar, violating their earlier assurance to give back his previous status as ruler of his territory. As mentioned before, Pazhassi Raja raised protest only when the British imposed additional dues upon him.

In the meanwhile, when Kerala Varma Pazhassi Raja refused to collect the revenue, there appeared Vira Varma, who claimed to be the actual ruler of Kottayam. He was the then ruler of Kurumbranad and uncle of Pazhassi Raja.[19] As Vira Varma offered collection according to the British stipulations, the British divested of the powers from Kerala Varma and signed settlements with Vira Varma in the year 1793. The revenue circle was consisted of the *Qasbas* of Kottayam, Pazhassi, Katirur, Kuttiyadi, Tamarasseri, Kurumbranad, and Parappanad.[20]

Though the Company had made settlements with Vira Varma, Pazhassi Raja did not permit him to collect revenue from Kottayam.[21] It was because of this the Raja himself was not ready to allow anyone to intrude into his territory, where he considered himself ultimately sovereign. Pazhassi Raja was not the only ruler to refute the direction of the British. Choily Nambiar[22] and Ravi Varma of Patinjare Kovilakam[23] [western branch of Zamorin's family] had refused to pay the revenue. As mentioned elsewhere in this study, the collections in the form of spices or in cash were very risky for any state at that time. There were also instances of representations for reduction of land tax by the local chiefs. That representation was jointly signed by, according to the British documents, Paul Naroote Ocuppa Nair, Bayoote Nair, Cootyan Nair, Carru Cootecur Nair and Cowle Callan [the original Malayalam names are yet tobe identified] etc. They wrote, "...We are now disposing of our cattle and the ornaments of our women and children to pay him this money and are in great distress, we therefore represent our situation to you in the *arzee* [memorandum] in the hope that justice will be done..."[24]

Besides, the contemporary records also speak of the inability of the British to collect the revenue properly. To the British, the Achans of

Palakkad, Edatara, Mannor, Congad and Kavalappara Nairs etc. had defaulted in their payments.[25] The Revenue Department Diaries give us an impression that the revenue arrears were a common phenomenon during the time.[26] Chovakaran Moosa's undertaking to pay the Beebi of Kannur's arrears for the year 1795-96 could also be noted.[27] There were reported cases of "deserting 'Coodiyans' and 'Mookistmaras' of Kadathanad to the countries of Cotiote and Payyormala on account of the *negdee* [tax] being rated too high."[28] The revenue statements reproduced in the Revenue Department Diaries are explicit that the revenue collection was a dire failure compared to the assessments made thereof.[29]

When the Rajas informed their difficulty in collecting the *jama* from their areas, Jonathan Duncan, the governor of Bombay, had directed the supervisor of Malabar to reduce their dues.[30] Mr. Farmer was transferred in the next year, and therefore, J. Stevens was appointed as his successor. Personally, Stevens was opposed to the reduction of dues, and he came to the conclusion that Duncan's measures to reduce the dues were against the Joint Commissioners' report and therefore, they should be nullified.

It was in this context that the Company made arrangements to the execution of quinquenial [for five years] agreements by the rajas and the chiefs in south Malabar in 1794.[31] Upon similar data, settlements were next effected with the Rajas in the north. With regard to Kottayam, the British signed an agreement with Vira Varma Raja and accordingly he held sovereignty over Kottayam. Nevertheless, in the next year itself Pazhassi Raja not only stopped the collection of revenue of Kottayam but also, once more took law into his own hands."[32]

As the British launched retaliatory steps, the Raja moved to the 'impenetrable' and 'tractless' forests of Wyand and thereafter led guerrilla warfare against the British troops. He could conquer the Kuttyadi pass in June 1796.[33] In the following month, after a meeting with Pazhassi Raja, Col. Dow had heeded to his request of returning the property which either had been confiscated or plundered from Kottayam. In due time came the orders from Bombay[34] and the Supreme government[35] regarding the Raja's reinstatement, highlighting the "restoration to his district and property". These orders of the governments, interestingly, were not communicated to the Raja by the local officials of the Company.[36] The question, why this important message was not appropriately intimated to the Raja, still remains as a riddle.

By this time itself, there emerged an insurgency situation throughout Malabar. The Company records are vociferous of this situation and each and every diary after 1796 exhibits concern of the British over revenue collection. For instance, the company insisted on measures on Cotiote [Kottayam] and Wayanad, as well as the realization of Company's revenue from Cotiote.[37] Fascinatingly, Tipu Sultan had engaged in intrigues with the French and he had raised claim over Wyanad and its revenue. The negotiation with Pazhassi Raja failed in 1797 and the British thought of measures for restoration of peace in Kottayam and Wayanad.[38]

The British thereafter was contemplating on formulating a conciliatory strategy towards Pazhassi Raja, but he had turned very adamant against the Company by this time. Accordingly, he declared ban on the passage of the troops of Tipu Sultan and the Company through Wayanad.[39] The disturbances in the regions of Wyanad and Kottayam were being characterised as 'anarchy' in British records. There is a reference to 200 Nair rebels headed by one of the members of Vellattiry family,[40] which illustrates the extensive co-operation from other rajas of Malabar.

In the meanwhile, in the context of Tipu Sultan's resilient claim over the proprietorship of Wyanad,[41] after a thorough examination, the Governor General endorsed the same and "allowed it to remain free to Tipu Sultan".[42] In response to the British proclamation forbidding people from assembling and assisting Pazhassi Raja, he was to seek aid from Tipu Sultan. Tipu Sultan had agreed to supply him with ammunition and to station 6,000 "Carnatics" under his Killidar at Karkan kotta.[43] Apart from this, Pazhassi had also contacted the Tamil rebels of Dindigal through the mediation of the Mappila rebels of Eranad.[44] At the same time, lack of sufficient substantiation with regard to prime motives of Tipu Sultan, especially the terms and conditions of this alliance with the Raja leaves one inconclusive. However, it was clear that the Raja had secretly assisted Tipu during the Fourth Anglo-Mysore war[45].

The following leaders who were the local chiefs along with the number of their army men (as found in the bracket) had maintained the support base of Pazhassi Raja across Malabar. The following influential chiefs such as Parappanad Raja (100 men), Kannavath Shekharan Nambiar (140), Elampulayan Kunhan (100), Kaiteri Ambu (100), Kaiteri Kumaran (100), Kaiteri Eman (006), Puttan Veettil Rairu (10), Meena Koran (10), Shekhara Varier (10), Paitalott Nair (05), Mylodan Kanchan Nambiar (10) etc. were readily offering their men. The solidarity of these people and guerrilla mode of depredations had actually challenged the British establishment.

Discomfited and exhausted by recurring defeats, the British sued for peace in July 1797. Accordingly, the government cancelled the lease of

Kurumbranad Raja and renewed it on behalf of Kerala Varma's elder brother, who had just returned from Travancore.[46] Apart from that, Pazhassi Raja was granted a pension of Rs.8000/- per annum and the plundered Pazhassi house was made good to him. When the Pazhassi Raja decided to accept the pension and other privileges offered by the British, his close associates such as Kaiteri Ambu stood steadfast against these inducements, and hence, this 'period of peace' did not last for long.

The fourth Anglo-Mysore war and subsequent victory of the British created an atmosphere of insurgency in Malabar again. According to the treaty of war, Wayanad and Coimbatore directly came under the British control. The death of Tipu Sultan in the battlefield (1799) made the atmosphere congenial to pursue the expansionist policies of the Governor General, Lord Wellesley. When the Mysore commission went to take possession of Wyanad, Pazhassi Raja stressed his claim over the district and persisted in keeping possession of it.[47] To sustain his pretensions, the Raja raised defence of a large number of men consisting of Nairs, tribals, Mappilas and Musalmans, the last being the portions of disbanded troops of the late Mysore Sultans. The British were aware that the tranquillity of Malabar and collection of revenue had been interrupted during the war.[48]

The insurgency turned into another phase when Pazhassi Raja descended the Ghats of Kuttyadi and there he joined with Unni Mootha Mooppan and many of chief landholders of Iruvazhinad such as Kamburath, Peruvayal and Kannavath Nambiars. In June-July 1800, the rebels had taken possession of the low country of Kottayam who attacked and destroyed a portion of Murdoch Brown's plantations at Anjarakkandy besides demolishing the British outposts at Kodolli and Manatana.[49]

In addition to this, the insurgents of North Malabar had been extended a strong support base from the Mappila rebels of South Malabar. Even during the time of Joint Commissioners' enquiries and settlements, they showed signs of protests and endeavoured to defend their existing systems. According to the British observation, the coastal Mappilas were active traders and well behaved but their fellow religionists who lived in the interior were incessantly engaged in marauding expeditions.[50] Unni Mootha Moopan of Elampilasseri, Athan Gurukkal of Manjeri, Chemban Pokker of Vellattiri's land [Valluvanad], Hydros Kutty of Chavakkad etc. were prominent leaders of the anti-British struggles[51]. Athan Gurukkal had some followers in different regions of south Malabar such as Kunhammed Kutty of Edavanna who was also very close to Wandoor.[52] Mannarkkad, Thamarasseri, Pulavayi, Vettatunad, Cheranad and Eranad were major centres of their activities. These rebels created chaos and confusion in the British circles than ever before.

While majority of the merchant class of Mappilas were supportive of the colonial state, the agricultural class among them staunchly resisted the British and because of which they were denigrated as 'outrageous', or 'ruffians' as reflected in the British records. To quote Joint Commissioners, The statement that, "...they never would voluntarily or quietly submit to pay the revenue..."[53] implies that the Mooppans, the erstwhile revenue administrators under Tipu Sultan, had challenged the British from collecting revenue. What is not part of the dominant historiography is Mooppans were previously great contenders of Tipu Sultan's invasions in Malabar and later close allies of the Pazhassi Raja, to lead a united struggle against the British.

The British records frequently characterise those rebellions as 'Moplah disturbances', and several records such as *Diaries* especially those belong to the last leg of eighteenth century and beginning of 19th century recurrently discuss the problem in detail. Those revolts in Southern districts, especially in Eranad, Valluvanad, Cheranad and adjoining areas practically eliminated the Company's government in those parts. Walter Ever, a former member of the Court of Directors described the gravity of situation like this: "From Tanoure [Tanur] to Chowghat [Chavakkad], the road from Calicut to Cochin upward 30 miles there is no government than in the deserts of Saudi Arabia".[54] The major objective of those rebellions actually was to retain the pre-British socio-economic system. According to K. K. N. Kurup, an authority on Pazhassi rebellions, there were traces of 'social banditry' in these instances of earliest resistances in Malabar.[55]

From the earliest days of establishment of British administration in the province, the Company keenly paid its attention on the 'depredations of jungle Mappilas' and from time to time they received fresh complaints of their revolts. Mr. Farmer had his own opinion to transfer the collections of their districts 'to the Company, which seemed the only way of reconciling and attaching them to the government'. Maj. Dow's proposal in this regard was that 'their [Mappilas] collections should be entrusted to men of their own tribe under proper restrictions'. And in order to expedite the measures to conciliate the rebels, it was agreed to give a general amnesty to Nairs and Mappilas for their all past offences up to 1st February 1793.[56]

However those measures were proved to be ineffective by receiving fresh reports of violence by Hydros, a rebel (robber, in the words of the British) in the districts of Vellattiri and Vettattunad, whose men had committed 'several inhuman murders and daring robberies besides alarming that part of the country in general, sending threatening letters to extort money and provisions from the plan of their houses burnt and themselves put to death'.[57] Major Dow was deputed to allure Hydros and to bring him of Calicut, but on the way he escaped and pursued his acts of violence against the British. Major Dow's project in this regard was "to adopt Tipu Sultan's plan by appointing the fittest persons in the different Mappila districts, Moopas or headman of their respective divisions entertaining (and placing them under the British superintendent of each jurisdiction) under such a proportionate number of armed Mappilas to assist in the collection of the revenues and in the preservation of peace and order in the districts". These measures and gestures of the British allow us to postulate that there was an insurgency situation in Malabar. And the British had followed various measures of inducement and use of force which varied according to person to person, and place to place.

When the earliest violence was reported, the supervisor had attempted to bring the afore-mentioned Hydros Kutty through the mediation of *quazi* (the religious head of a particular region) of that part of the country. The *quazi* informed that it was not an easy job. Mr. Stevens, superintendent of the Southern district, reported at the same time that Unni Mootha Mooppan was the chief of all Mappila Mooppans. He had possessed a fortified house in the jungle, about fourteen miles away from Cherpulasseri, the seat of the southern superintendency. He, as the British apprehended, would assist in chastising the other disturbers of the peace but being himself in reality the secret spring and mover of every disorder.[58] Previously, Unni Mootha had resorted to raise stiff resistance to Tipu Sultan's army and in 1786-87, Arshad Beg was forced to take him with 100 followers.

Since the possibility of an amicable solution was more or less proved to be improbable, the British were planning an armed attack. The offer of a general pardon to the rebellious Mappilas was treated with neglect especially by Unni Mootha, which again created an atmosphere of confrontation. His army consisted of exclusive Mappilas, several Carnatic sepoys and, moreover, he had the habit of correspondence with the power above the ghats [probably the Mysore], who had thousands of his dependents.

But as per Maj. Dow's orders, Captain Burchall marched to Unni Mootha and after surrounding his fortified place of abode passed almost the entire day in unsuccessfully endeavouring to induce him to come into his camp and return with him to Cherpulasseri. Though fierce battle continued until the night, Unni Mootha escaped when the "moon was going down". Maj. Dow's recommendations with regard to the containing future depredations were first, to appoint proper persons of their own tribe in conjunction with the government officers, to collect the revenue from them and secondly, to disarm them, as soon as it could be done safely to prohibit them from going about armed.[59]

In this way, the British were compelled to make an interim agreement on 8th May 1794 with Unni Mootha Mooppan by Maj. Murray[60] with a view to secure peace to the country in his small district of Elampulasseri by offering him an allowance of Rs.1000/- per annum. But he renewed his pretensions to a share of the revenue and began using black mail.[61] Consequently, the supervisor there upon offered a reward of Rs.3000/- for his capture. Capt. Mc. Donald had seized and demolished his stronghold on the forest-clad hill of Panthallur near Malappuram. Later on Unni Mootha Mooppan was pardoned and was restored to his estate of Elampulasseri. Though he was pardoned, the British records refer to Unni Mootha's insurgencies in the coming years as well.

Another person who led strong resistance was Athan Gurukkal of Manjeri, who was erstwhile revenue Collector of the Zamorins in pre-British times. When he and his father, Moideen Kutty Gurukkal resisted the Mysorean impositions in 1784, they were deported to Srirangapatanam by the Mysore state. His father was unfortunate to die there; and when the British captured Malabar in 1792, Athan Gurukkal was appointed as the head of police establishment in Eranad.[62] But this affectionate relation with the British did not last for long. As in the period of Tipu Sultan, the Gurukkal raised protest against the overburden of the collection. During the time of Tipu Sultan, the land lords were all along with Gurukkal because of high rate of revenue. Likewise, when the British increased the rate of revenue, Gurukkal, along with other local chiefs, had staunchly fought against the British.

Another reason for his anti-British rebellions was the British perception about Gurukkal's ever increasing influence over the people of his region. In 1799, Gurukkal had absolutely turned against the British as a result of murder of Unni Mootha's brother by the British (Unni Mootha was brother -in-law of Athan Gurukkal). The British version of explanation as the very reason for the resistance from Athan Gurukkal was the spirit of revenge for the punishment inflicted by the regular judicial process on the above mentioned relative, Adam Khan, who had been executed for murder.

The grand alliance of the great rebels such as Unni Mootha, Athan Gurukkal, Chemben Pokker etc. became alarming after an abortive attempt had been made by the Assistant Collector, Mr. Baber to seize Chemban

opinion the government could very well demand 35 percent to 40 percent of the agricultural produce. He also felt that the produce of various kinds of trees was calculated very low.[73]

The assessment on land ordered by Macleod was so high that people were forced to sell their moveable property to pay the tax of the previous year.[74] The new rates introduced by Macleod, indeed, put a heavy burden on the tax payers of Malabar. It is argued that the calculation of the actual produce and the snap survey (which was conducted in hurry and completed within 40 days) were really unscientific. The proclamation of *paimash* has caused the spreading of rebellion further. The rebels advanced above the ghats and the Panamaram fort was destroyed by rebel leaders Edachena Kunkan and Talakkal Chandu.

Below the ghats, especially in Kurumbranad, the rebellions caused the British troops and every surviving officer had to fly. The prominent rebel leader below the ghat was Kunhi Moideen Mooppan of Elathur, who not only excited the people and fought against the Company's authority, but also induced the Wayanad rebels to descend to Kurumbranad.[75] There are references to Pazhassi's regular contact with the Kurumbranad jungles, the Avinjat Nayar of Payyormala and Raja of Kadathanad, both being suspected of aiding him.[76]

Since the armed rebellion gained momentum by proclamation of Macleod's Paimash, the rebels dared to capture Kozhikode prison on 1st March 1803. Out of 210 prisoners, fifty were killed by the British sepoys, thirty eight were taken and the rest were freed.[77] Taking responsibility of the deterioration of law and order, Mr. Macleod relinquished his office in favour of Robert Rickards, who declared certain revenue relaxations to appease the farmers in the region.

As part of ameliorating the peasants of Malabar, Rickards allotted one third of the net produce to the cultivators as was the custom. However, those measures were proved to be insufficient to put down the rebellion completely. Revolts were continuously reported from the places such as Pazhassi, Chirakkal, Cannanore, Tellichery and Dharampatanam.[78] In the course of time (March, 1803), Mr. Rickards was called back as the Collector. The sub collector was Thomas Harvey Baber, whose efforts in driving rebels are oft-quoted. The repeated resignation or withdrawal of the Company personnel can be seen as the symptoms of lack of organisational skills, stability and confidence of the Company. All the events lead us to think that every moment they were in trouble due to the insurrections.

By 1804, the Company had made an attempt to mollify the former Rajas by offering *Malikhana* (pension) to them. At the same time, a new band of native troops called *kolkars* was organized by Captain Watson. The *kolkars* were equally mobile and with an equal knowledge of the people, language and the country hunted down the small batches of Pazhassi adherents. As most of the *kolkars* had familiarity with the hill tracts and climate they could advance in many parts by conquering or killing the high profile rebel leaders such as Talakkal Chandu in the next year. Apart from the *kolkars,* the British had been assisted by many quarters, especially by the native revenue officers and upper caste associates, which led them to the victory.

Though the British could brutally suppress the rebellion and punish the rebel leaders across Northern and Southern parts of Malabar, the rebellion obviously could convey a message to the British that their future as administrators was not so secure. It might be incorrect to generalize that the elite section of the society was solely associated with the British. Several rebel leaders such as Kannavath Nambiar, Avinjatt Nair etc. stood against the British, where as those who benefited from the British became their supporters. Though one section of elite people was associated with the British, the other section had raised strong resistance against the British. There are always complexities and divergent forces within the society.

Conclusion

The anti-British resistance commanded by local chiefs and Mappilas in Malabar is quite remarkable, due to several reasons. First of all, the insurgency situation throughout Malabar followed by the completion of the takeover of Malabar can be seen as tangible evidence against the Revisionist historians' position that the colonial administration over India was made possible with the consent of the people rather than imperial designs. In other words, they argue that the people of the colonies never fought against the British and were just collaborators of colonial state. However, in the case of Malabar, as it is obvious, even long after its takeover in 1792 the British could not develop an established form of government at least until 1805, when Pazhassi Raja was assassinated. And more importantly, the revolts were not occasional or isolated ones.

Mapping of the storm centres of insurgency may help us to understand the extent and gravity of the uprisings. Almost every locality of Malabar can be found as covered by any form of revolts. If we take four of the present districts of Malabar, the following were significant spots: In Kannur there were Manathana, Mattannur, Pazhassi, Kurungoth, Irikkur, Kuthuparamba, Periya, Payyannur, Tellichery etc.; in Waynad, Manantavati, Ganapati Vattam (Sulthan Bathery), Edathara, Pulpally, Karimpuzha, Tirunelli, Panamaram, Lakkidi etc.; in Malappuram, Pantallur, Elimpulasseri, Manjeri, Tanur, Mannarkkad, Angadipuram etc.; in Kozhikode, Thamarasseri, Kurumbranad, Kuttyadi, Athyodi jungles, Peruvayal, Kozhikode etc., were major centres. Apart from these regions, the rebels of Dundigal, Coimbatore, Tirunelveli, Erode, Satyamangalam and some places in Karantaka were also closely linked with Malabar rebels (see the Map II). This actually gives us the picture of a wider regional distribution of the rebellion covering a wide area transgressing the language barriers. In such a way the rebellions in Malabar had linked fairly well with the South Indian resistance movement.

Secondly, the tendency of characterization of the revolts of Pazhassi Raja and others as the first 'national' and the upheavals as 'the first war of independence' etc. stand far from the reality. It is highly probable that whether those initial responses of the individual rulers can be termed as nationalistic. While taking such a position we have to keep in mind that it was a period in which the modern concepts of 'nation state' and 'nationalism' were absent at that time in India. Historically speaking, we cannot trace any traits of nationalism in the last part of eighteenth century or until the latter half of the 19th century itself. The theory of 'restorative revolts' by Kathleen Gough is not acceptable because, the revolts led by Pazhassi and others were not aimed at restoring the previous system as such, instead, they were fighting for maintaining their own position under the British revenue regime. In order to state the character of these insurrections, further studies are necessary. As a preliminary hypothesis, it is assumed that the principal organisers of the insurrections were local chiefs who were either pre-modern landlords or those privileged as revenue collectors under the Mysore and the British, who fought along with their militarized dependents and characterization at a broader 'peasant' rebellion, which demands further explorations.

The propensity to portray Pazhassi Raja as the personification of Hindu pride and valour is far from historical reality and to be resisted historically. Equally important is the Hindutva propagandist argument that Muslims were passive to the Pazhassi resistance, which also proved to be blatantly false. Indeed, such historical constructs contradict the large corpus of the archival records and which establish the secular nature of the resistance where the Mappila chiefs had a predominant role. It helps us to maintain that there was generally an insurgency situation in the early years of establishment of British power in Malabar. The British apparently had struggled very hard to overcome the peoples' resistance and because of this, they resorted to violence through the agency of a police state. To be precise, the earliest phase of anti- colonial resistance movement in Malabar reflects the mentality of the people, where they fought together transcending religious and language barriers.

Notes

1. Kanakalatha Mukund, *The View from Below: Indigenous Society, Temples and Early Colonial state in Tamil Nadu, 1700 – 1836*, Hyderabad, 2005, p. 26.
2. *R. J. C.,* Paras 135-37, pp. 163-64.
3. When the Raja stood against new British revenue, the British were in contact with him. After a prolonged discussion, the Raja had agreed firstly, the entire pepper production (at least 500 *kanti*s) was to be handed over to the British at the rate of Rs.90/- per *kanti*; secondly a sum of 20,000/- rupees either in cash or natural produce was to be paid in two installments one year in arrears. But in the coming year, the Commissioners unilaterally made amendments to the previous treaty, according to which the Raja was compelled to pay Rs. 50,000/- along with at least 700-800 *kanti*s of pepper. The Commissioners also compelled him to abolish the custom of *Purushantharam* and acceptance of all gifts and presents, as applicable to the other Malabar Rajas. But the Keralvarma Pazhassi Raja felt humiliated and refused to accept all those unjust impositions.
4. See for example, inward letters in the Political Department for March and October, 1804, Vol. 2275; Inward letters from July to September 1801, Serial No. 2272 General No. 20638.
5. *R. J. C.,* Para 215, p. 254; Para 291-92, p. 332.
6. *Ibid.,* p. 333.
7. S. P. D. D., Nos. 88 (1800), 89 (1800), 96 (1800) etc.
8. K. M. Panikkar, *Kerala Simham* (Mal.), [The Lion of Kerala], Thrissur, 1968.
9. K. Rajayyan, *South Indian Rebellion; The First War of Independence 1800-01*, Mysore, 1971.
10. The writings of Prof. K. K. N. Kurup, such as *Pazhassi Samarangal* [Pazhassi Rebellion], *Pazhassi Samara Rekhakal,* transcends the boundary of scientific history and he seemingly presents a narration of Pazhassi rebellions with a tinge of Hindu nationalism. For example, he writes "inspired by the *kshathra dharma* he [Pazhassi] could organize the people against Mysore and by which he was loved by them" (K. K. N. Kurup, *op. cit.,* p.24). He is also vociferous in linking the revolts with the peasant consciousness in Malabar.
11. *R. J. C.*, Para 136, p. 163.
12. Logan, *Treaties and Engagements*, p. 151.
13. Kathleen Gough, "Indian Peasant uprisings", in A. R. Desai ed., *Peasant Struggles in India,* Delhi, 1979, pp. 85-126.
14. K. K. N. Kurup, *Pazhassi Samara Rekhakal, op. cit.,* pp. 128-29; see also, K. K. N. Kurup, 'Pazhassi Revolts' in P. J. Cheriyan, ed., *Perspectives in Kerala History,* Thiruvananthapuram, 1999, pp. 402-07. It is doubtful that such a class

of peasantry was emerged in the period under discussion. His comparison of Pazhassi revolt with Taiping revolts also seems to be illogical.

15. Margret Frenz, *From Contact to Conquest,* New Delhi, 2003, p. 106.
16. Dr. K. S. Mohan, *Pazhassi Raja, Porattathinte Nalukal* (Mal.) [Pazhassi Raja: The Days of Struggle], Kochi, 2007, p. 95.
17. Kerala Varma belonged to the Western branch of Kottayam royal family, whose headquarters was at Pazhassi, 6 K.M. south of Mattannur - Kuthuparamba route of the present district of Kannur. It was because he resided at Pazhassi that he came to be called as the Pazhassi Raja. Included in the Tellichery division, Kottayam is an area of forest-clad hills, rich in pepper and other spices. He belonged to the lineage of Patinhare Kovilakam (western palace), Rajas of the Zamorin family in the last quarter o the eighteenth century. For more details see T.P. Sankaran Kutty, *A Tragic Decade in Kerala History*, Trivandrum, 1977, fn. 1, pp. 2-3; Dr. K. S. Sreekumar ed., *The History of Freedom Movement in Kerala,* The Regional Records Committee, Trivandrum, 2000 (1970), p. 21.
18. *Ibid.*
19. According to the general perception, Vira Varma was adopted to Kurumbranad and accordingly he became the ruler.
20. Logan, *Malabar*, Vol. I, p. 499.
21. K. K. N. Kurup, *op. cit.,* p. 36.
22. S. P. D. D., No. 50, 1796.
23. R. J. C., Para 482, p. 490.
24. R. D. D., No. 15, 1796, p. 72.
25. *Ibid.,* p. 94.
26. *Ibid.,* p. 123.
27. Copy of the translation of Moosa's engagement to pay the Beebi of Cannanore's revenue arrears for the year K. E. 970 (1795), *Ibid.*
28. Letter from William Handley to Kadathanad Raja, dated, 27th February, 1796; *Ibid.,* p.196.
29. For example, according the revenue statement of Cotiote it had to pay an amount of Rs.40964.1.14 and had only paid Rs.7000 in cash and Rs.12, 450/- in pepper. The Balance amount was Rs.21, 514. Similarly in the case of Chirakkal, against the total settled amount of Rs. 72,408.3.57, an amount of Rs.4000 had been found remained arrears see, *Ibid.,* p. 303.
30. Duncan's direction was that to collect half of the rent at the rate of Rs.41/- for 1000 *idangazhis* instead of earlier agreements of half of the produce. K. K. N. Kurup, *op. cit.,* p. 38.
31. Logan, *Malabar, op. cit.,* p. 501; Logan, *Treaties*, ii. LXXX to LXXXII, LXXXIV to LXXXVII.
32. Logan, *Malabar*, p. 503.
33. *Ibid.,* p. 511.
34. Logan, *Treaties*, ii., CXXII.
35. *Ibid.,* i., XCV.
36. Logan, *Malabar,* p. 512.

37. S. P. D. D., No. 55, 1797.
38. *Ibid.,* No. 57, 1797.
39. *Ibid.,* No. 78, 1799.
40. *Ibid.,* No. 78, 1799.
41. Letter from Tipu Sultan to the Governor General, 26th April, 1798 in Kabir Kausar, *Secret Correspondence of Tipu Sultan,* New Delhi, 1980, pp. 228-29.
42. Letter from Governor General to Tipu Sultan, 7th Aug. 1798, *Ibid.,* pp. 234-5.
43. Logan, *Malabar*, p. 516.
44. K. K. N. Kurup, *op. cit.,* p. 50.
45. Logan, *Malabar*, p. 514.
46. Dr. K. S. Sreekumar, ed., *op. cit.,* p. 22.
47. Logan, *Malabar,* p. 527.
48. S. P. D. D., No. 80, 1799, pp. 4227-35.
49. C. A. Innes, *Malabar Gazetteer,* Trivandrum, 1997, (1908), p. 45.
50. Logan, *Treaties,* ii, CLXXXVIII.
51. For a detailed analysis of the resistance of the Mappila Chiefs of South Malabar, See, M.P. Mujeebu Rehiman, 'Counter Voices to the Early British State: Unni Mootta Mooppan and Chemban Pokker, the Primitive Rebels from South Malabar' , *Society and Culture,* Govt. Arts and Science College, Calicut,Vol.7, issue1, January 2016 pp. 169-189.
52. Inward letters From July to September, 1801, Back No. 62, Shelf. 1447, Serial No. 2273, General 20638, pp. 1-3.
53. *R. J. C.*, Para 292, p. 332.
54. Walter Ewer to Henry Dundas, 17th July, 1797, Home Misc. Vol. 438 (India Office Library and Records, London), pp. 194-95, cited in K. K. N. Kurup, Modern Kerala Studies in Social and Agrarian Relations, New Delhi, 1988, p. 63, fn. 6.
55. Prof. K. K. N. Kurup is of having the argument that there were some traces of social banditry in those revolts.
56. R. J. C., Para 215, pp. 254-255.
57. *Ibid.,* pp. 255-56.
58. *Ibid.,* p. 329.
59. *Ibid.,* p. 339.
60. Logan, *Treaties,* ii. LXXVIII.
61. Logan, *Malabar,* p. 501.
62. *Ibid.,* p. 522.
63. S. P. D. D., No. 88, 1800, pp. 732-37.
64. K. Rajayyan, *South Indian Rebellion, the First War of Independence, 1800-1801*, Mysore, 1971, p. 181.
65. S. P. D. D., No. 99, 1800.
66. Logan, *Treaties,* ii. CCXVI.

67. Board of Revenue, 4th May, 1801, Proceedings, Vol. 282, pp. 5265-6, cited in K. Rajayyan, *op. cit.,* p. 175.
68. C. K. Kareem, *Kerala and Her Culture An Introduction,* Trivandrum, 1971, pp. 20-21.
69. K. K. N. Kurup, *op. cit.,* p. 101.
70. A. P. Abdurahiman, 'Palassi Rebellion: The Role of Coastal Merchants', *Journal of Kerala Studies,* Vol. I, No. 2&3, Jan. 1974, pp. 295-98.
71. T. P. Sankaran Kutty Nair, *op. cit.,* p. 15.
72. Logan, *Malabar,* p. 543.
73. A. P. Abdurahiman, 'Macleod's Paimash and the Malabar Rebellion of 1803' *Journal of Kerala History,* Vol. IV, March, 1977, p. 65.
74. Collectorate Records, Vol. 2311 (Revenue), fn. 81, quoted in *Ibid.,* p. 66.
75. A. P. Abdurahiman, *op. cit.,* p. 69.
76. Logan, *Malabar,* p. 532.
77. W. Macleod to the Chief Secretary, 2nd March, 1803, Foreign Secret Consultations, 14th May and 2 March, 1803, Foreign Secret Consultations, quoted in K. K. N. Kurup, 'Pazhassi Rebellion' in P. J. Cheriyan, ed., *op. cit.,* p. 405.
78. Dr. K. S. Sreekumar, ed., *op. cit.*, p. 24.

Conclusion

The economy and society of Malabar were in the course of transition during the latter half of the eighteenth century due to various factors. The political structure also was in the transformation as the Mysorean rulers and the British made intervention in that sphere. The present book is an attempt to address the existing theories and arguments and to find a logical explanation to various issues regarding society and economy in Malabar in the eighteenth century. The most domineering of which in fact is the British interventions with regard to land ownership and related issues.

In the first phase of its administration, the British introduced a revenue policy in tune with the colonial perception, which in every sense was anti-people and diametrically opposed to the existing practice. Permanent settlement was introduced aiming at the creation of the class of *zamindars* or landed aristocracy in order to get a permanent source of revenue. In Malabar, a section of people, particularly the elite class of *janmis,* were transformed to the absolute owners of land. This transformation was based mainly on the colonialist perception of property right. According to the European perception, right to property was a natural one. The British administrators who introduced reforms in property right were influenced by the thoughts of John Locke, for whom, the private ownership was a law of the nature. He firmly believed that one individual's human rights included, along with liberty, owning and disposing of the property that one had gained by mixing one's labour with the land. According to the European perception, each and every individual has a right to property and which was alienable as well. But the right to property that existed in pre- British Kerala was quite opposite to the perceptions of the British. The people of Malabar had right to hold the land on the basis of a written deed (*karanam*) and such a right was to be acquired by the individual by his own effort. It was actually not the property right in western terms, but a sort of right of control. Accordingly, the land under one's control was not saleable or transferable. But all these traditional concepts and practices related to property were subjected to drastic change under the nascent colonial legal framework.

The transactions in land thereafter were put under strict scrutiny of the state, for the purpose, permanent registration of land was introduced in Malabar in the year 1794. Occupation of waste land was another step from the part of the Company towards introduction of private property in land. Those waste lands were assigned to somebody, and revenue was imposed upon that person as land owner. All those reforms paved the way for the introduction of a new 'revenue regime' in Malabar.

The ideas of utilitarianism, liberalism and the doctrine of rent developed by Malthus, James Mill and Ricardo etc. had largely influenced the British in the formulation of their revenue legislations. According to Ricardo, rent was the share of surplus produced on fertile soils. Since the rent was appropriated by the landlords, it does not help the process of productive accumulation and since the landlords turned out to be the unproductive class, it was necessary for the state to appropriate this rent by abolishing intermediaries. For Mill, the rent belonged to the state, which in fact was the actual owner of all land. This doctrine of rent provided the rationale for a high revenue demand by the British.

Major discussions and debates on the theme in Europe had largely influenced in formulating a revenue policy in British Malabar. As a preliminary step, the British conducted an extensive survey of land in order to understand the nature of ownership in land. Colonial reports from W.G. Farmer onwards postulated that the Brahmins or *jenm-kars* were the actual owners of land, or those having absolute property in land. With the report of Warden, the British accepted that the *janmis* were the sole owners of land.

The anti-British sentiment and resistance from the part of the local administrators [*natuvazhis*] and other influential chiefs of Malabar were unambiguous response to the new revenue reforms by the British. The loss of confidence and lack of influence in the circles of British power structure was the result of the said resistance. In this context, Kathleen Gough's characterisation of Pazhassi revolts as 'restorative revolts' is to be examined. Because, the revolts led by Pazhassi Raja and others were not aimed at restoring the previous system as such, instead, they were fighting for a sphere of their own influence within the British revenue regime.

Those who have attempted to study the history of eighteenth century Malabar have focused mainly on the establishment of British power over the territory and subsequent results. Most of those studies share the idea that by the year 1792 a colonial state was established in Malabar. But the British records itself stand against this general perception and there are contradictory evidences to offer a divergent argument. Precisely, though the British had conquered the land of Malabar by 1792 and it took at least 13 years for them to exercise power in the real sense. In comparison to other places of India, the case of Malabar is not exceptional. For example, the settlement of 1765 had been established in British Bengal; but Orissa remained unconquered until 1803. And in the case of Benares, though the British had obtained administrative powers in 1775 in Benares, they couldn't exercise any direct political authority for quite some time. From 1788 to 1795, the British in Benares had no advancement. In the case of Madras also, the British could make a breakthrough only by 1821 with the introduction of the *ryotwari* settlement even though it had established the direct administration in 1782. Likewise, in a period between 1792 and 1805, virtually, there existed no state in Malabar. If anything was possible for the British state, it was only a 'revenue regime'.

Before entering into the revenue settlement, the British had started to survey and cartographical representation of the whole territory which they conquered. Initially, the information was gathered by the army and naval forces, which later on was undertaken by the officials accompanying the Resident. James Rennel was the first cartographer of India who surveyed Bengal and neighbouring regions. His surveys were largely benefited by later revenue assessors. Likewise, in Malabar, the Vettattunad escheats were surveyed by Capt. Moncrief and Col. Sartorious surveyed the rivers of the country and Lt. Monier Williams prepared the first map of Malabar under Moncrief's supervision. These surveys on the west coast were mainly intended to identify the resources such as timber, spices and forest resources.

Colonial reports, right from the Joint Commissioners' report to Buchanan's *Journey* are obvious documents of colonial 'gaze' on the people and its resources of Malabar. Profound observations of Buchanan is the typical example of such an official genre of colonialist writing. His writings highlight the British intentions of transformation of the existing landscape. William Thackeray, author of another report, speaks of utilization of natural resources especially of rivers and possibility of widening and connecting them. The establishment of plantations in cinnamon, coffee, pepper, nutmeg, spices, etc. can be seen as result of these surveys and travels. Those works were, of course, the intellectual base for the establishment of colonial state in Malabar.

The ecological imbalances that arose due to colonial intervention in Malabar is an area least explored. Protracted warfare and introduction of plantation had started to affect nature badly. The teak forests of Eranad and

Valluvanad *taluks* were subjected to indiscriminate felling of teak, which according to C.A. Bayly, had resulted in depletion of the water level in the area. It is a fact that the army of Arthur Wellesley had caused to destroy the trees in the hill tracts of Waynad, when they waged a prolonged war with Pazhassi Raja. However, this period was only the starting point of such destructive activities.

The policies and administrative strategies formulated by the British in India were not the result of a slow and steady process, but with a very clear plan. To a section of historians, this project of colonialism was more a trial and error method than a pre-planned agenda of administration. However, this argument cannot be accepted as shown by Dirks and others. Of course, colonial powers had the object of conquest at the very beginning itself. Though there was confusion about the method and *modus operandi*, the colonial ambition of conquering a vast land was not at all set aside. There was no thought of giving up the project of Indian conquest at any point of time.

It is true that theoretical and philosophical questions predominant in Europe had a considerable role in the British policies promulgated in India. On many occasions, the attitudes and mentalities of the British public and the intelligentsia had influenced those debates. For instance, until 1790's the Home administration of the Company and the British public at large remained opposed the expansionist wars and further annexations of territories in India. Many a time impediments from within or outside had hampered the advancement of the company's rule in India. As a result, in the initial phase, the Company's policies were not so clear and the lack of clarity led the British to resort to variety of policies.

As mentioned, the early experimentation of the British state in Malabar, of course, was leading to the establishment of a revenue regime. For the "effective" administration, the British had to learn more and more about the people of the land and they used all state modalities to transform knowledge into power. In order to introduce a revenue system, the British had to construct knowledge about India. But the arguments of scholars such as B.S. Cohn, that for the Company, to create Orientalist knowledge about India was more important than collection of revenue - is actually against reality. It is a fact that there is no knowledge without a purpose. In the case of the British, knowledge was often used as a tool for governing the people. It was the Orientalist epistemology that became the steering force of the Company in the whole course of its rule. As William Jones had rightly observed, "all Orientalist studies in the eighteenth century had a political slant". In the case of the British, knowledge was often used as a means of governing the people.

What the British introduced in Malabar was a variant of Madras *ryotwari* system. According to Madras *ryotwari*, the state's share was fixed as the half of the next produce of the land after deducting the expenditure of cultivation. The actual cultivator in turn, was to be assured of the other half of the net produce. However, the Malabar *ryotwari* was entirely different one, according to which, the *janmi* was considered as the sole legal proprietor of the land.

The question regarding the existence of land revenue in pre-Mysore Kerala has been addressed by the present study. According to some contemporary chroniclers and modern historians, there was no organised and systematic revenue system in the period. Actually, there were two or more than two types of dues which had to be paid to the landholders namely, *paattam* and *vaarum*, a share to the overlord or local chief. The terms such as *melvaarum*, *Melpaathi*, *melodi*, etc. indicate the share of a fraction of produce from land usually collected by the rulers, the temples or chieftains. As those dues showed the features of both tax and rent, as some scholars pointed out, it may be better understood as 'rent-tax'.

However, the first systematic land survey and settlement in Malabar was conducted by Tipu Sultan, known as *jamabandy* settlement. The Mysore state in Malabar had converted state's grain share into money at certain rates. Likewise, the Mysorean administrators surveyed the land and fixed the land tax on the basis of the produce, where such a practice was unfamiliar to the rulers and people of Malabar. Survey of the land appears to have entrusted with *kandezhuthu, Melkangana kanakku* (Menon, Menokki etc.), but the point is that there was no centralised and uniform collection only localised collection. The new system of tax, *huzur niguti*, was collected from the *janmi's* share of rent. And the government made direct relations with the tenants. This was the period from which direct interventions of the state into production and its assessment was begun. Apart from that, since Hydar Ali's times itself, the right of *janmis* had been taken or absorbed by the government and the Mappila *kaanakkaars* started to disregard the dominance of the *janmis*.

The British Joint Commissioners, after an extensive collection of information by the *Sheristadars*, made a proclamation that *janmis* were the sole owners of land and *kaanakkaars* as the owners' lessees, though which invited a series of land disputes and complications. The British by fixing ownership was transforming land to a commodity and they were seeking a class of supporters of administration. The newly introduced reforms were found tough for smooth functioning and the implementation of which was made with the support of the newly established judiciary.

Apart from the changes in ownership, there were also some new changes in measurement and classification of land. In pre-colonial times, the procedure of measurement of land was dependent on the type of land, which means the paddy fields were measured, based on their sowing capacity, *parambas* and *purayidams* on the areas of tree planted or *kuzhi* and the areas of forest trees or *kutti*. This classification was replaced by the measurements of feet, square feet, acres and hectares which made the measurement procedures uniform. If the earlier classification was based upon land use, the British classification was only on the basis of physical extent of land alone.

The British plan of establishing a monoculture plantation was evident as early as Buchanan's journey (A. D. 1800-01). In Buchanan's enquiry, non-remunerative trees were to be felled down and forest's value had to be calculated in terms of saleability. In the coming years the British took his observations as a guideline for extension of plantation, especially the teak plantation. The British policies, particularly the revenue policy invited a series of protests from the part of rulers and local chiefs of Malabar. The government had to overcome resistance from various corners. The fierce and prolonged revolts waged by the ruler of Kottayam, Pazhassi Kerala Varma Raja in the north and the Mappila chiefs in the south were historic. It has to be noted that even though Malabar was taken over by the British in the year 1792, until 1805, (when Pazhassi Raja died) they couldn't make any considerable advancement in the region due to strong resistance of the indigenous people.

Historiographically, the British writings always followed a way of demonstrating the resistance movements by the indigenous people in a derogative manner. The Report of Joint Commissioners depicted Pazhassi Raja as 'the most intractable and unreasonable of the Rajas'. The Mappila rebels were represented as 'bandits' and 'robbers' in British writings. The same report deliberated Mappilas of south Malabar as 'jungle Mappilas' and 'robbing Mappilas', 'who never would voluntarily or quietly submit to pay the revenue'. Interestingly, the early nationalist historians were enthusiastic to characterise Pazhassi Raja as the 'Lion of Kerala' and his rebellion as the first war of independence in Kerala, while no serious attempt was made to highlight the Mappila resistance, which gained momentum in collaboration with Pazhassi Raja's battles against the British.

Likewise, it is unfortunate to see a renowned historian like K.K.N. Kurup succumbed to the neo-nationalist enthusiasm in characterising Pazhassi Raja as a 'Hindu-Peasant-Nationalist'. Most of his works in this direction is almost authentication of the commonsensical perception that Pazhassi Raja's struggles were part of a growing nationalist consciousness in Malabar. It is now obvious that, attributing nationalism in Pazhassi Raja's struggles is meaningless because, prior to the Mysorean occupation, the Raja was in alliance with the British and was fighting against Tipu Sultan. Contrary to his calculations, the British neglected him after their victory over Tipu Sultan and only from then onwards he was moving against the British. Besides, even in the course of hostility, the British offered some privileges to Pazhassi Raja and he had signed a settlement with them, though which was in fact not recognised by his comrades. Significantly, attributing nationalism to the early phase of the anti-colonial resistance may not be fair, since the ideas of nation or nationalism were yet to emerge in India after a long time. However, such struggles should be given due respect and representation in the history of India's anti-colonial history but not losing the rigour of historical research.

The issue of peasants' participation in the revolt, and 'popular support' as formulated by scholars must also be put under serious scrutiny. It is a fact that most of the leaders of the revolt were those who lost their powers and privileges under the British. The resistance was against the British and the British policies. What actually existed in Malabar during the period was an insurgency situation. Serious enquiries have yet to be undertaken to gather substantial source materials in order to verify whether Pazhassi Raja's resistance movement can be termed as 'popular revolt' or 'peasant revolt'.

Recently, another stream of historical writing is looming large, which is premeditated to appropriate history and career of Pazhassi Raja. Most of the arguments presented in the guise of facts lack corroborative source materials. It follows a methodology of presenting legends as history. If the religious idioms like 'temple', 'deity', or 'oracles' were made use of by a ruler like Pazhassi Raja, it cannot be understood simply in religious or communal terms. Rather, it must be seen as a part of larger political act in order to get the people sensitized by his anti-colonial struggles, and history of similar movements proves that such acts were common across India.

Historiographical representation also presents a confusing discourse on the matter of the support base of the rebels with regard to their religious identity. This argument, in a nutshell, proposes that the support base of the Pazhassi Revolts constituted only the Hindu population and the Mappilas during period were against the Raja and his revolts. However, a curious student of history can conclude that available evidence stands antithetical to such an argument. In fact, as we could see elsewhere, on many occasions, the Mappila chiefs had extended their support to the Raja's army. The British records speak extensively of Pazhassi Raja and his men who were assisted by Unni Mootha Mooppan at Kuttiyadi. There are also references to Athan Gurukkal, Chemben Pokker, Unnimootha Mooppan and several others who had fought against British as close associates of Pazhassi Raja.

Until the fall of Pazhassi Raja, Mappila rebels of South had associated directly or indirectly in his major operations. The Mappila leaders of the north like Chaladi Thangal, Hydar Kunhikkutty, Elampulam Kunhan, Vavantullan Kunhi (sic), Kunhi Moideen Mooppan of Elathur, etc. were very allies of the Raja in his resistance against the British. Though Chovvakkaran Moosa and Mucky were the principal mappila merchants of the British in Malabar, they had supplied rice, gunpowder and other essentials to the Pazhassi raja and rebels. There are ample and solid evidence to state that religion was not an obstacle for Mappilas in aligning with the anti- British rebellion.

The intervention of Mysore state in Malabar was a crucial factor which caused some changes in the existing society, economy and polity as well. However, that short period of Mysoreans has been often discussed with religious overtones. From the colonial administrative historians to the nationalist writers, the cause of Mysorean invasion of Malabar was one and the same, the religious factor. The economic and strategic factors had not been taken into account. What is actually found missing in those writings is the actual motivation of the rulers for invading an alien land, Malabar. For Mysore, Malabar was a foreign land with rich resources such as spices, timber, forest resources etc. and a land with extensive coastal area, which could be utilised for extension of their power to the southern region of India, apart from its strategic and commercial importance. The Mysore rulers never fought battles in the sake of religion. Though they were pious Muslims, their associates and ministers were mostly Hindus. No space was there for religious bias in Mysore state. There are instances of grants of land, gold and money extended to temples, maths and priests from the royal treasury of Tipu Sultan. When Maratha army destroyed the math of Sankaracharya, Tipu Sultan was extending financial and moral support to the priest. And in a similar vein, was Tipu Sultan hostile to Muslim rulers such as Nizam of Hyderabad for his alliance with the British. The same is the case of Tipu Sultan's expulsion of the Mahdi Muslims from his troops, for disobeying his instruction to follow moderate religious rituals. It was culminated in incarceration of their leaders such as Mahtab Khan and Alam Khan.

Tipu Sultan's attempt to intimidate Mappila merchants and by which extract spices by imposing trade monopoly can also be seen as a part of a wider objective. Indeed, the religion never played a major role for Mysore rulers and it was subordinate to political factors. If they were conscious of religion, they would not have been hostile to the Mappila merchants. The Mysore rulers were politically ambitious enough to fight wars with several rulers of South India. And they were not reluctant to adopt any extreme measures against those who challenged their power. For instance, Hydar set fire to an extensive village in Jagir (area including Chingalpet and Madras). Jagir was under the control of Muslim rulers. Hydar set fire to the extensive farmland and houses in order to intimidate both the ruler and the people of that area, by which the Mysore army could establish its supremacy. The same method was followed in Malabar too, which categorically shows that religion played little role in political conquests.

The Mysore rulers fought with the Malabar Rajas as their enemies, who were followers of a different belief system and cultural pattern. It is quite natural to feel that the religious and cultural differences of indigenous people and rulers of Malabar were obsolete and so that they were contemplating on introducing certain reforms especially in connection with the caste system, customs, dress code etc. But we do not have ample evidence to believe that all those reforms were introduced in religious terms.

Towards formulating a logical explanation for resistance from the part of Brahmins and Nairs against Mysore state, the revenue reforms of the Mysore could come to the centre stage. Revenue reforms was a bolt from blue for those elite class, because, they were destined lose their age-old privileges. Apprehensive of losing their position and power, the *Janmis, Naduvazhis,* and *Nairs* raised fierce resistance against the Mysore rulers. The case of Mappila chiefs called Mooppans of Malabar also was not different. The Mooppans and Gurukkals had raised strong protests without any consideration of religion. If religion was a deciding factor, this sort of protest couldn't have been taken place. Apart from that, when an alliance was formed by the British and Marathas against Tipu Sultan, Hyderabad Nizam was the prominent figure, where the religion was a non-issue. As explained before, the attitude of Mysore rulers was the same towards the Nawab of Jagir and Mappila merchants of Malabar. So it can be argued that the religion in pre-modern times cannot be seen as a factor of polarisation as in the present. To be precise, contrary to colonialist and some indigenous/ nationalist writers' perception, the Mysore's invasion of Malabar was purely driven out of economic and political factors, and never religious. They had attempted to conduct experiments in revenue system, trade and state craft including conduct of first survey, introduction of *huzur niguti*, direct payment etc. had far reaching impact upon society, economy and polity of Malabar. In short, during the early phase of its rule in Malabar, the East India Company had to go through a tortuous path. Apart from the differences of opinion in Britain, the Company had to face a series of resistance from the indigenous rulers and chiefs. Though Pazhassi revolts and Mappila resistances came to an end by 1805, new flames of powerful and protracted voices of dissent and new challenges had to be faced by the British in the near future. Of course, colonialism had made a rupture in the political economy of Malabar, but it was founded upon the brutal suppression of relentless voices of people's dissent.

Glossary

adiyar	agrestic bondmen
amil	local tax collectors
amsam	administrative unit (an order above *desam*)
angadi	bazaar, market
artham	security
arzee, arji (harji)	Petition
atiyayma	servility
attaikkol	annual revenue
avakasom	right
brahmaswam	the brahmin property
cartaz	Portuguese permit to trade in the Indian Ocean
changatam	temple servants
chanta	market place/weekly bazaar
chekon	ezhava warrior
cherikkal	royal land (pandaravaga/ kandulavu)
chunkam	Toll
desam	village
desavaazhi	village head, local authority responsible for the natuvazhi
devaswam	temple property
fanam	gold or silver coins of different value
gurukkal	trainer of kalari
hobali, hovali	district
idangazhi	liquid measure on the west coast 1 *idangazhi* = 1.8696 litres
illam	nambutiri houses
jama/jumma	assessment of revenue
jamabandi	tax assessment, state revenue of land

janmam	birth, hereditary ownership
janmam-kaanam-maryadai	ownerwhip-lease regulations
janmappanayam	mortgage of a property, upon which an additional advance is given.
Jati	caste
jivitam	life time
kachams	strict rules and regulations by brahmins and naduvazhis
kalari	school of martial art
kammalars	artisans
kaanakkaaran	leaseholder
kaanam	purchase of janmam, mortgage, credit
kanti	a unit of measure for weight, between 500lb and 560lb
kaaraalan	tenant of temples
karanavar	male head of the family/ Taravadu
katamai	compulsory duty
kavu	shrine
khudadad sarkar	God's government/state
kizhiyakkam	brahminical codes
kolkar	native militia organised by the British
kovilakam	branch of the royal family
kudiyan	inhabitants, lease holders
kur	seniority rank
kuzhikkaanam	rents for cultivation of jungle land
makkathayam	inheritance by son
malikhana	pension
marumakkathayam	inheritance by sister's son
maryada	social custom
mela	periodical fair
menon	belongs to elite nayar family, accountant by profession
moopans	headman (revenue collectors)
muppu	seniority
mura	rank
nadu	district

naduvazhi	head of a natu
niguti, negdee	Tax
nirattipper	lands transfer with libation of water
otti	a piece of land
paimash	measurement of land
panayam	pledging of land
para	liquid measure: 1 para equals 10 *itangazhis*
parambu	elevated land or garden land
parankis	portuguese
paattam	lease / Rent
paattamkar	leaseholder
pedi	Fear
purayitam	household
rakshabhogam	protection money
ryot	peasant
sambhandham	Nair women's marriage relation with Brahmin
sanketam	protection force under temples
serishtadar	administrative official
swarupam	territorial unit
tahsildar	head tax official
tara	administrative unit
taravadu	family unit forming a household and unit of of landownership
taavazhi	collateral of the branch of a family unit (taravadu), ownership of this branch.
thangal	muslim spiritual leader/ Sayyids
theendal	pollution by caste
theruvu	street
tukri	division, district
tukridar	overseer of division or district
uralan	temple trustees
variyam	temple committee
varrum	share of produce
verumpaattam	simple lease

Bibliography

Primary Sources

Reports of a Joint Commission of Bengal and Bombay Appointed to inspect into the state and conditions of the Province of Malabar, 1972-1973, Kerala State Regional Archives, Kozhikkode.

Jonathan Duncan's Report, 1793, Kerala State Regional Archives, Kozhikkode.

Revenue Department Diaries (from 1779 to 1801), Maharashtra State Archives, Mumbai.

Secret and Political Department Diaries (from 1767 to 1810), Maharashtra State Archives, Mumbai.

Tellicherry Consultations (from 1725 to 1751), Kerala Studies Section, Kerala University Library, Trivandrum.

Letters from Tellicherry (from 1721 to 1751), Kerala Studies Section, Kerala University Library, Trivandrum.

Letters to Tellicherry (from 1726 to 1750), Kerala Studies Section, Kerala University Library, Trivandrum.

Minutes of the Board of Revenue (1818), Maharashtra State Archives, Mumbai.

Published

Aitchison, C. U., *A Collection of Treaties Engagements and Sanads Relating to India and Neighbouring Countries,* Vol. IX, Calcutta, 1926 (1876), Bombay University Library, Mumbai.

Appadurai, Arjun, *Economic Conditions in Southern India, 1000-1500,* Madras, 1990 (1936).

Baden- Powell, B.H., *The Land system of British India: Being a Manual of the Land Tenures and the Systems of Land Revenue Administration Prevalent in the Several Provinces,* 3 Vols., Delhi, 1990 (1892).

Buchanan, Francis, *A Journey From Madras through the countries of Mysore, Canara and Malabar*, 1800-01, Vol.2, Delhi, 1988 (1807).

Conner and Ward, *A Descriptive Memoirs of Malabar,* Thiruvananthapuram, 1995 (1906).

Fay, Eliza, *Original Letters from India, (1779-1815),* London, 1986 (1925).

Innes, C. A., *Malabar Gazetteers*, Trivandrum, 1997 (2nd Reprint).

Kausar, Kabir, *Secret Correspondence of Tipu Sultan,* New Delhi, 1980.

Kirk Patrick, William, *Select Letters of Tipu Sultan,* London, 1811.

Logan, William, *A Collection of Treaties Engagements and other papers of importance Relating to the British Affairs in Malabar,* Thiruvananthapuram, 1998(1879).

—, *Malabar*, Vol. 1, Madras, 1951, (1887).

Thackeray, William, *Report on the Revenue Affairs of Malabar and Canara, 1807*, Madras, 1911.

Walker, Major, *Report on the Land Tenure of Malabar*, 1801.

Zeinuddin Sheikh, *Thuhfat al- Mujahiddin,* tr. by S. Muhammad Husayn Nainar, Calicut, 2006.

Malayalam

Kurup, K. K. N., ed., *Kavalappara Papers*, Calicut, 1984.

—, ed., *Kutali Grandhavari,* Calicut, 1995.

Narayanan, M. G. S., ed., *Vanjeri Grandhavari*, Calicut, 1987.

Namputiri, N. M., ed., *Vellayude Charithram,* Sukapuram,1998.

Scaria, Joseph, ed., *Thalasseri Rekhakal,* Kottayam, 1996.

Secondary Sources

Unpublished Doctoral Theses

Ganesh, K. N. , 'Agrarian Relations and Political Authority in Medieval Travancore, (AD 1300 - 1750)', Unpublished Ph.D Thesis, Jawaharlal Nehru University, New Delhi, 1987.

Mohandas P., 'A study of the Colonial Investments in Malabar and the Nilgris in the 19th century', unpublished Ph.D. thesis, University of Calicut, 2005.

Swai, Bonaventure, 'Trade and Politics in eighteenth century Malabar', mimeo, Unpublished, Dar- es Salam, 1979.

Books

Alavi, Seema, ed., *Eighteenth Century India*, Delhi, 2002.

Alexander, P. C., *Dutch in Malabar,* Annamali, 1946.

Ali, B. S., *British Relations with Hydar Ali, 1760- 1782,* Mysore, 1963.

Arasaratnam, Sinnappa, *Maritime India in the Seventeenth Century,* Delhi, 1994.

Ayyar, Krishna, K.V., *The Zamorins of Calicut*, Calicut ,1999 (1937).

Baden- Powell, B.H. , *The Indian Village Community*, London, 1896.

—, *The Origin and Growth of Village Communities in India*, London, 1899.

Bagchi, A. K., *Capital and Labour Redefined: India and the third world*, Delhi, 2002.

Balakrishnan, P. K., *Tipu Sulthan* (Mal.), Kozhikode, 1996 (1959).

Balakrishnan, P.K., *Jati Vyavasthithiyum Kerala Charithravum* (Mal), Kottayam, 1983.

Bayly, C. A., *Indian Society and Making of the British Empire*, Delhi, 1987.

—, *Rulers, Townsmen and Bazars, North Indian Society in the Age of British expansion*; Delhi, 1992.

Beaglehole, T. H., *Thomas Munro and the Development of Administrative Policy in Madras, 1792-1818*, Cambridge, 1966.

Bouchon, Geneveve, *Regent of the Sea: Cannanore's Response to Portuguese Expansion, 1507-1528,* Delhi, 1988.

Brittlebank, Kate, *Tipu Sultan's Search for Legitimacy: Islam and Kinship in a Hindu Domain,* Delhi, 1997.

Chaudhuri, K. N., *The Trading world of Asia and the English East India Company, 1660-1760*, Cambridge, 1978.

Cheriyan, P. J., ed., *Perspectives on Kerala History*, *Kerala Gazetteer*, Vol. II, Part II, Thiruvananthapuram, 1999.

Cohn, Bernard, S., *An Anthropologist Among Historians and other Essays*, Delhi, 1990.

—, *Colonialism and its forms of Knowledge*, Delhi, 1997.

Dale, Stephen Frederic, *Islamic Society on the South Asian Frontier, The Mappilas of Malabar, 1498 – 1922,* Oxford, 1980.

Day, Francis, *The Land of Perumals or Cochin: Its Past and Present,* Madras, 1863.

Desai, A. R ed. *Peasant Struggles in India,* Delhi, 1979.

Dobb, Maurice, *Studies in the Development of Capitalism,* London, 1970.

Fernandes, P., *Storm over Srirangapattanam,* Bombay, 1969.

Fisher, Michael H., ed; *The Politics of the British Annexation of India, 1757-1857*, Delhi, 1993.

Forest, D., *Tiger of Mysore,* London, 1970.

Frank, Andre Gunder, *Re-Orient: Global Economy in the Asian Age,* 1998.

Frenz, Margret, *From Contact to Conquest, Transition to British Rule in Malabar 1792- 1805*, New Delhi, 2003.

Frykenberg, R. E., ed., *Land Control and Social Structure in Indian History,* Delhi, 1979 (1969).

Fuller, C. J., *The Nayars Today,* Cambridge, 1976.

Furber, Holden, *John Company at work, A Study of European Expansion in India in the eighteenth century*, 1948.

—, *Bombay Presidency in the Mid Eighteenth Century*, Bombay, 1965.

Gabriel, Theodore, *Hindu Muslim Relations in North Malabar, 1498-1947*, New York, 1996.

Galetti, A., et al., *The Dutch in Malabar,* New Delhi, 1984 (Reprint).

Ganesh, K.N., *Keralathinte Innalekal,* Trivandrum, 1997 (1990).

Gangadharan, C. H., *Mayyazhi* (Mal.), Mahe, 1987.

Gangadharan, M., *The Malabar Rebellion,* Kottayam, 2008.

Gopal, M. H., *Tipu Sultan's Mysore,An Economic Study,* Bombay, 1971.

Gopalakrishnan, P. K., *Keralathinte Samskarika Charithram*, (Mal.), Trivandrum, 1994 (1974).

Guha, Ranajit, *A Rule of Property for Bengal,* New Delhi, 1981.

—, *Dominance without Hegemony*, New Delhi, 1998.

Gundert, Herman, *Keralappazhama* (Mal.), Kozhikode, 1997 (Rpnt)

Gupta Ashin Das, *Malabar in Asian Trade*, Cambridge, 1967.

Gurukkal, Rajan, *The Kerala Temple and Early Medieval Agrarian System,* Sukapuram, 1992.

Habib, Irfan, *Agrarian System of Mughal India, 1550- 1707,* Bombay, 1963.

—, *Essays in Indian History, Towards Marxist Perception,* Delhi, 1995.

—, ed., *Resistance and Modernisation under Hydar Ali and Tipu Sultan,* New Delhi, 1999.

Haney, Lewis H., *History of Economic Thought*, 1949.

Haridas, P. J. ed., *Keralavum Swathantrya Samaravum* (Mal.), Trivandrum, 2000.

Haridas, V. V., *Zamorines and the Political Culture of Medieval Kerala,* Orient Blackswan, Hydarabad, 2016.

Hassan, Mohibul, *History of Tipu Sultan*, Delhi, 2006 (1951).

Irschick, Eugene, F., *Dialogue and History*, Delhi, 1994.

Iyer, R. Mahadeva., *Land Revenue History*, 1915.

Kareem, C. K., *Kerala under Haider Ali and Tipu Sultan*, Ernakulam, 1973.

Kumar, Dharma, *Land and Caste in South India,* Cambridge, 1965.

Kumar, Dharma and Meghnad Desai, ed., *The Cambridge Economic History of India, Vol. II, c.1751-1970,* 2005(1983), New Delhi.

Kunju, Ibrahim, A. P., *Kerala-Mysore Relations*, Trivanrum, 1975.

Kurup, K. K. N., *Aspects of Kerala History and Culture*, Trivandrum, 1977.

—, *William Logan: A study in the Agrarian Relations of Malabar*, Calicut University, 1981.

—, *History of Tellicherry Factory, (1683 -1794)*, Calicut University, 1985.

—, *Modern Kerala: Studies in Social and Agrarian Relations,* New Delhi, 1988.

—, *Pazhassi Samarangal* (Mal.), Trivandrum, 1988 (1980).

—, *Pazhassi Samara Rekhakal* (Mal.), Calicut, 2004.

Kutty, Sankaran T.P., *A Tragic Decade in Kerala* History, Trivandrum, 1977.

Kutty, Ummer A.P., *Keyimarute Charitram* (Mal.), Tellicherry, 1995 (1916).

Lombard Denys and Jean Aubin, ed., *Asian Merchants and Businessmen in the Indian Ocean and Chinese Sea*, Delhi, 2000.

Marshall, P.J., *East India Fortunes: The British in Bengal*, New Delhi, 1976.

—, *Bengal; the British Bridge head, Eastern India, 1740-1828*, Delhi, 1990.

Masani, K. P., *Britain in India,* London, 1970.

Mathew, K. S., *Portuguese Trade with India in the Sixteenth century,* New Delhi, 1983.

Mathews, Johnsy, *Economy and Society in Medieval Malabar (AD 1200-1600)*, Changanesseri, 1996.

Mayer, Adrian, C., *Land and Society in Malabar,* Oxford, 1952.

Menon, K. P. Padmanabha, *History of Kerala,* 4 vols., New Delhi, 1989.

Metcalf, Thomas R., *Ideologies of the Raj*, New Delhi, 2005 (1998).

Miller, Ronald Eric, *Mappila Muslims of Kerala: A Study in Islamic Trends,* Hydarabad, 1990.

Misra, B. B., *The Central Administration of the East India Company,1773-1834*, London, 1959.

Mohan, K. S., *Pazhassi Raja, Porattathinte Nalukal* (Mal.), Kochi, 2007.

Moreland, W. H., *Agrarian System of Moslem India,* Delhi, 1968.

—, *From Akbar to Aurangazeb: Study in Indian Economic History,* Delhi, 1968.

Mukherjee, Nilmani, *The Ryotwari System in Madras, 1792-1827*, Calcutta, 1962.

Mukherjee Rudrangshu and Lakshmi Subramaniam, ed., *Politics and Trade in the Indian Ocean World*, Delhi, 2003.

Mukund, Kanakalatha, *Trading World of the Tamil Merchant,* Chennai, 1999.

—, *The View from Below: Indigenous society, Temples and Early Colonial state in Tamil Nadu, 1700 – 1836*, Hydarabad, 2005.

Nair, Madhavan, K., *Malabar Kalapam* (Mal.), Kozhikode, 1993.

Nair, Ramachandran, S., *The State and Economy in Colonial British Kerala,* Trivandrum, 1998.

Nair, Sivasankaran, K., *Nieuhoff Kanda Keralam* (Mal.), Trivandrum, 1996.

Nambiar, E. K. G., ed., *Agrarian India, Problems and Perspectives*, Calicut University, 1997.

Namputiri, N. M., *Samutiri Charithrathile Kaanappurangal* (Mal), Sukapuram, 1987.

—, ed., *Vellayude Charitram*, (Mal.), Sukapuram, 1998.

—, *Mamamkam Rekhakal*, (Mal.), Sukapuram, 2005.

—, *Malabar Patanangal: Samutiri Nadu*, (Mal.), Trivandrum, 2008.

Nambutiripad, E. M. S., *Kerala Yesterday Today and Tomorrow,* Calcutta, 1968 [1967].

Narayanan, M. G. S., *Kerala through Ages,* Trivandrum, 1976.

—, *Perumals of Kerala; Political and social conditions of Kerala under the Chera Perumals of Makotai (800 - 1124 AD),* Calicut, 1996.

Nightingale, Pamela, *Trade and Empire in Western India, 1784-1806*, New Delhi, 1970.

Panikkar, Gopala, T. K., *Malabar and its Folk: A Systematic Description of the Social Customs and Institutions of Malabar,* Madras, 1983 [1900].

Panikkar, K. M., *Kerala Simham* (Mal), Thrissur, 1968.

Panikkar, K. N., *British Diplomacy in North India,* Delhi 1968.

—, *Peasant Protests and Revolts in Malabar,* New Delhi, 1990.

—, *Against Lord and State: Religion and Peasant Uprisings in Malabar,1836 – 1921,* Delhi,1992.

—, *Ibn Batuta Kanda Keralam* (Mal.), Kottayam, 1993.

Philips, C. H., *The East India Company 1784-1834,* London, 1940.

Pillai, Elamkulam, P. N. Kunjan, *Janmi Sampradayam Keralathil*, (Mal), Kottayam, 1959.

—, *Studies in Kerala History*, Kottayam, 1970.

Pillai, Velu T. K., *Travancore State Manual*, Vol. II, Trivandrum, 1940.

Polanyi, Karl et. al., *Trade and Markets in Early Empires*, Free Press, New York, 1957.

—, *Primitive, Archaic and Modern Economies: Essays of Karl Polanyi,* Boston, 1968.

Poonen, T. L., *A Survey of Rise of Dutch Power in Malabar(1603- 78),* University of Travancore, 1948.

Prakash, Om, *European Commercial Enterprises in Pre- Colonial India,* Cambridge, 1998.

Radhakrishnan, P., *Peasant Struggles, Land reforms and Social Change: Malabar 1836- 1982,* New Delhi.

Rajayyan, K., *South Indian Rebellion, The First War of Independence, 1800-1801*, Mysore, 1971.

Rajendran, N., *Establishment of British power in Malabar (1664 to 1799)*, Allahabad, 1979.

Ravindran, T. K, *Malabar under Bombay Presidency*, Calicut, 1969.

Ravindran, T. K, *Cornwallis System in Malabar,* Calicut, 1969.

Rehiman, M.P. Mujeebu, *The Other side of the Story: Tipu Sultan, Colonialism and Resistance in Malabar,* Kottayam, 2016.

Roll, Eric, *A History of Economic Thought*, Calcutta, 1980 (1938).

Sen, S. P., *The French in India,* Calcutta, 1947.

Sharma, K. L., ed., *Caste and Class in India*, Jaipur, 1994.

Sreekumar, K. S., ed., *The History of Freedom Movement in Kerala,* The Regional Records Committee, Trivandrum, 2000 (1970).

Sridharan, M. P., *Papers on French Colonial Rule in India,* Calicut, 1997.

Srinivas, M. N, *India's Villages,* Bombay, 1960.

Steensgard, Neils, *The Asian Trade Revolution of the Seventeenth Century,* Chicago, 1973.

Stein, Burton, *Thomas Munro, the Origins of the Colonial State and His Vision of Empire*, Delhi, 1989.

—, *The Making of Agrarian Policy in British India, 1770 - 1900,* Delhi, 1992.

Stokes, Eric, *Utilitarians in India*, Delhi, 1959.

Subramaniam, Sanjay, ed., *Merchants, Markets and state in Early Modern India*, Delhi, 1990.

—, *The Career and Legend of Vasco Da Gama,* Cambridge, 1997.

Taylor, Meadows, *Tipoo Sultan, A Tale of Mysore War*, Madras, 2001.

Tharakan, Michael P. K., *Forest Wealth and Ritual Status: Gleanings from Kollangode Records,* Trivandrum, 1993.

Thompson, Edward and G.T. Garrett, *History of British Rule in India*, Vol. 1, New Delhi, 1999.

Varghese, T. C., *Agrarian Changes and Economic Consequences, Land Tenures in Kerala, 1850-1960*, Bombay, 1970.

Varier, M. R. Raghava, and Rajan Gurukkal, *Kerala Charithram,*(Mal.), Sukapuram, 1992.

Varier, M. R. Raghava, *Village Communities in Pre Colonial Kerala,* Mysore, 1994.

—, *Madhyakala Keralam Sambattu Samuham Samskaram* (Mal.), Trivandrum,1997.

Veluthat, Kesavan, *Brahmin Settlements in Kerala*, Calicut, 1978.

Veluthat, Kesavan and P. P Sudhakaran eds., *Advances in History, Essays in Memory of Prof. M. P Sreedharan*, Calicut, 2003.

Wallerstein, Immanuel, *The Modern World System,* Vol. I, Orlando, 1974.

Articles

Abdurahiman, A. P., 'Palassi Rebellin: The Role of Coastal Merchants', *Journal of Kerala Studies,* Vol. I, No. 2&3, Jan. 1974.

—, 'Macleod's Paimash and the Malabar Rebellion of 1803,' *Journal of Kerala History,* Vol. IV, March, 1977.

Alavi, Hamza, 'India and the Colonial mode of Production', *Social Register,* London, 1965.

Banerjea, Ruchira, 'A Wedding Feast or Political Arena? Commercial Rivalry between the Ali Raja and the English factory in North Malabar in the eighteenth century', in Rudrangshu Mukherjea and Lakshmi Subramaniam, ed., *Politics and Trade in the Indian Ocean World*, Delhi, 2003.

Bhattacharya, Neeladri, 'Colonial State and Agrarian Society', in B. Stein ed., *The Making of Agrarian Policy in British India, 1770 - 1790*, Delhi 1992.

Bouchon, Geneveve, 'A Microcosom: Calicut in the sixteenth Century', in Denys Lombard & Jean Aubin, ed., *Asian Merchants and*

Businessmen in the Indian Ocean and Chinese Sea, OUP, Delhi, 2000.

Chakrabarty, Subhra, 'The English East Indian Company and the Indigenous sloop Merchants of Bengal: Akrur Dutta and his family, 1775-1857', *Studies in History*, 20, 1ns, 2004.

Davis, Donald, R., 'Recovering the Indigenous Legal Traditions of India: Classical Hindu Law in Practice in Late Medieval Kerala', *Journal of Indian Philosophy*, 27, 1999, pp. 159-213.

Embrie, Anslee T., 'Land holding in India and British institutions', *in* R.E. Frykenberg ed., *Land Control and Social Structure in Indian History*, Delhi, 1979 (1969).

Cohn, Bernard S., 'Structural Change in Indian Rural Society 1596 – 1885', in R.E. Frykenberg ed., *Land Control and Social Structure in Indian History*, Delhi, 1979 (1969).

Gough, Kathleen, 'Indian Peasant uprisings' in Desai A.R ed. *Peasant Struggles in India,* Delhi, 1979.

—, 'Agrarian Society in Kerala (1500-1800)' in P.J. Cheriyan, ed., *Perspectives on Kerala History*, *Kerala Gazetteer*, Vol. II, Pt. II, Thiruvananthapuram, 1999.

Ganesh, K. N., 'Ownership and control of land in Medieval Kerala: *janmam - kaanam* relations during the sixteenth - eighteenth centuries,' *IESHR*, 28, 3, (1991).

—, 'Agrarian Relations in Kerala: An over view', in E.K.G Nambiar, ed., *Agrarian India, Problems and Perspectives*, Calicut University, 1997.

—, 'Structure of Political Authority', in P.J. Cheriyan, ed., *Perspectives on Kerala History*, *Kerala Gazetteer*, Vol. II, Pt. II, Thiruvananthapuram, 1999.

—, 'European Perceptions of Kerala landscape: From Barbosa to Buchanan', in Kesavan Veluthatt, P.P Sudhakaran eds, *Advances in History, Essays in Memory of Prof. M.P Sreedharan*, Calicut, 2003.

Gupta, Ashin Das, 'Malabar in 1740', *Bengal Past and Present,* LXXX, 1960.

Gupta, Sulekha Chandra, 'Retreat from Permanent Settlement and Shift towards a new Land Revenue Policy', in in Burton Stein ed., *The Making of Agrarian Policy in British India, 1770 - 1900*, Delhi, 1992, p. 66.

Gurukkal, Rajan, 'The Formation of Caste Society in Kerala: Historical Antecedents', in K. L. Sharma ed., *Caste and Class in India*, Jaipur, 1994.

Kurup, K. K. N., 'Pazhassi Rebellion' in P.J. Cheriyan, ed., *Perspectives in Kerala History,* Thiruvananthapuram, 1999.

Marshall, P. J., 'Economy and Political Expansion, the case of Oudh', in M. Fisher, ed., *The Politics of the British Annexation of India, 1757-1857*, Delhi, 1993.

Menon, Dilip, 'Houses by the Sea: State Formation Experiment in Malabar 1760-1800', *Economic and Political Weekly,* 1999.

Nambutiri, N. M., 'A Malayalam Chronicle on Hydar's Invasion of Kerala,' Indian History Congress, Bombay, 1980.

Parthasarathi, Prasannan, 'Merchants and the Rise of colonialism,' in Seema Alavi, ed., *Eighteenth Century India*, Delhi, 2002.

Rajendran, N., 'Shifting Balance of Pepper trade in the late Eighteenth century', in *Eighteenth Century India, papers in honour of Prof. A.P. Ibrahim Kunju*, Calicut, 1981.

Raju, S., 'Organization of Medieval Self forms: *Swapurm* and *Muppu-vazhcha*', Lateral Study Series, 15, S.S.S. M.G. University, Kottayam, nd.

Rehiman, M. P. Mujeebu 'Tipu Sultan's invasion of Malabar: A Reappraisal', in Dr.V.Kunjali ed., *Kerala Society: Historical Perceptions*, University of Calicut,2002.

—, 'Colonial perception of Land Ownership in Kerala: The Case of Janmam', *Calicut University Research Journal*, Vol.4, No.2, June, 2004, pp. 30-39.

—, 'Bigotry Historiography and Ideology: Gleanings from an 18th Century Chronicle' , *Calicut University Research Journal,* Vol.5 Aug 2005, pp. 96-103.

—, 'Merchants Colonialism and Indigenous Capital: The case of Chovakkaran Moosa and the East India Company', *Arts and Ideas* Vol.3, Nos. 1&2, Thrissur, June, 2007, pp.129-139.

—,'Pepper Timber and the Ports: Towards an Economic Interpretation of Mysore's Engagements in Malabar', *Journal of the Institute for Research in Social Sciences and Humanities,* Vol 9, Nos 1&2, January-Dec 2014, pp. 39-60.

—, 'Counter Voices to the Early British State: Unni Mootta Mooppan and Chemban Pokker, the Primitive Rebels from South Malabar', *Society and Culture,* Govt. Arts and Science College, Calicut, Vol.7, issue: 1, January 2016, pp. 169-189.

Shea, T. W., 'Barriers to Economic Development in Transitional Societies: Malabar, a case study', *Journal of Economic History,* XIX, 1959.

Stokes, Eric, 'Traditional Resistance Movements and Afro-Asian Nationalism: The Context of the 1857Mutiny Rebellion in India' in idem, *The Peasant and the Raj,* Cambridge, 1978.

Subramaniam, Sanjay and C. A. Bayly, 'Portfolio Capitalists and the Political Economy of Early Modern India', in Sanjay Subramaniam, ed., *Merchants, Markets and state in Early Modern India*, Delhi, 1990.

Swai, Bonaventure., 'Notes on Colonial state with special reference to Malabar in eighteenth and 19th Centuries', *Social Scientist*, Vol. 6, July 1978.

—, 'From Kolathunad to Chirakkal: British Merchant Capital and the Hinterland of Tellicherry, 1694- 1766', *Studies in History,* Vol.1, No.1, January-June 1985.

Tharakan, P.K. Michael, 'Development of colonial Economy in Kerala (1500-1947)' ,in P.J. Cheriyan, ed., *Perspectives on Kerala History, Kerala Gazetteer*, Vol. II, Pt. II, Thiruvananthapuram, 1999.

Veluthat, Kesavan, 'Further Expansion of the Agrarian society: the Political Forms', in Cheriyan P.J., ed., *Perspectives on Kerala History*, *Kerala Gazetteer*, Vol. II, Part. II, Thiruvananthapuram, 1999.

Index

B

K

N